Backstop

Backstop

A History of the Catcher and a Sabermetric Ranking of 50 All-Time Greats

WILLIAM F. MCNEIL

Foreword by Pete Palmer

McFarland & Company, Inc., Publishers
Jefferson, North Carolina, and London

LIBRARY OF CONGRESS CATALOGUING-IN-PUBLICATION DATA

NcNeil, William.
    Backstop : a history of the catcher and a sabermetric ranking
of 50 all-time greats / William F. McNeil ; foreword by Pete
Palmer.
        p.   cm.
    Includes bibliographical references and index.

    ISBN 0-7864-2177-0 (softcover : 50# alkaline paper)

    1. Catchers (Baseball)— United States.   2. Catching
(Baseball)— Statistics.   3. Catchers (Baseball)— United States—
Biography.   I. Title.
    GV872.M35   2006
    796.357'23 — dc22   2005031105

British Library cataloguing data are available

On the cover: Ivan Rodriguez *(Ivan "Pudge" Rodriguez Foundation)*

Manufactured in the United States of America

McFarland & Company, Inc., Publishers
  Box 611, Jefferson, North Carolina 28640
  www.mcfarlandpub.com

To my wife Janet.
She has always been there for me unconditionally.
I owe her a debt of gratitude I can never repay,
and I love her more than she will ever know.

ACKNOWLEDGMENTS

Pete Palmer (who wrote the foreword to this book) was a tremendous help in the execution of this study. He may not have agreed with my approach, my formulas, or my results, but he made himself available whenever I needed him. I bombarded him with hundreds of questions and requests for information, and he always responded in a timely manner. He answered my questions courteously, and he provided me with the information I requested. He is a credit to the human race and a valuable asset to the Society for American Baseball Research (SABR) and to the baseball world in general.

I would also like to thank Vic Wilson and Bill James for their correspondence, Steve Milman for the use of his research material, and Gene Tenace, Jay Sanford, John Outland, Linda Butt, Roy Hartnett, Sheila Hartnett Hornof, the Ivan "Pudge" Rodriguez Foundation, the New York Yankees, the Boston Red Sox, the Montreal Expos, the Texas Rangers, and the Cincinnati Reds Historical Library for photographs.

CONTENTS

FOREWORD

Bill McNeil, with his many years of experience as an observer and a writer, has tackled one of baseball's most difficult questions—who was the game's greatest catcher? Statistical methods have been developed that are reasonably accurate for batting and pitching, as well as, to some extent, fielding for infielders and outfielders, but catching is a puzzle. A catcher has to call a good game, know the hitters, distract the hitters, work the umpire, work with his pitchers, keep the defense alert, not let pitches get by him, back up first base, catch pop-ups, field bunts, keep runners close to their bases, and then throw them out if they try to steal. He has to crouch down on every pitch, rifle the ball back to the pitcher maybe 10,000 times in a season, and then get up there and hit.

Bill has chronicled the changing role of catchers over the years, profiled all the best ones, reported the findings of others and then come up with his own technique for doing the job. Although his conclusions do not completely agree with my own research, I can't quarrel with the results. His methods are carefully thought out, as good as any and better than most.

He has presented a good mix of historical and biographical data, including some information on the evolution of the game itself, which should be interesting to any fan. *Backstop* is a serious study of a difficult subject. It will make a valuable addition to any baseball library.

Pete Palmer

A longtime chairman of SABR's Statistical Analysis Committee, Pete Palmer has been co-editor of The ESPN Baseball Encyclopedia *and several editions of* Total Baseball. *With John Thorn, he co-authored* The Hidden Game of Baseball.

Although a few debates turned violent, most of them were kept on a friendly note, with both sides putting forth their arguments as to why one player or another deserved (or didn't deserve) a place on the team. Surprisingly, the All-Star teams have remained relatively stable since the 1930s. Babe Ruth has remained a fixture in the outfield and is generally accompanied by Ted Williams and either Joe DiMaggio or Willie Mays. The infield usually consists of Lou Gehrig at first base, Rogers Hornsby at second, and Honus Wagner at shortstop. The third base position, which belonged to Pie Traynor for years, is now a tossup between Brooks Robinson and Mike Schmidt. Walter Johnson is still considered to be the top right-handed pitcher in baseball history, while Lefty Grove has been challenged by Sandy Koufax for the southpaw slot.

The All-Star catching position has seen the most changes over the years and seems to be awarded to the best catcher of the era. Since the 1970s, that has been Johnny Bench. The catcher on the first All-Star team was Buck Ewing, a member of the New York Giants and one of the 19th century's first superstars. Ewing sparkled at the plate and in the field. The early 20th-century All-Star teams normally included either Ray Schalk of the Chicago White Sox, who caught from 1912 to 1929, or Wally Schang, who caught for six teams between 1913 and 1931. All-Star teams of the 1920s and '30s recognized catchers like Gabby Hartnett, Mickey Cochrane and Bill Dickey. In the '50s and '60s it was Yogi Berra and Roy Campanella. And now it is Johnny Bench.

Television began to dominate the baseball scene during the last half of the 20th century, and the players suddenly became more than professional athletes. They became matinee idols. Bench, who entered the major leagues in 1967 was big, handsome, strong, and a shameless self-promoter. The new TV mentality infected all segments of society and changed baseball's All-Star teams from talent contests to popularity contests. For the most part, active players and recently retired players capture the votes of the electors at the expense of players of earlier eras. One glaring example is the recently constructed All-Century team, voted on by more than 1,000,000 fans, most of whom were under 35 years of age and had never seen any players who played before 1970. Baseball legends such as Christy Mathewson, Lefty Grove, and Stan Musial were ignored by the voters. Honus Wagner was out-polled by Ozzie Smith, Walter Johnson was beaten by Nolan Ryan, and Nap Lajoie finished behind Rod Carew. Johnny Bench was voted as the top catcher with Yogi Berra as his backup. Bench was the only world-class catcher most fans ever saw play, while Berra was a major celebrity and popular author.

In the few cases where All-Star teams were selected statistically, only offensive measurements were used. But offense tells only half the story. Defense is as important as offense in measuring a player's overall skills. To date, there has never been a study that combines a player's offensive statistics with his defensive statistics to arrive at a measurement of his overall ability. A player's skills in the field are vitally important to the success of his team, and in the case of the catcher, his defensive contributions may be as important as his offensive contributions. It is extremely difficult to evaluate any position on a baseball team both offensively and defensively, but catching is probably the most difficult position to evaluate at the present due to a lack of defensive statistics available for the position. Sabermetrics, the mathematical and statistical analysis of baseball records made popular by Pete Palmer and Bill James, provides many sophisticated formulas for measuring the offensive contributions of major league players as well as formulas for measuring the defensive contributions of position players, but as yet, there are no satisfactory formulas for measuring the defensive skills of catchers because of the unique problems associated with the position.

Since the catching position seemed to be the most contentious position on All-Star teams, and since no scientific study had ever been conducted to identify baseball's greatest all-around catcher by combining a player's offensive statistics with his defensive statistics, this study was undertaken to correct that oversight. First, a set of offensive statistical formulas were devised, which were individually adjusted for both era and park factors so that all players would be measured on the same basis. The statistics, which fall under the definition of Sabermetrics, included an adjusted on-base percentage, an adjusted slugging percentage, sacrifice hits, stolen bases, and double plays grounded into. Next a set of practical statistical formulas were developed to measure a catcher's defensive contributions to his team, including his adjusted fielding average, passed balls, adjusted caught-stealing percentage, adjusted wild pitches, and adjusted assists other than caught-stealing assists. Finally, each player's offensive rating and defensive rating were combined to arrive at a final rating that would recognize baseball's greatest all-around catcher.

There have been many great catchers over the years. Fourteen of them reside in the Baseball Hall of Fame in Cooperstown, New York. Some catchers have been defensive magicians, some have been offensive powerhouses, and some have combined both skills in equal amounts. This study compared the top 50 catchers ever to play the game, and in addition to identifying baseball's greatest all-around catcher, it also identified the number one offensive catcher and the game's best defensive catcher. The selections will no doubt create lively discussions among baseball fans as each fan tries to justify his man's claim to the title. It is hoped that this study will also lead to a more sophisticated evaluation system developed by the game's foremost historians and statisticians to improve the evaluation of the best all-around catchers in baseball.

Johnny Bench once said, "I can throw out any runner alive." Joe McCarthy claimed that Gabby Hartnett was the perfect catcher. Ty Cobb said Roy Campanella was the best catcher. Paul Richards thought Mickey Cochrane was number one. Similar comments have been made about Yogi Berra, Bill Dickey, and Mike Piazza. But only one man can be number one. And his identity will be revealed in the following pages.

Part I

◆ ◆ ◆

Meet the Candidates

♦ 1 ♦

THE CATCHER—
BASEBALL'S QUARTERBACK

A baseball team consists of nine men, all with one objective in mind: to beat the other team. The pitcher is one of the most important players on the team, because without superior pitching, a team cannot win. The Boston Red Sox of 1933 to 2003 are a perfect example of that theory. They have continually stocked their lineup with powerful hitters from Ted Williams and Bobby Doerr to Manny Ramirez, yet they usually fall to the pitching-rich New York Yankees, who showcase names like Allie Reynolds, Ron Guidry, and Roger Clemens. Connie Mack, "The Grand Old Man of Baseball" was correct when he noted more than 80 years ago, "Pitching is 80 percent of the game."

John B. Foster, however, in his 1921 book *How to Catch*, suggested the catcher was the most important man on the field. "There is one fact that makes the catcher's position stand out conspicuously. He has no assistance. He is the guardian of home plate, the sole fielder in his territory, the receiver of the pitcher's severe delivery, and, as he faces the field, the watchman for all of his team. He can see the incidents of the game to better advantage than the basemen and the outfielders. The catcher is the brain center of the team. From his position behind the plate he has a clear view of all the infielders and outfielders and knows if they are in the correct position or not. He also carefully observes every batter to learn their weaknesses, and he confidently handles the pitching staff, making every pitcher feel he is in control of the game.... The good catcher keeps the batter off balance at all times, keeps him guessing as to what pitch will come next. This is one of the catcher's most important responsibilities." The catcher not only decides what pitch should be thrown, but also decides on the location of the pitch. In addition to that, he positions his infielders depending on the individual batter and the pitching sequence to be used, and he calls for pitchouts and pickoff plays at strategic times to keep the other team off balance. He is involved in every pitch during the game.

He is also responsible for all the defensive plays around the plate, including fielding bunts or topped hits, catching pop flies or foul balls, backing up first base on ground balls to the infield, backing up third base on outfield plays, throwing out prospective base stealers, and blocking the plate to prevent a runner from scoring. "Two physical attributes needed by a catcher," according to Foster, "are a strong arm and a quick release. He must be a good thrower, one who can get the ball to the bases in the quickest time, with the least effort and the lowest altitude from the ground. Almost all good catchers are snap throwers. They do not use a high, round-arm, overhand motion. When there is a runner on base, it is the catcher's responsibility to watch him closely, and if he believes the runner is about to try to steal, he can signal the pitcher to throw the ball well out, and knowing that the batter cannot reach it to hit it, has a fair chance to trap the runner."

Two of baseball's legendary catchers, Mickey Cochrane and Gabby Hartnett, authored a book, titled *How to Catch*, in 1941. Their instructions mirrored Foster's, with a few exceptions. From a physical standpoint, the two veterans said, "Since a catcher must receive pitches of all descriptions, high, low, inside, and wide, during a game, he should possess a sizable physique ... that will enable him to handle them all. It is true that several of the greatest backstops in history were comparatively small men. However, [size] is a decided asset to the young player who desires to make catching a career. It is also important that a catcher have a good throwing arm and rather large hands. He is always a threat to hostile base runners if he can throw to bases with speed and accuracy. He must have perfect coordination of his hands, arms, feet and body and be physically equipped with plenty of endurance."

From a playing standpoint, the catcher's "heart must be in the game, his mind must function constantly, and he must hustle.... The experienced catcher has stored away in his mind a vast fund of information covering the strong points and the weaknesses of each hitter who steps to the plate.... Experience proves every good hitter has a favorite type of pitch, which he hits most effectively. 'Wait for the good pitch' is the sound philosophy of these good hitters. Make these hitters hit YOUR best pitch.... Catchers should always shift quickly to catch or block pitches that are wide of the plate. In shifting, merely step sideward to right or left in relation to the pitch. They should not try to catch wide balls by merely reaching for the ball alone. Go out after the ball.... On balls hit to the infield, it is a good practice to go down to first with the runner unless there are runners on second or third base. This gives you an opportunity to back up the first baseman on all plays, recover balls that are missed and overthrows of the base....

"The catching position is the most physically demanding position on the team, in addition to being the nerve center of the team's defense. The catcher has to squat down behind the batter more than 150 times a game, causing severe wear and tear on his knees, yet he must always be ready to engage in bone-breaking collisions at the plate as runners trying to score attempt to knock the ball loose from his hands. He is prone to broken fingers from pitched balls as well as other assorted bumps, bruises, and cuts to his body from pitches and wayward bats. The injuries a catcher suffers are such that it is rare if a catcher plays in every game during the season. More often than not, he will miss 30 or 40 games due to injury, or fatigue.

"The catcher is also the team psychologist, able to discern subtle changes in a pitcher's demeanor or approach to the game. If a pitcher gets angry, loses confidence, or appears to be tiring, the catcher must be ready to act. And each pitcher has to be handled differently to get the most out of him. Some pitchers need to be coddled, some flattered, some cajoled, and some need to be verbally challenged. The catcher must know which pitchers respond to which tactic."

The best catchers are also experts at distracting the batter from the job at hand. They keep up a steady stream of chatter, inquiring about the batter's family or how he likes his new team. Roy Campanella was particularly playful behind the plate, one time pouring dirt in Willie Mays's shoes and another time making Stan Musial hold his awkward corkscrew batting stance for several minutes before giving his pitcher the sign. Gabby Hartnett was so chatty and friendly that many a batter was busy listening to his remarks when the third strike crossed the plate. Branch Rickey told a story of an at-bat he had while playing for the St. Louis Browns. "When I came to bat in the second inning, Ossie Schreckengost, the famous catcher for the Philadelphia Athletics, spoke kindly to me, calling me by my first name. 'When did you get back, Branch?' I was pleased with the old catcher's inquiry, and I said, 'Just this morning, Ossie.' The call was two and two when he said to me, 'You have been to see your mother, haven't you?' I said 'Yes, I have,' but I didn't turn toward him. Then he said, 'How is she, Branch?' I turned to look at the old fellow squatting so low behind me and I said, 'She is better, thank you.' When I looked up, Chief Bender had started his pitch. I froze and took the strike dead through the middle. 'Ha ha!' said Schreck. You could have heard him in the outfield. 'Ha ha! I struck you out.'" Rickey was a catcher himself, but not one of the better catchers. In fact, in one game in 1907 he allowed 13 stolen bases, a major league record.

"The first qualification of a major league catcher," according to Rickey, "is a strong throwing arm — strong enough to throw to second base" without excessive movement of either the arm or the body. Roy Campanella could rifle the ball to any base without getting out of his crouch. His snap throw, starting just behind his ear, was short, quick, accurate, and powerful. Rickey continued, "Body checking should be the habitual practice of every catcher.... The catcher seldom has an excuse for the low-pitched fast ball getting by him.... A passed ball catcher is not a catcher.... A catcher must be nimble with cat-like reflexes to pounce on a bunt, spin after a pop fly, or dive for the tag after an errant throw to the plate.... Most of all, the catcher needs strength and stamina to block the plate from runners coming in to score.... Another very necessary quality of a good catcher is the ability to back up plays. On balls hit to the infield, where the batsman is obviously out at first base, the catcher must extend himself. His running speed becomes important. It's a great asset if he is fast enough to retrieve a wild throw even as far as the near-right-field foul territory.... The catcher is in position to be the field general. He sees exactly where seven men are standing and he should be the master defensive tactician of the game.... A great catcher like Campanella or Cochrane or Delancey or Kling or Dickey practically runs the game."

Organized baseball has been played for more than 160 years, and for the first 20 to 25 years, the catcher stood a good eight to 10 feet behind the batter and caught the ball on a bounce. Later he moved closer to the plate, but because he had no protective equipment to cover his face or his body, he was considered to be somewhat lacking in common sense. A popular poem of the day, penned by George Ellard, the organizer of the original Cincinnati Red Stockings, defended the courage of the catcher.

> We used no mattress on our hands
> No cage upon our face.
> We stood right up and caught the ball
> With courage and with grace.

James "Deacon" White was the first major league catcher to play directly behind the plate. As a member of the Boston Red Stockings of the old National Association in 1875, the husky White challenged the practice of the day by crouching within two feet of the batter. However, he might not have been as foolhardy as first thought, because he soon changed positions and played most of his career as a third baseman. White went on to have a fine major league career, playing 15 years and batting .303. Gradually other catchers moved in close to the plate when runners were on base, in order to prevent stolen bases. Jonathan F. Light, in his book *The Cultural Encyclopedia of Baseball,* cited a newspaper account of 1860s catcher Nat Hicks of the New York Mutuals, when he began playing close behind the batter. "Player after player went down before his unfaltering nerve, and although struck four times during the game — once squarely on the mouth by the ball, and once on the chest and twice with the bat — he could not be driven away from his position." Before that, catchers played farther back to catch the ball on one bounce, which could be recorded as an out on a foul tip." The courageous Hicks lasted only two years in the National League, catching a total of 53 games while hitting a barely visible .227.

Light also reported on another dangerous facet of the catching game. "Nineteenth-century catcher Silver Flint once was in a train wreck. When a physician saw his mangled fingers after the accident, he started to splint them until Flint supposedly told him that they got that way from catching for the Chicago White Sox." As one 19th-century wag said, "Shaking hands with a catcher is like shaking hands with a bag of peanuts."

The need for protective equipment for the catcher was obvious, and over a period of 30 years, catcher's mitts, chest protectors, shin guards, and catcher's masks were invented to keep the catcher from bodily injury. The first catcher's mask was invented by Fred Thayer of Harvard University in 1876 and worn by teammate Jim Tyng. It was a modified fencing mask and often caused as many injuries as it prevented. Prior to the facemask, a catcher only had a rubber mouth guard to protect his teeth. In 1884, a sheepskin chest protector was developed by Keystone of Philadelphia catcher Jack Clements. It was originally worn under the uniform shirt by players who were embarrassed to be seen wearing any protective device. Clements was a unique individual in his own way. He was one of the few left-handed catchers ever to play major league baseball, and his career lasted 17 years, including 1073 games caught.

Fielders' gloves came into use in the 1880s, but it wasn't until the 1890s that they were generally accepted. At first, it was considered unmanly to wear a glove. A.J. Spalding patented the first catcher's mitt in 1891. Shin guards were introduced into major league baseball in 1906 by Philadelphia Phillies catcher Red Dooin, who wore them underneath his uniform to escape the ridicule of the fans. Roger Bresnahan of the New York Giants was the first player to wear them outside his uniform, in 1907, and according to Couzens, he was almost laughed off the field by the fans.

Once catcher's masks, mitts, and chest and shin guards were made part of a catcher's repertoire, his game improved significantly. As Foster noted, "Catchers should stand as close to the batter as possible for several reasons: to catch a curve ball as soon as it breaks to prevent passed balls or wild pitches, to improve his chances of catching a foul tip, and to give the pitcher a better target to shoot for." Most of Foster's tips on catching are still valid, with one exception. The catcher's mitt used in 1921 was a rigid, overstuffed glove that made it difficult to catch a pitched ball. The catcher could not close the glove to trap the ball as he does today. He had to keep his bare hand positioned next to the glove so he could cover the ball as soon as it hit the glove, to prevent it from popping out. This practice resulted in frequent broken fingers and bruised knuckles if the catcher moved his bare hand to the glove too soon. Catchers also suffered badly swollen hands from catching fastballs day after day. Many of those injuries became permanent. Today, with the big, soft gloves, catchers trap the ball in the area between the thumb and the index finger so the ball never comes in contact with the hand itself.

Protective equipment was only partially successful in preventing injuries, as catchers even today suffer painfully broken fingers from foul tips, as well as an assortment of other injuries resulting from collisions and other accidents. Wes Westrum suffered ten broken fingers during his career, not an unusual number, and as he recalled, you played with broken fingers rather than turn the job over to some ambitious young hotshot in the minors waiting for his opportunity. Roy Campanella suffered many painful injuries over his career, including a chipped bone in the heel of his left hand and a damaged nerve in 1954. The injuries seriously affected his batting average, which plummeted to .207, but he still controlled the game and gunned down 58 percent of the runners who dared challenge his arm. Johnny Bench suffered through a series of painful injuries to his feet, his hands, his elbow, his knees, and his shoulder. He was eventually moved to third base so as to keep his big bat in the lineup. Los Angeles Dodgers catcher John Roseboro suffered a gash on his head in 1965 when San Francisco Giant batter Juan Marichal clubbed him with a bat after Marichal thought the Dodger catcher's return throws were too close to him. Steve Yeager was struck in the throat by a splintered bat, which barely missed an artery, in 1976. Yeager subsequently invented a throat guard to be attached to the bottom of the facemask. And Ray Fosse, the catcher for the Oakland Athletics, may have had his career shortened by a collision at home plate during the 1970 All-Star game. Fosse suffered a fractured shoulder when Pete Rose barreled into him in the 12th inning while scoring the winning run in a 5–4 National League victory. The 6'2", 215-pound Fosse never again showed the batting skills or power he had before the accident.

The first National League baseball game was played at the Jefferson Street Grounds in Philadelphia on April 22, 1876, between the Philadelphia

Athletics and the Boston Red Caps. The Red Caps won the game 6–5. Over the next quarter of a century, Major League Baseball produced many great players, including catchers Mike "King" Kelly and Buck Ewing. The two superstars were big men, standing 5'10" tall and weighing a hefty 190 pounds in an era when the average major league player stood about 5'7" tall and weighed 150 pounds soaking wet.

Like many of the players of their day, Kelly and Ewing played every position on the team. Both players were considered catchers, although Kelly played more games in the outfield than he did behind the plate. King Kelly was the

King Kelly was the most colorful baseball player of the 19th century.

flashier of the two. He was primarily an offensive player who led the league in doubles and runs scored three times each and batting once. And he was a daring base runner who once stole 84 bases in 116 games. He averaged more than 60 stolen bases and 127 runs scored for every 550 at-bats. When he retired in 1893, he left behind a career batting average of .307. His counterpart, Buck Ewing of New York Giants fame, was a better all-around player. He was also a renowned slugger who averaged 25 doubles, 18 triples, and seven home runs for every 550 at-bats, to go along with a .303 batting average. And he averaged 34 stolen bases with 113 runs scored. He was outstanding on defense as well, leading the league in assists three times and in double plays twice. All in all, Buck Ewing was the prototype catcher of the 19th century and usually the catcher on the all-time All-Star teams selected during the dead-ball era.

When the 20th century got under way, the philosophy of the baseball owners changed. Where big, powerful sluggers dominated the game during the 1880s and '90s, the owners now considered them to be defensive liabilities and began to staff their rosters with smaller, faster, more defensive players. This strategy carried over to the catching position, where the top players of the era included Ray Schalk and Johnny Kling, both of whom stood 5'9" and weighed in the neighborhood of 160 pounds. The speedy Schalk was the first catcher to back up first base on balls hit to the infield. The defensive moves gradually began to pay dividends. Stolen bases, which reached a high of 259 stolen bases per team in 1894, had dropped to 120 per team in the American League by 1918, and two years later, the National League average settled in at 121 stolen bases for every 154 games. A sign of the times occurred in 1914 when Les Nunamaker of the Yankees threw out three Indians attempting to steal in one inning. In fact, of the more than 3000 runners who challenged the arms of American League catchers that year, 45 percent of them were tossed out. And in 1916, Ray Schalk, the top gun of major league catchers, nabbed 51 percent of the 231 prospective base stealers who dared challenge his arm. These statistics should be kept in mind when reviewing the embarrassingly low caught-stealing records of today's catchers, who claim their poor performance is the result of the large number of runners attempting to steal today as compared to 50 or 60 years ago. The history of the game disproves that claim. It shows that a catcher's caught-stealing percentage does

Ray Schalk may have been the greatest defensive catcher in baseball history.

not depend entirely on the number of runners who test his arm. It also depends on a catcher's skill at throwing the ball. Ivan Rodriguez, for instance, has thrown out almost 50 percent of the runners attempting to steal, about 20 points higher than the league average.

In 1920, baseball owners, who noticed the electrifying effect Babe Ruth's home runs had on the paying public, juiced up the ball and sat gleefully back and watched the fans pour through the turnstiles to watch home runs leaving the yard at a record pace. In 1919, the 16 major league teams averaged 28 home runs a year. In 1920, the average had jumped up to 39 home runs per team, and by 1930 it had reached 98 home runs per team per year. As the offense became more oriented toward long-ball, the stolen base trailed off somewhat, but still remained a potent weapon, with such fleet-footed runners as Ty Cobb, Max Carey, Ben Chapman, and Frankie "The Fordham Flash" Frisch burning up the basepaths.

The general feeling in baseball, even into the 1920s, was that hitting varied significantly with the position played and that catchers were not expected to contribute very much offensively. F.C. Lane, in his book *Batting*, published in 1925, quoted Hugh Jennings, who said, "Outfielders must hit and so must first basemen. Their positions are not so difficult in a fielding sense and give them opportunity to develop their batting eye…. You can forgive a catcher for not hitting because he has so much else on his mind." Catcher Bill Fischer seconded that opinion. "The pitcher and catcher are mostly pretty useless with the willow."

But that situation changed dramatically during the 1920s, thanks to a new breed of catchers led by Gabby Hartnett, Mickey Cochrane, and Bill Dickey. With the advent of the long ball, catchers were expected to contribute offensively as well as defensively. The first of the great all-around catchers entered the scene in 1922. Charles Leo "Gabby" Hartnett arrived in the Chicago Cubs' spring training camp on Catalina Island, California, fresh out of Class A ball in Worcester, Massachusetts, and proceeded to set the league on its heels with a combination of a powerful throwing arm and a mighty bat. He was soon recognized as the greatest all-around catcher ever to play the game. And he was just the first of the world-class catchers to play the game. He was followed by Mickey Cochrane of the Philadelphia Athletics in 1925, Bill Dickey of the New York Yankees in 1928, and Ernie Lombardi of the Brooklyn Dodgers in 1931. Lombardi was traded to the Cincinnati Reds a year later, where he became a legend.

The catchers of the early days, even after the introduction of the lively ball, still took pride in their defensive skills. Several of them, in fact, put on demonstrations of catching baseballs dropped from great heights. Pop Schriver of the Chicago Cubs caught a ball dropped from the top of the Washington Monument in 1894, and Gabby Street of the Washington Senators duplicated the feat in 1908. Baltimore Orioles catcher Wilbert Robinson, during his managerial days with the Brooklyn Dodgers, accepted a challenge thrown at him by his players to catch a ball dropped from a low-flying plane during spring training in Florida. Unfortunately for Robinson, one of the players was the fun-loving Casey Stengel, and Casey quietly substituted a ripe grapefruit for the baseball. On the appointed day, a large crowd of people gathered on the beach, and Uncle Robby positioned himself in the sand, ready for the historic feat. The plane, flown by aviatrix Ruth Law, descended to a height of 400 feet and dropped the object toward the waiting catcher. The grapefruit broke through Robinson's glove and exploded against his chest, sending him hurtling to the ground, oozing grapefruit juice. Thinking he had been fatally injured, he began to scream, "My God, I've exploded. The damn thing has blown me apart. Help me! I'm dead." Robinson lay on his back whimpering for several seconds, then slowly opened his eyes and looked up at the sea of smiling faces looking down at him. The wide grins told Uncle Robby he had been had.

Other great catchers came along over the decades. Lawrence "Yogi" Berra, a stocky, clumsy outfielder who was equally clumsy behind the plate, was taught the fine points of the position by Dickey and evolved into one of the all-time greats. In addition to his defensive strengths, Berra might have been the game's greatest bad-ball hitter and one of its most dangerous clutch hitters. Roy Campanella followed Berra to the majors, debuting with the Brooklyn Dodgers in 1948. Unlike Berra, the 26-year-old Campanella had been a professional baseball catcher for more than ten years, including nine years in the highly rated Negro leagues. He was agile and graceful and possessed one of the strongest throwing arms in major league history, which, combined with a quick snap throw, made him the most feared catcher ever to play the game. Johnny Bench, another all-around backstop, joined the Cincinnati Reds in 1967 and went on to win the National League Rookie of the Year honors the following year, followed by two MVP Awards. As the millennium came to a close, catchers were being selected primarily for their hitting prowess, with long-ball hitting a top priority. Defense was a secondary consideration. There are three active catchers who are earning a well-deserved reputation for their backstopping talents. Charles Johnson is recognized for having one of the strongest throwing arms in the major leagues as well as for carrying a powerful bat. Ivan "Pudge" Rodriguez is a polished all-around receiver, a perennial .300 hitter with good power, who has the highest caught-stealing percentage of any catcher since Campanella and Berra. Mike Piazza has some defensive shortcomings, particularly in throwing out prospective base stealers, but he has no equal with a bat in his hand. In fact, he is already being recognized as the greatest hitting catcher in baseball history, combining a .311 batting average with 35 home runs a year.

Over the years, sportswriters, managers, players, coaches, and fans, have all taken a crack at selecting their all-time All-Star team. The practice began shortly after professional baseball was introduced and has continued to the present day. The 1930 All-Star squad consisted of Lou Gehrig on first base, Rogers Hornsby at second, Honus Wagner at shortstop, Pie Traynor at third, and Babe Ruth, Tris Speaker, and Ty Cobb in the outfield. Eventually Cobb was replaced by Ted Williams on many teams, and the

LARRY BERRA

Yogi Berra directed the New York Yankees to 14 American League titles.

center field spot was filled by either Joe DiMaggio or Willie Mays. Lou Gehrig still has a firm hold on first base, Rogers Hornsby remains the top second baseman, and Honus Wagner has no equal at short. In the 1970s, Traynor was replaced by Brooks Robinson, who has been challenged by Mike Schmidt over the past decade. Walter Johnson is still considered to be the greatest right-handed pitcher ever to play the game, and the south-paw slot is a close call between Lefty Grove and Sandy Koufax.

The most contentious position on the team is catcher, where no less than eight catchers were voted to the position over the past 100 years. The whim of the voting public changes with the times and normally favors the most recent candidate. In the early days, around the turn of the century, Buck Ewing was the catcher on most All-Star teams. Between 1915 and 1925, the popular choice was Ray Schalk. In the 1930s Gabby Hartnett, Mickey Cochrane, and Bill Dickey filled the bill. Yogi Berra and Roy Campanella captured the top spot during the '50s and '60 s, and they were succeeded by Johnny Bench. During the last half of the 20th century, the voting mentality took another turn when television changed major league

Johnny Bench was the anchor of the Big Red Machine of the 1970s. *Courtesy Cincinatti Reds Historical Library.*

baseball players from athletes into celebrities. And that situation was reflected in the final selections for the All-Star teams, which became more of a popularity contest than a measure of a player's skill. Most voters today seem to vote on a player's reputation rather than on his achievements.

Gerald Couzens, in his book *A Baseball Album*, presented an all-time All-Star team that was selected by baseball fans, writers, and sportscasters, for the major league baseball offices. The finalists for catcher were Bill Dickey, Mickey Cochrane, and Roy Campanella, with Cochrane receiving the most votes. By 1997, the old guard had changed, and new blood was selecting All-Star teams. The Baseball Writers Association of America made their choices for the "best ever" and selected Bench as the catcher, followed by Berra and Campanella. Neither Dickey nor Cochrane were anywhere to be seen. Probably fewer than 10 percent of the writers had ever seen Berra or Campanella in action and not more than two or three percent had ever seen Dickey or Cochrane.

In 1999, major league baseball was at it again. This time, they balloted fans only, to select an All-Century team. Needless to say, anyone who played prior to 1960–1970 was a forgotten asset, unless they happened to be from a high-profile population center like New York City. Johnny

Bench, TV's darling, was elected to the catching position, followed by another famous celebrity, Yogi Berra, who had many folksy books, TV appearances, and commercials to his credit. Some indication of the validity of the All-Century team can be seen in the selections. Baseball legends such as Christy Mathewson, Lefty Grove, Stan Musial, Honus Wagner, and Warren Spahn were ignored by the voters. They had to be added to the team by a hastily convened special committee, to try to give the poll some credibility.

Johnny Bench seems to be the catcher of choice for All-Star team balloting in recent years, supplanting Berra, Campanella, Dickey, and Cochrane. The reasons for Bench's success are many and varied. To begin with, he was the first catcher to usher in the television era, so he was seen by more people than any catcher in baseball history. And he was a notorious self-promoter, flashy, friendly, and always ready to tell a reporter or a TV interviewer how great he was. The Oklahoma native often boasted that he could throw out any runner alive and once said when people talk about great catchers, they start with him. In addition, he was also the recipient of ten consecutive Gold Gloves for defensive excellence, which guaranteed his place as baseball's greatest defensive catcher. But it was all sound and fury, signifying nothing, as will be discussed in the chapter on the best defensive catchers. The Gold Glove Award is, like the selection of an All-Star team, primarily a popularity contest, voted on casually by managers and coaches who are more concerned with the pennant race than they are in voting for the best defensive players in their league. One baseball historian noted that once a player won a Gold Glove, it was easy for him to win another, and before long it would become a habit. The same players are selected year after year. The 2000 American League award for the shortstop position was given to Alex Rodriguez, which raised eyebrows around the baseball world. Rodriguez was probably the greatest all-around shortstop in the American League, but he was not considered to be in the same class defensively as Omar Vizquel, who committed only seven errors all year. Rodriguez's powerful offense (41 homers, 132 RBIs and .316 batting average) may have been the deciding factor in his winning the supposedly defensive award.

Occasionally an All-Star team was selected statistically by a baseball magazine, but in those cases, only offensive statistics were used to compare the players. What was his batting average? How many runs did he score? How many did he bat in? How many home runs did he hit? How many bases did he steal? Those questions are all valid, but so are questions regarding a player's range, his throwing arm, his fielding average, and his ability to throw out a base runner. Unfortunately, a player's defense has never been taken into consideration, except for a few unsubstantiated general comments.

In recent years, Pete Palmer has introduced to the American baseball public a new statistical system called a "linear weights" measurement, where he compares every event in a game in terms of runs. The system became the anchor of a new mathematical system called Sabermetrics, a revolutionary device for comparing both the offensive and defensive skills of position players as well as pitchers. It has been used extensively in recent years to rate one player against another, but as yet, it cannot be used to rate catchers because of the dearth of valid statistics about the position. A catcher's defense cannot be easily measured because it has been obscured by such things as a spiraling strikeout rate, as well as changes in the field dimensions that have reduced a catcher's ability to catch foul balls. Also, one of the catcher's most important skills, his ability to throw out prospective base stealers, has never been compiled. In recent years, thanks to Pete Palmer, and a host of other energetic researchers, these data are beginning to surface.

This book is the first to study catchers statistically, both offensively and defensively. The top catchers in baseball history were screened to arrive at a group of 50 candidates who appeared to be the most dominating players at their position. Some potential candidates could not be included in the study because they played in the dead-ball era, and their statistics, particularly their defensive statistics, could not confidently be measured and converted to the same basis as the modern catchers. There were other great catchers who could not be included in the study because they played out their careers in other leagues, such as the Japanese Leagues and the Negro Leagues.

In succeeding chapters, the greatest catchers ever to play the game will be profiled up close and personal, covering their on-field achievements as well as their off-field lives. The latest technological advances in baseball statistics will be reviewed, and their applicability to this study of the game's greatest catchers will be determined. The most appropriate offensive and defensive formulas for comparing one catcher with another will be selected, and those statistics will be presented and tabulated. The study will identify the best offensive catcher in major league history as well as the best defensive catcher. And finally it will celebrate the greatest all-around catcher ever to play the game.

♦ 2 ♦

GREAT CATCHERS WHO ARE OUT OF THE LOOP

During the dawn of baseball in the nineteenth century, players had to be more versatile than players today. Rosters were smaller and players had to fill in for their teammates in case of injury or some other emergency. Most catchers played behind the plate less than half the time, moving to another position in case of an injury, either to themselves or to another player. Such was the case with great receivers like Buck Ewing, who caught in 48 percent of the games in which he played, and King Kelly, who caught just 40 percent of his games. Catchers were particularly vulnerable in the 1800s, since they didn't have adequate protection for their hands, their faces, or their bodies. And since most of them were in the lineup for their defense, they periodically sat out games to rest and to nurse their wounds. But those few catchers who like Ewing and Kelly, were great hitters in addition to being outstanding defensive players, "rested" by playing in the outfield or at first base.

Deacon White was just one of the dozens of outstanding catchers who should be recognized for their skills behind the plate, but who cannot be included in this search for baseball's greatest all-around catcher, for various reasons. White, like Ewing, Schalk, and others of their time, played baseball during the dead-ball era, and their statistics, particularly their defensive statistics, cannot be judged on same basis as the modern catchers. Other great catchers played their entire careers outside the umbrella of organized American baseball, in the Japanese leagues and the Negro Leagues, and their statistics also cannot be compared to modern major league catchers. And although the likes of Josh Gibson, Katsuya Nomura, King Kelly, and Ray Schalk cannot be included in this study, their achievements should be recognized.

Charlie Bennett of the Detroit Wolverines was the best catcher of his era. The 5'11", 180-pound backstop came out of New Castle, Pennsylvania, to star for the great Wolverine teams of the 1880s. Playing alongside future Hall of Famers Dan Brouthers and Sam Thompson, Bennett was the acknowledged field leader of the team. He was behind the plate on June 12, 1883, when J. Lee Richmond tossed the first perfect game in major league history, defeating the Cleveland Blues 1–0. As reported by John R. Husman in SABR's *Nineteenth-Century Stars*, Richmond said years later that Bennett was "the best backstop that ever lived. He went after everything, he knew no fear and he kept his pitcher from going into the air." *The Sporting News* noted, "He has not a whole or straight finger in the lot. Every joint is swollen or misshapen."

The Detroit Wolverines captured the National League pennant in 1887 and went on to beat the St. Louis Brown Stockings of the American Association, 10 games to five, in a 10-city traveling World Series. Bennett handled the receiving chores in eleven of the games, taking flawlessly the slants of Lady Baldwin, Pete Conway, and Charlie Getzien. He also hit a respectable .262 and scored six runs. His career ended in tragedy when, during a hunting trip to Kansas in the winter of 1894, he tried to catch a moving train, missed the step, and fell underneath the train, severing both legs. Over the course of a notable fifteen-year career, Charlie Bennett was behind the plate in 90 percent of the games he played, caching 954 games, batting .256. He also led the league in fielding percentage seven times, tied with Gabby Hartnett for the most years leading the league in fielding.

A contemporary of Bennetts arrived in the major leagues in 1885 and carved out a memorable career for himself behind the plate. His name was James "Deacon" McGuire, and he crouched behind the plate for the first time in 1884 with the Toledo Blue Stockings of the American Association. Interestingly, he shared catching duties with Fleetwood Walker, generally recognized as the first black player to play in the major leagues. While Walker was limited to one season in the big time because of his color, McGuire went on to establish a major league record for catchers, playing 26 years. During that time he played for no fewer than twelve teams, demonstrating his durability by playing in more than 100 games in a season five times, at a time when the season was only 130 games. In 1895 he caught every inning of every game. He still holds the major league record for assists by a catcher with 1859. His long service behind the plate was evident in his gnarled fingers, every one of which had been broken at one time or another.

Although the 6'1", 185-pound McGuire was recognized as a defensive specialist, he also carried a potent bat, accumulating 1729 base hits, including 398 for extra bases, while hitting .278. He batted over .300 six times during his career, which witnessed some of the more significant changes in the game of baseball and in the protective equipment worn by the catcher. He played when pitchers were allowed to throw overhand for the first time, when the distance from the pitcher's mound to the plate was extended from 55 feet to 60 feet, six inches, in 1893, and when catchers first wore a chest protector, a catcher's mitt, and shin guards. Father Time caught up with the venerable catcher in 1906, when he was 42. But he was pressed into service four more times over the next six years, donning the pads for the last time in 1912. He was 48. Like Bennett, Deacon McGuire caught in 90 percent of the 1781 games in which he played. He was the first catcher to catch more than 1000 games in a career, and his 1611 games behind the plate were the major league record until it was broken by Ray Schalk in 1926.

During this same period, baseball's first superstar emerged from the sandlots of Paterson, N.J., to star for the Chicago White Stockings and Boston Beaneaters. Michael Joseph "King" Kelly was born in Troy, N.Y. on December 31, 1857, but grew to manhood in the Garden State before moving to Ohio to play for the Buckeyes in the International Association in 1877. A year later, he joined the Cincinnati Red Stockings, where he played for two years before joining Cap Anson's Chicago team. Kelly rose to stardom in the Windy City, sparking his team to five National League titles an one world championship in seven years. He also played on pennant-winning teams of the Boston Red Stockings in the Players League in 1890 and the Beaneaters in 1891.

The tall, rugged, mustachioed Irishman cut a handsome figure on a ball field, and thrilled the fans with his exciting play, much as Jackie Robinson would do sixty years later. Like Robinson, King Kelly could play any position, and over the course of his career, he played them all at one time or another. He was an outstanding defensive player with a strong throwing arm that served him well whether he was playing the outfield, shortstop, or catcher. During his career he played 759 games in the outfield and 582 games behind the plate. He was the first catcher to use finger signals to communicate with his pitcher. He also had a quick mind that on one occasion forced a league rule change. Sitting on the bench during a game, he watched as a batter hit a foul pop-up out of the reach of his team's catcher. Leaping to his feet, he yelled, "Kelly now catching for Boston," and made the catch. The play was legal at the time, but was banned at the next league meeting.

King Kelly's greatest assets were his lightning-fast bat and his blazing speed. The 5'10½", 185-pound right-handed hitter was a consistent .300 batter, who led the league in batting twice, hitting .354 in 1884 and a sizzling .388 in 1886. He also showed the way in runs scored four times and averaged 0.93 runs per game over his career, the fourth highest mark in major league history, behind Hamilton, Gore, and Stovey. Kelly was most dangerous after he got on base, terrorizing the opposing pitcher with his electrifying speed and bringing the fans to their feet with the now famous chant of "Slide, Kelly, Slide." In the days when only one umpire officiated a game, Kelly routinely went from first to third on an infield grounder without bothering to touch second, while the umpire was watching the play at first. He would also race home from second base without passing third on hits to the outfield. He was the game's most exciting player and the greatest player of his era. As late as 1921, Al Spink, the legendary baseball writer, called him the greatest player that ever lived.

Off the field, the swashbuckling Kelly cut a handsome figure in his tailored suits, top hat and patent leather shoes. The King was larger than life, often partying from dusk to dawn in the bars of Chicago and Boston. He spent money like the proverbial drunken sailor, buying drinks for the house and consuming more than his share in the process. He was so beloved in Boston that the fans presented him with a horse and carriage so he could ride to the park in style. King Kelly retired from baseball in 1894 at the age of 36 and died of pneumonia in Boston the same year. Cap Anson, his manager for seven years, was quoted in *Baseball's Hall of Fame: Cooperstown* as saying that Kelly was "as great a hitter as anyone, and as great a thrower, both from the catcher's position and the field, more men being thrown out by him than any other man." The King was voted into the Hall of Fame in 1945.

William "Buck" Ewing was a contemporary of King Kelly and, like Kelly, one of the greatest players of the nineteenth century. Also like Kelly, he was a versatile player who played every position on the team at one time or another. The Ohio native broke into major league baseball with the Troy Trojans in 1880 at the age of 20. Three years later he joined the New York Gothams, where he became a legend. During the course of his 18-year career, Ewing played 636 games behind the plate, 253 games at first base, 235 in the outfield, 127 at third base, 51 at second, 34 at short, and nine on the mound. He was a jack of all trades and master of at least one — catching. He was generally recognized as the best catcher of his era. According to Gary Spoerle, he was the first player to crouch behind the plate and one of the first to keep a book on the weaknesses of opposing batters. He had a rifle for a throwing arm, and since he was one of the first catchers to throw from a crouch, he had extra valuable seconds to gun down the runner, yet according to his infielders, his throws were light and easy to handle. He was also adept at picking runners off base with his quick, accurate throws, and on some occasions he would fake a passed ball, then throw out the runner who tried to take advantage of it.

Buck Ewing took such a beating behind the plate that he was forced to play other positions occasionally and to watch from the bench when the injuries became too severe. He never caught more than 97 games in a season and only played in about two-thirds of his team's games. Still, he led the league in putouts once, assists three times, and double plays twice, during the 1880s. The injuries took their toll on Ewing's body over the years, and after 1990, he played primarily in the outfield or at first base.

Ewing was not a one-dimensional player, however. He was also one of the best power hitters of his generation. Over the course of his career, he hit over .300 eleven times, including nine years in a row, finishing with a career average of .303. He averaged 25 doubles, 18 triples, and seven home runs for every 550 at-bats. He led the league in triples in 1884 with 20, and his career average of 18 triples a year is one of the highest averages in baseball history, trailing only Joe Jackson's 19. His seven home runs were also high for the era and would convert to about 25 during the lively ball era, with a possibility of 45–50 homers as a high in any one year. Fittingly, Buck Ewing was one of the first players elected to the Baseball Hall of Fame by the Veterans Committee in 1939.

Another of the early-day Jacks-of-all-trades was Roger Bresnahan. The pugnacious Irishman was called the "Duke of Tralee" because he told everyone he was born in Ireland, although the records say he first saw the light of day in Toledo, Ohio. The stocky, 5'9", 180-pound firebrand began his professional career as a pitcher with Lima in the Ohio State League at the tender age of 16. One year later he was on the mound for the Washington Senators of the National League, where he racked up a perfect 4–0 record, but he was shipped back to the minors the next year after a contract dispute. When he returned to the big time as a member of the Baltimore Orioles, he was converted into a catcher by his manager, John McGraw. From that time to the end of his career he spent 68 percent of his playing time behind the plate, although he played every position on the team at least once. He was a fixture in center field for several years due to his speed.

When McGraw moved to the New York Giants in 1902, he took Bresnahan with him. The Duke of Tralee had his finest season with the bat in 1903. The fleet-footed catcher batted leadoff, hit a lusty .350, and stole 34 bases in 113 games, while directing his ace pitchers Joe McGinnity and Christy Mathewson to 31–20 and 30–13 records, respectively. In spite of the performances of those three players, the Giants still finished six and a half games behind the pennant-winning Pittsburgh Pirates. They came

Roger Bresnahan (left) was arguably the greatest all-around catcher of the early
20th century.

back the next year to capture the National League pennant, but they refused
to play the American League champion Boston Pilgrims in the World
Series. In 1905, they won it all, beating the Philadelphia Athletics four
games to one in the Fall Classic, with Bresnahan catching Christy Mathewson's three complete-game shutouts, and leading both teams at bat with
a .313 average, the only player to break the .300 mark.

   Over his 17-year career, Roger Bresnahan caught 974 games and batted .279, all the while battling opposing players and fans and taunting
umpires unmercifully. He was frequently ejected from games, suffering
numerous fines and suspensions for his behavior. The husky catcher was
the first player to wear a batting helmet on the field after suffering a bean-

ing in 1905, and was the first player to wear shin guards on a regular basis. The batting helmet idea didn't catch on for another half-century, but shin guards soon became a standard piece of equipment for catchers. Bresnahan was named to the Hall of Fame in 1945.

As the twentieth century began, major league club owners changed their emphasis from big sluggers to small, fast, defensive players. The era of "Big Dan" Brouthers, Sam Thompson, and Roger Connor was over. They were viewed as clumsy oafs who could hit home runs but were defensive liabilities. This change was probably brought about by the performance of the famed Baltimore Orioles, who were the dominant team of the 1890s, winning three pennants and finishing a close second twice with rabbits like John McGraw, Hughie Jennings, and "Wee Willie" Keeler. The Orioles beat their opponents with speed, defense, and aggressive base running. They popularized the Baltimore chop, an intentional chop hit that resulted in a high bouncer that the fast Oriole hitters usually beat out. They also utilized the sacrifice bunt, the hit-and-run, and the stolen base effectively, and they seldom beat themselves. Most catchers between 1900 and 1920 fit this mold.

Jimmy Archer was a catcher in the major leagues for twelve years between 1904 and 1918. For three of those years he was a teammate of Roger Bresnahan. Unlike Bresnahan, he was actually born in Ireland, and his family moved from Dublin to Toronto, Canada, when he was a child. The tall, slender Archer suffered a freak accident while working as a barrel maker in Toronto that left his right arm permanently bent, but stronger than a healthy arm. The injury reportedly gave Archer the strongest throwing arm in the major leagues. During his career he tossed out 645 would-be base thieves for a caught-stealing rate of 48 percent. He threw out 81 prospective base stealers in 1912, including 19 New York Giants in 22 games. Jimmy Archer was one of the first catchers to throw from a crouch, using a powerful snap throw that not only cut down base thieves, but also allowed him to pick runners off base at a rapid pace.

Another of the great catchers of the first two decades of the twentieth century was Johnny Kling of the Chicago Cubs. As noted by Milton J. Shapiro, "He was known as Mr. Brains of the old Chicago team, helping them to pennants in 1906, 1907, 1908, and 1910. Kling had an arm like a whip, in that department rating above Bresnahan. His handling of pitchers and overall field generalship were superb." The 5'9½", 160-pound backstop, known as "Noisy" because of his constant chatter behind the plate, enjoyed a 13-year career in the National League, catching 1168 games and batting a respectable .271 with 123 stolen bases.

Johnny Kling's defensive statistics include leading the league in putouts six times, fielding percentage four times, assists twice, and double plays once. He holds the National League record for the most consecutive seasons leading the league in fielding, with four, tied with Gabby Hartnett. The man from Kansas City cut down opposing runners trying to steal 48 percent of the time during the regular season, compared to a league average of 45 percent. He duplicated his percentage in 21 Series games, tossing out 19 of 40 runners. Chicago Cub pitchers certainly appreciated their catcher. Ed Reulbach said he was one of the greatest catchers who ever wore a mask, while Mordecai "Three-Finger" Brown said he couldn't remember Kling ever calling the wrong pitch.

The Boston Braves had a defensive magician of their own, a gangly redheaded receiver by the name of Hank Gowdy. The freckle-faced son of a railroad yard foreman from Columbus, Ohio, he stood 6'2" and tipped the scales at a light 182 pounds. As Al Hirshberg noted, "Shy, soft-spoken and awkward in street clothes, he was poetry in motion in a baseball uniform." And he had a rocket for an arm, tossing out an estimated 51 percent of all the runners who challenged him, one of the top four or five caught-stealing percentages in the history of major league baseball. From 1910 to 1930, Gowdy caught 897 games, batted a respectable .270, and led his team defensively.

He was a member of the "Miracle Braves" in 1914, the team that fought its way to the pennant by winning 34 of their last 44 games, climbing from last place on July 15 to first place on September 8. They left the New York Giants in their dust, racing to the National League pennant by a whopping 10½ games. Hank Gowdy sparked his team to a four-game sweep of Connie Mack's powerful Philadelphia Athletics, scorching the ball at a .545 clip, one of the highest World Series batting averages ever. His six base hits included three doubles, a triple and a home run. Gowdy played in two more World Series, with the New York Giants in 1923 and '24, and was the goat in the '24 affair. In the twelfth inning of Game 7, Gowdy tripped over his facemask while chasing a foul pop-up off the bat of Muddy Ruel. Ruel subsequently doubled and carried the championship run across the plate on a single by Earl McNeely.

Gowdy's career covered 17 major league seasons, with one year out for military service during World War I. He was the first major leaguer to enlist after the war began in 1917, and he saw action in France. He would later defend his country again in World War II. On the baseball field, the big catcher caught two no-hitters, as well as the longest game ever played, the 26-inning duel between Joe Oeschger and Brooklyn's Leon Cadore. While the Dodgers used two catchers in the game, Gowdy squatted behind the plate for the entire 26 innings, going one for six with the bat and handling the deliveries of Oeschger to perfection.

Ray Schalk came on the major league scene in 1912 and stayed around for nineteen years. Over that period he caught a total of 1726 games, a major league record until Gabby Hartnett broke it in 1939. He still holds several major league records, including the most seasons leading the league in fielding (eight), the most years leading in putouts (nine), the most no-hitters caught (four), the most double plays (226), and the American League mark for assists (1811). He also set a major league record for putouts, but that record has since been broken.

Schalk was a lightweight as far as catchers go and one of the smallest men in the major leagues, standing just 5'9" tall and weighing a feathery 155 pounds, but he was a giant on the field. He was as tough as nails and one of the most durable catchers in baseball history, catching more than 100 games a year twelve times. In addition to being a great field general, he was the best of his time in gunning down would-be base stealers with a 48 percent caught-stealing percentage. He was even better in World Series play, nailing 51 percent of the 39 runners who tried to steal on him. He was also one of the fastest catchers ever to play the game and the first catcher to back up plays at first base and third base. He even combined with Eddie Collins to make several putouts at second base.

The Illinois native was not much of a hitter, compiling a .253 batting average in 5306 career at-bats, but he was an outstanding base runner who stole 176 bases during his career, including 30 in 1916, both major league records for catchers. He hit a solid .286 in two World Series, including the 1919 Black Sox scandal, when he hit .304. Ray Schalk was the premier defensive catcher of his time, and he may well have been the greatest defensive catcher in the history of baseball.

Wally Schang was a contemporary of Ray Schalk, catching 1439 games between 1913 and 1931. Like Schalk, he had a strong throwing arm, which nabbed 48 percent of all the runners who tried to steal on him. Overall, he was not in Schalk's class as a defensive catcher, but he was a much better hitter than the Chicago White Sox receiver. He had a career batting average of .284, averaging 27 doubles, nine triples, and six home runs for every 550 at-bats. During his 19-year career, he played on six pennant winners with the Boston Red Sox and New York Yankees, winning three world championships in the process. On May 12, 1915, catching for the Philadelphia Athletics, he threw out six St. Louis Browns attempting to steal. Five years later, playing with the Boston Red Sox, he had eight assists in a game against the Cleveland Indians. Both of them are still American League records. He also holds the AL record for most errors in a career with 218.

There was one baseball player who might have risen to the top of the catching profession under different circumstances. Jimmie Foxx joined

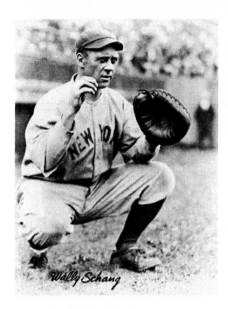 

Left: Wally Schang was a rarity in the early 20th century — a catcher who could hit. *Right:* Jimmie Foxx, one of baseball's greatest first basemen, began his career as a hard-hitting catcher for the Philadelphia Athletics.

the Philadephia Athletics in 1926, after leading all Eastern Shore League catchers in assists as a 16-year-old. Unfortunately for Foxx, Connie Mack already had a catcher named Mickey Cochrane, so the man known as "The Beast" shifted to first base, where he went on to become one of the two greatest first basemen in major league history, along with Lou Gehrig. Over a 20-year career, Foxx batted .325 and hit 534 home runs, a total exceeded only by Babe Ruth at the time. Although he is not eligible to be compared with the greatest catchers in baseball history, having caught a total of just 108 games, his offensive and defensive statistics will be presented in later chapters for comparison purposes and for a peek at what might have been.

Outside the major leagues, in other professional leagues in the U.S. and Japan, there were a number of great catchers who went unnoticed because their exploits were not covered in the mainstream American press. Perhaps the greatest of these catchers, and maybe the greatest all-around catcher in baseball history, in or out of the majors, was a handsome, carefree backstop named Josh Gibson, who played baseball twelve months of the year for 16 years. He caught for such teams as the Homestead Grays and the Pittsburgh Crawfords in the Negro Leagues during the summer, then traveled to Cuba, Mexico, Puerto Rico, and the Dominican Republic,

for the winter leagues. He was a sensa-
tion wherever he played. His career batting average in the Negro Leagues was a
sizzling .351 with 51 home runs for every
550 at-bats. He hit .353 with 34 homers
a year in Cuba, .355 with 27 homers in
Puerto Rico, and .373 with 54 homers in
Mexico. In the book *The King of Swat*, it
was estimated that Gibson would have
batted .312 in the major leagues with a
monstrous 61 home runs for every 550
at-bats, dwarfing Babe Ruth's 50 homers,
Mark McGwire's 52, and Barry Bonds's
41. In addition, the big catcher had good
foot speed, averaging 14 triples a year
and leading the league in that department three times. He even showed the
way in stolen bases at least once.

Unlike many of the modern major
league sluggers, Josh Gibson was not a
free swinger. He was a dangerous contact hitter with quick wrists. His short,
compact stroke allowed him to hit the

Josh Gibson is recognized as
the greatest catcher in Negro
League history.

ball anywhere around the plate, making him a difficult batter to fool. He
seldom struck out. Like Joe DiMaggio and Ted Williams, Gibson had years
where he had more home runs than strikeouts. In Mexico, for instance,
over a two-year period, he hit 44 home runs with just 31 strikeouts in 450
at-bats, while stroking the ball at a .393 clip.

Gibson was not a one-dimensional player, however. He was also an
outstanding defensive catcher as well. Walter Johnson, who saw Gibson
play in Washington many times, claimed he made catching look easy, as
if he were relaxing in a rocking chair behind the plate. When he was young,
Gibson was reportedly weak on pop flies around the plate, but hours of
practice corrected that deficiency. He was an imposing figure behind the
plate, standing 6'2" in height and weighing in at a muscular 217 pounds.
He always had a strong, accurate throwing arm, was a good handler of
pitchers, and was like a brick wall blocking the plate against runners trying to score. Roy Campanella, one of the finest all-around catchers in
major league history, played with and against Gibson for nine years in the
Negro Leagues and in foreign winter leagues, and he said that Gibson was
a better catcher than he was. He also said that Gibson was the greatest

hitter he ever saw, even better than Ted Williams, Stan Musial, and Willie Mays.

Raleigh "Biz" Mackey is generally recognized as one of the Negro Leagues' greatest all-around catchers. He could do it all, both offensively and defensively. Although he didn't have Josh Gibson's power, he still wielded a potent bat, hitting .322 over a celebrated 28-year career, with 11 home runs for every 550 at-bats. He was Roy Campanella's mentor, teaching the 15-year-old Philadelphian all the tricks of the trade. John Holway quoted Campy as saying he watched "how [Mackey] blocked the plate, how he shifted his feet for an outside pitch, how he threw with a short, quick, accurate throw without drawing back ... In my opinion, Biz Mackey was the master of defense of all catchers." And Negro League veterans used to say, "If you want to see what Biz Mackey was like as a catcher, just watch Campanella. Campy is a clone of Mackey."

The 22-year-old Mackey joined the Indianapolis ABCs of the Negro National League and soon began to establish a reputation for himself as one of the finest receivers in the game. He moved on to the Philadelphia Hilldales in 1923 and spent the next thirteen years there. He clouted a monstrous .364 in '23 and followed it with averages of .363 and .356. The jovial backstop appeared in two Negro League World Series against the Kansas City Monarchs. He hit just .241 in 1924, as the Hilldales lost to the Monarchs in the 10th and final game. The next year, Mackey ripped the ball at a .360 clip, with three doubles, a triple, and a home run, and the Hilldales got a measure of revenge, whipping the Monarchs five games to one.

Mackey, like many of the Negro League players, traveled the baseball circuit, playing in the Negro Leagues in the summer, then moving to warmer climes for four months of winter ball. He hit .309 in the tough Cuban Winter League in 1924–25, but played in the highly regarded California Winter League, against major league players and players from the AAA Pacific Coast League, most other years between 1920 and 1945. The tall, husky backstop punished the white pitchers on the coast to the tune of .366, the sixth highest career average in CWL history. He batted a torrid .455 against Hollis "Sloppy" Thurston, a 20-game winner with the Chicago White Sox in 1924, .382 against former New York Giant pitcher Ferdie Schupp, and .370 against Herm "Old Folks" Pillette. Biz Mackey finally hung up his catcher's mitt and his spikes in 1945 at the age of 48. In his last Negro League season, he stung the ball at a .307 clip for the Newark Eagles.

Across the Pacific Ocean, the Japanese leagues produced a catcher who was the equivalent of the great catchers in the U.S. His name is

Katsuya Nomura, and he played in the Japanese leagues for 27 years, during which time he set the all-time professional baseball record for most games played by a catcher — 2918. MLB receiver Carlton Fisk is second with 2226. Nomura is the greatest catcher in the history of Japanese baseball and a legend around the world. His 657 career home runs are the most home runs hit by a catcher in professional baseball history, second only to Sadaharu Oh in Japan and the eighth highest total in the annals of professional baseball. His offensive achievements include nine Japanese league home run championships, including eight in a row. He is tied for the most home runs in a season in the Japanese Pacific League, with 52. He also captured six consecutive RBI titles and one batting championship. He won the triple crown in 1965 with a batting average of .320, 42 home runs, and 110 runs batted in. He was a five-time recipient of the Pacific League Most Valuable Player award. When he retired in 1980, the 5'9", 187-pound backstop held the Japanese league record for most total games played (3017), and most career at-bats (10,472). He accumulated 2901 base hits, 1988 runs batted in, and 1509 runs scored. His average season batting statistics are mirror images of those of Roy Campanella, the Hall of Fame catcher of the Brooklyn Dodgers.

Name	AB	R	H	D	T	HR	RBI	BB	SO	BA
K. Nomura	550	79	152	21	1	35	104	66	78	.277
R. Campanella	550	82	152	23	2	32	112	70	65	.276

Katsuya Nomura was primarily an offensive player. He was slow afoot and had a below-average caught-stealing percentage, throwing out just 31 percent of the runners who tested his arm. But he was the most durable catcher in the annals of professional baseball, holding the all-time records for games played and years played. He once caught every inning of a 150-game season, including 16 doubleheaders, and he played in every game during six seasons. He is a member of the Japanese Baseball Hall of Fame.

There were many outstanding defensive catchers in the major leagues in the early twentieth century as is evidenced by the above biographies, but that situation changed drastically over the years. Between 1900 and 1920, catchers were small and fast and primarily defensive specialists. Then, in 1919, a husky young pitcher-outfielder named Babe Ruth blasted 29 home runs for the Boston Red Sox. One year later, the Babe, now a full-time outfielder with the New York Yankees, put 54 balls into orbit, sending baseball fans into a frenzy. And the lively ball era was under way. In 1922, a 21-year-old catcher from Millville, Massachusetts, named Charles Leo "Gabby" Hartnett joined the Chicago Cubs and began to revolutionize the catching position. He was the first of a new breed of receivers, blessed with enormous defensive talent and carrying dynamite in his bat. The period from 1920 to 1960 was the golden age of catchers, as well as of baseball in general. Subsequent chapters will follow the evolution of catchers through the golden age who not only excelled on defense, but could also wield a bat with the best of them, to the "big bomb" era of the 1980–2000 period, when catchers were sought primarily for the offensive contributions, often at the expense of their defense.

◆ 3 ◆

FROM HARTNETT TO
LOMBARDI—1920 TO 1940

Every era has had its great catchers. There has never been an era without several world-class receivers. What does change, however, is the emphasis on different aspects of the game. For instance, from 1900 to 1920, pitching dominated the game and teams played for one run at a time. Under those conditions, owners and managers were interested in catchers with strong throwing arms who could thwart the opposition's attempts to score runs. After 1920, when the lively ball came into play, a new breed of catcher arrived on the scene, still with strong defense, but also with a powerful bat and long-ball capabilities. The decades from 1920 to 1940 may well have been the golden age of catching as dozens of world-class receivers made their debuts in the Big Show, and many of them even competed against each other for starting jobs on major league rosters.

Muddy Ruel

The first catcher of note in this era was Herold Dominic "Muddy" Ruel, a slightly built right-handed hitter who stood 5'9" and weighed 150 pounds in his prime. He was one of the early defensive specialists, the last of the old dead-ball era backstops. Ruel was born in St. Louis, Missouri, on February 20, 1896, and quickly picked up his nickname by playing sandlot baseball games using a mud-reinforced baseball. He came right off the hard-packed playing fields of St. Louis to play for his hometown Browns in 1915 at the age of 19. After bouncing back and forth between the major leagues and minor leagues for several years, the 26-year-old backstop settled down in Washington, where he became a star.

Ruel quickly established himself not only as one the game's premier defensive players, but as a pesky hitter as well. Behind the plate, he had few equals during his 19-year big-league career. He led the American League in fielding average, putouts and assists three times each. He had one of the best career fielding averages in the annals of the game; his .982 percentage was six points higher than the league average. He was always among the league leaders in caught-stealing percentage, fewest passed balls allowed, and total assists, and he had above-average speed and range. He was also durable, catching more than 1400 games during his career, including eight years of 100 or more games caught. As a hitter, he batted a respectable .275 and three times went over the magic .300 mark. He was a dependable contact hitter who struck out only 29 times a year while driving in 65 runs for every 550 at-bats. He didn't hit with power, averaging only 27 extra-base hits a year and showing just four home runs in 4514 at-bats, but he managed to coax 73 bases on balls to keep the opposing pitcher honest. Ruel's best year was the championship year of 1924, when he hit a solid .283 in 149 games with 57 RBIs. He also led the league in putouts, double plays, and assists.

During his Washington years, Muddy Ruel caught the great Walter Johnson while guiding his team to two American League pennants and one world championship. Johnson, a 35-year-old veteran who had just suffered through a losing season when Ruel arrived, was revitalized by the aggressive young catcher. Over the next three years, Johnson would go 17–12, 23–7, and 20–7, capturing two American League pennants along the way. Ruel and Johnson were the heroes of the 1924 Series, with Johnson gaining the victory in Game 7, and Ruel scoring the championship run in the 12th inning. Coming to bat in the bottom of the 12th with the score tied, one man out, and the bases empty after Johnson had pitched four scoreless innings in relief, Ruel hit a pop-up behind the plate, but was given a second life when New York Giants catcher Hank Gowdy stepped on his mask while chasing the ball and dropped it. Ruel didn't miss again. He doubled past third and came around to score the championship run on a single by Earl McNeely.

Following his baseball career, Ruel who had obtained a law degree from Washington University during his playing days, worked for a time as a coach for the Chicago White Sox and later as a legal advisor to baseball commissioner Happy Chandler. He also managed the St. Louis Browns for one season and served as general manager of the Detroit Tigers, until ill health forced his retirement from the game.

Bubbles Hargrave

Eugene Franklin Hargrave was born in New Haven, Indiana, on July 15, 1892. He began his professional baseball career in 1911 as a catcher-outfielder for Terre Haute in the Central League, where he spent three years refining his catching technique and learning to hit. After stinging the ball at a cool .309 clip in 1913, his contract was sold to the Chicago Cubs, but he didn't impress the Windy City brass, and he was released after hitting just .207 in 41 games over two years. Returning to the minor leagues, he bounced around the American Association for five years, fine-tuning his batting stroke. He finally put it all together in 1919 and had two excellent years with St. Paul, batting .303 that year and .335 the following year, with 36 doubles, 12 triples, 22 home runs, and 109 runs batted in in 142 games.

The Cincinnati Reds bought Bubbles Hargrave's contract from St. Paul in 1921, beginning a successful nine-year major league career. He was an outstanding receiver for the Reds, hitting over .300 for six consecutive years and posting a fine .983 fielding average, eight percentage points above the league average. In 1923, he enjoyed his finest season with the bat, hitting .333 with 23 doubles, nine triples, 10 home runs, and 78 RBIs in 118 games. Three years later, he became the first catcher to lead the league in batting, with a .353 average in 105 games. Ernie Lombardi duplicated the feat twelve years later.

Hargrave retired from baseball in 1934 after spending the last four years in the minors. His career totals showed 852 games played, with 786 base hits in 2533 at-bats, for a .310 batting average. He is one of only five major league catchers to retire with a .300 batting average. The others are Dickey, Cochrane, Phelps, and Lombardi. The 5'10", 175-pound right-handed batter averaged 34 doubles, 12 triples, six home runs, and 82 RBIs for every 550 at-bats.

Bob O'Farrell

Bob O'Farrell, the man who would eventually lose his job to Gabby Hartnett, was a world-class backstop in his own right. He played in the National League for 21 long years, catching a total of 1338 games between 1915 and 1935. The rugged 5'10", 185-pound catcher was born in Waukegan, Illinois on October 19, 1896, and began his professional baseball career 18 years later with Peoria in the Three-I League. He was a catcher even then and impressed all who saw him with his defensive skills. He was called up to the Chicago Cubs for two games at the end of the season and banged out his first major league hit at the age of 18. Two years later he was back to stay.

O'Farrell spent the next six years in a Cubs uniform, establishing himself as one of the top receivers in the National League. He led the league in putouts and assists twice each over that period and even chipped in with two .300 seasons at the plate, hitting .324 in 128 games in 1923 and .310 in 131 games the next year. He also displayed some power at the plate in '23 with 25 doubles, four triples, and 12 home runs in 452 at-bats. An injury shelved him for several weeks the following season, and when he returned to the diamond, Gabby Hartnett had his job. The next summer, he was traded to the St. Louis Cardinals, who were in the process of building a championship club under general manager Branch Rickey and manager Rogers Hornsby. O'Farrell gave the hard-hitting Redbirds the field leadership they needed to scale the heights. The talented catcher guided their pitching staff to a National League pennant by two games over Cincinnati. His contributions didn't go unnoticed, as the baseball writers on the

selection committee voted him the National League's Most Valuable Player based on his field leadership, his outstanding defensive contributions, and his strong year with the bat. He hit a solid .293, with 30 doubles, nine triples, and seven home runs, while driving in 68 runs in 147 games.

The 1926 World Series provided Bob O'Farrell with his greatest day in baseball. St. Louis faced the powerful New York Yankees of Babe Ruth, Lou Gehrig, Tony Lazzeri, and Bob Meusel, and battled them to a standstill through six games. Grover Cleveland Alexander, the old warhorse, had stopped "Murderers' Row" 10–2 in game six and was in the bullpen for the finale. In the bottom of the seventh inning of Game 7, with the Cardinals protecting a slim 3–2 lead, the Yankees loaded the bases with two out

Bob O'Farrell starred for the Chicago Cubs and St. Louis Cardinals in the 1920s. *Courtesy John Outland.*

and the dangerous rookie Tony Lazzeri coming to the plate. Hornsby wasted no time in reaching into his bullpen and beckoning Alexander to the mound. The crafty 39-year-old veteran fanned the young second baseman in one of the classic one-on-one matchups in World Series history. Alexander was still on the mound in the bottom of the ninth when, with two men out and the bases empty, he walked Ruth on a full count. Inexplicably, the Bambino took off for second base on the first pitch to Meusel, and Bob O'Farrell calmly gunned him down at second to end the Series. O'Farrell batted .304 for the Series and had eight assists in seven games, including two caught-stealing assists in four chances.

O'Farrell moved on to the New York Giants in 1928, then had short stints with the Cubs, Cardinals, and Reds. The old veteran closed out his major league career in 1935 at the age of 38, leaving behind a noteworthy 21-year career, which included a total of 1338 games caught, with a tough .273 batting average. The aggressive O'Farrell was dominant in all phases of the defensive game. He led all modern catchers in assists per game, with 113 for every 154 games played, and his 59 caught-stealing assists are third all-time behind Muddy Ruel and Gary Carter. He also posted a .976 fielding average, which was one point higher than the league average, and a 48 percent caught-stealing rate, which was three percent above the league average. His six passed balls per year were among the lowest totals recorded by the leading catchers.

Gabby Hartnett

The first of the truly great all-around catchers to arrive on the scene in the twentieth century was a skinny young Irishman from Millville, Massachusetts. Charles Leo Hartnett was born on December 20, 1900, and by 1922 he was catching for the Chicago Cubs. From the beginning, the "Hartnett Arm" intimidated base runners around the National League. In his first full year as the Cubs' first-string catcher, in 1925, he gunned down 56 percent of the runners who tried to steal on him. And he kept it up over the next decade and a half, never allowing more than 52 stolen bases in any one year. His career average of 43 stolen bases allowed per year was 15 less than the league average. Not only did Gabby shoot down potential base stealers, he also picked runners off base at a record pace. He was completely fearless when it came to throwing the baseball around the infield, and as a result, he led the league in assists three times between 1924 and 1928, but he also led the league in errors three times. Once he matured and became more disciplined, he became the most dominant catcher in the major leagues. From 1928 to 1938, Gabby Hartnett led the league in fielding percentage seven times, including four years in a row, both National League records. He also led the league in assists four times, putouts twice, and double plays six times, another league record. And he routinely set the pace for caught-stealing percentage year after year. Although no complete statistics have been compiled as yet, showing his position in the league, he almost assuredly led the league in that category most years if not all, based on his career caught-stealing percentage of 53 percent, which is second only to Roy Campanella of Brooklyn in major league history.

Considering his dominant defensive posture, Gabby Hartnett would have been a welcome addition to any team even if he hit .250 with little power. But the 6'1", 218-pound right-handed slugger was a much better

hitter than that. In fact, he was one of the top hitting catchers in the history of the game. In 1924, he slugged 24 home runs, becoming the first major league catcher to hit more than 20 homers in a season, and he did it in just 398 at-bats. His best all-around season was 1930, when he led the league in fielding percentage, putouts, assists, double plays, and caught-stealing percentage, while stroking the ball at a .339 pace, with 37 homers and 122 runs batted in. During his career, he topped the .300 batting mark five times, while averaging .297 with 20 homers and 101 RBIs for every 550 at-bats. His career slugging percentage of .489 is third in major league history behind Mike Piazza and Roy Campanella.

The Chicago Cubs played in four World Series between 1929 and 1938, although Hartnett missed most of the '29 season because of a mysterious sore arm. The Cubs won the pennant in 1932 and again in 1935, with Hartnett hammering the ball at a .344 pace, with 13 homers and 91 RBIs in 116 games.

Gabby Hartnett is generally recognized as the Chicago Cubs' greatest catcher. *Courtesy Linda Butt.*

He also showed the way again in assists and fielding percentage and probably in caught-stealing percentage as well. His outstanding all-around season earned him the National League's Most Valuable Player trophy. But for the third time, the world championship eluded the Cubbies, and they were defeated by the Detroit Tigers four games to two. Gabby faced his American League counterpart, Mickey Cochrane, in the Series and may have had a slight edge in the individual competition. Gabby batted .292 with a homer and two RBIs, while Cochrane hit .292 with no homers and one RBI. On defense, Hartnett tossed out one out of two prospective base stealers, picked off one runner, and fielded flawlessly. "Black Mike" gunned down two out of three runners and was charged with one error in six games.

Two years later, Gabby Hartnett batted a career high of .354 in 110 games, with 12 homers and 82 runs batted in, but the Cubs, who had been leading the league since early July, faded in September and finished three games behind the pennant-winning New York Giants. The Chicago catcher did reach a milestone during the season, however. On September 27, he caught his 100th game of the season, the 12th time he had accomplished that feat, tying him with Ray Schalk for the major league record. The Cubs' failure to win the pennant in 1937 spelled doom for manager Charlie Grimm, and when the team found itself mired in fourth place in mid–July of 1938, eight games behind the Giants, the axe fell. Grimm was fired by owner Philip K. Wrigley and replaced by the veteran Gabby Hartnett. It was the defining moment in the career of 37-year-old Hartnett. He inherited the club on July 21 and spent the next six weeks restoring the confidence and morale of the team. Finally, in September, Hartnett had his team ready to go, and they came roaring down the stretch, winning 24 of 29 games over the final four weeks of the season. They closed to within half a game of the league-leading Pittsburgh Pirates with just six games left to play, with the first two against the Bucs in Wrigley Field. On September 28 the two teams squared off in a memorable pitching duel, and after eight and a half innings, with darkness settling over the field, the Cubs came up to bat for the last time before the game would be called. With two men out and no one on base, Gabby Hartnett stepped to the plate and ripped an 0–2 pitch from Mace Brown into the left field stands for a game-winning homer, putting Chicago in first place. The dramatic four-bagger has gone down in legend as "The Homer in the Gloamin." Chicago polished off the demoralized Pirates by a 10–1 score the next day and went on to capture the National League pennant by two games. Unfortunately, they couldn't sustain the magic, and they fell to the Bronx Bombers in the World Series, four games to none.

Gabby Hartnett was definitely one of the greatest catchers ever to play the game, and his peers were outspoken about his outstanding skills. Pitcher Charlie Root was quoted in *Heroes Behind the Mask* as saying, "The thing about Gabby is, he's always alert ... I bet he's broken up more steals and hit-and-run plays by calling for pitchouts than any other catcher in the game." He was often called "the master of the pitchout." Paul Richards, who caught in the major leagues in the 1930s and '40s and managed in the majors for twelve years, was quoted in *The Donald Honig Reader* as saying, "The best throwing arm I ever saw on a catcher probably belonged to Gabby Hartnett. And he was accurate. He was just a great throwing catcher. The fans used to come out early to watch infield practice just to watch Hartnett throw the ball around. That's quite a tribute to a fellow's throwing arm, wouldn't you say?"

Joe McCarthy had the final say. Marse Joe, who managed both Hartnett and Dickey and who saw Mickey Cochrane, Roy Campanella, Yogi Berra, and Johnny Bench play hundreds of times, gave his vote to Hartnett. According to McCarthy, "Gabby Hartnett was the perfect catcher." And he was elected to the National Baseball Hall of Fame in Cooperstown, New York, in 1955.

Mickey Cochrane

Another future HoF catcher appeared on the major league scene three years after Hartnett arrived. His name was Mickey Cochrane, and he was a Johnny-come-lately as a catcher. Born Gordon Stanley Cochrane in Bridgewater, Masachusetts, on April 6, 1903, the small-town boy grew up loving all sports—hunting, fishing, football and basketball, but mostly baseball. He dreamed of being a major league manager when he was just ten years old. He began his professional baseball career with the Dover Dobbins in the Eastern Shore League, playing under the name King, and he was the catcher for the team only because they had a vacancy to fill at that position. Mickey Cochrane didn't like catching, as reported by Charles Bevis. "I want to play somewhere in the infield or outfield ... I didn't want to be a catcher. It was thrust upon me.... It was the one position I actually despised." His inadequacy as a catcher didn't go unnoticed, either, as a local sportswriter constantly reminded him of it in print, with statements like, "King, the Dover catcher, missed his usual number of foul flies." And the owner of the Dobbins, after watching Cochrane catch, told his manager, "If he's a catcher, I'm Little Red Riding Hood." Fortunately for Dover, Cochrane's bat and flying feet more than offset his deficiencies behind the plate. He slugged the ball for a .322 average, scored 56 runs, and swiped 14 bases in 65 games, and the Dobbins walked off with the league title.

His performance in Maryland brought him to the attention of the Portland Beavers of the highly rated Pacific Coast League, who signed the youngster for $325 per month and a whopping $1000 signing bonus. Once again he was slotted in as a catcher, and he worked hard to smooth the rough edges in his catching style. However, as Westbrook Pegler pointed out in the *Chicago Daily Tribune*, "He knew he wasn't a catcher, and it didn't take him long to convince the management ... and if he held one pitch out of three, the papers ran off extras. He was one of the worst catch-

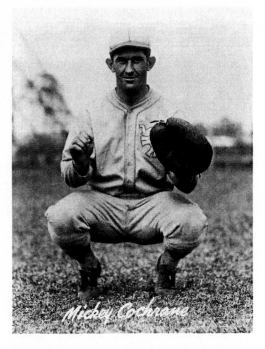

Mickey Cochrane was the spark plug of the Philadelphia A's 1929–31 American League championship team.

ers in the U.S.A." Two advantages he had as a receiver, however, were a strong throwing arm and the guts of a burglar, so very few runners took liberties with his arm. Eventually first-string catcher Tom Daly came to his rescue. Noting that Cochrane was using a small, hard mitt, Daly "told him to get a big, soft mitt, which would soak up the ball instead of bouncing it off. That made the difference. He had been a fairly good catcher after all." And, as at Dover, the kid from Bridgewater could run like the wind and hit like Ty Cobb. The strong PCL pitching didn't intimidate him at all, and he finished the season with a .333 batting average and 56 runs batted in in 99 games.

In 1925 Mickey Cochrane became the property of the Philadelphia Athletics, managed by Connie Mack, and he ended up catching by default. He was tried at several positions, including third base, with less than favorable results. As one Philadelphia scout had noted, "He can't field a ball at any position, but he can hit and he's a fierce competitor." Mack finally decided his new player might do less damage defensively behind the plate. The A's already had a stylish catcher by the name of Cy Perkins, a 29-year-old veteran with a shotgun for a throwing arm, who nailed 47 percent of all runners who tried to steal on him. Perkins had caught 100 or more games a season for the six consecutive seasons before Cochrane arrived, but he was a light hitter, and Mack was looking for more offensive power in his lineup. He saw a lot of promise in his new recruit, but as Pegler reported, Connie said, "...for a little while ... I was afraid someone had taken advantage of my trust. The boy was full of energy, but my goodness, he wasn't a catcher. But there was something in the way he tried that made me think we could do something with him. Besides, he could hit and run and he had the strength to work all day. So we taught him a few things about catching and he came on so fast that it wasn't long before I had to take Perkins out and use a better man. He never will be the artist that Cy was, but he gets results." The Bridgewater comet was so fast he often batted leadoff for the Philadelphia club, a rarity for catchers, who are noted for their sluggish footwork.

Mickey Cochrane soon became the nerve center of the powerful A's. He was the team leader, fiery and aggressive, and one of the game's genuinely poor losers. His dark demeanor on the field gave rise to one of his nicknames, "Black Mike." Teammate Doc Cramer was quoted in *The Ballplayers* as saying, "Lose a one-to-nothing game ... and you didn't want to get into the clubhouse with Grove and Cochrane. You'd be ducking stools and gloves and bats and whatever else would fly." In his rookie season of 1925, Cochrane whacked the ball at a .331 clip and, surprisingly, led the league's catchers in fielding percentage, and the revitalized Mackmen jumped up from fifth place in the league standings to second. After two more second-place finishes and one third-place finish over the next three years, Philadelphia strung together three straight pennants between 1929 and 1931, capturing the world championship in both 1929 and 1930.

Two years later, Connie Mack broke up the team, sending Lefty Grove to Boston and Mickey Cochrane to the Detroit Tigers as player-manager for $100,000 and a second-string catcher. The arrival of Cochrane and Goose Goslin, with the development of Eldon Auker and Schoolboy Rowe, carried the Tigers from a fifth-place finish in 1933 to pennants in both 1934 and '35, with the fiery Cochrane batting .320 and .319. Black Mike's cohorts dropped a four-games-to-three Series to St. Louis's famous Gashouse Gang in '34, but bounced back the next year to beat Gabby Hartnett and the Chicago Cubs, four games to two. Ever the bench jockey, Cochrane greeted the Chicago team's arrival on the field with the barb, "Hello, sweethearts, we're going to serve tea this afternoon. Come on out and get your share." The Tiger manager scored the world championship-winning run in the bottom of the ninth inning of Game 6 after beating out an infield hit. He scored on a base hit by Goose Goslin.

Mickey Cochrane's playing career came to a sudden end on May 27, 1937. In a game in Yankee Stadium, Black Mike lost sight of a Bump Hadley pitch in the late afternoon New York sun, and the ball crashed into his temple, sending him to the ground with a fractured skull. Mickey Cochrane never played another major league game. When he retired, the smooth-swinging 5'10", 180-pound left-handed hitter had the highest career batting average ever compiled by a catcher, .320. It is also number 47 all-time. He was not a home run hitter, but he pounded out more than his share of singles and doubles, averaging 34 doubles, six triples, and twelve home runs for every 550 at-bats. Cochrane's other statistics include 1451 games caught, 1652 base hits, 1041 runs scored, and the top on-base percentage among catchers, .419. He played in at least 100 games his first eleven years in the majors, and he led the American League in putouts six times and assists and double plays twice each. He was a two-time Most Valuable Player, with Philadelphia in 1928 and with Detroit in 1934. But perhaps his greatest assets were the intangibles. As Al Hirshberg noted in his book, *Baseball's Greatest Catchers*, he "never stopped fighting, never stopped moving, never stopped goading or scolding, or exhorting or cajoling his teammates to victory. He was a rare combination of mechanical genius and inspirational leader. Cochrane, who could handle pitchers, receive, run, throw, hit, lead and think, was a born winner." And he received his greatest honor in 1947 when he was voted into the Hall of Fame, the first modern catcher to enter those immortal portals.

Bill Dickey

Another legendary catcher began his major league career during the 1920s. William Malcolm "Bill" Dickey didn't have the fire of either Gabby Hartnett or Mickey Cochrane, but he quietly led his team to victory year after year. Bill Dickey was born in Bastrop, Louisiana, on June 6, 1907, but he grew up in Kensett, Arkansas, about fifty miles northeast of Little Rock, where his father was a conductor on the Missouri and Pacific Railroad. John Dickey encouraged his three sons to become baseball players, and they all took to the game like fish to water. Originally they all played several positions, but eventually Bill Dickey became a catcher because, as he said, "I guess I was always too slow to play anywhere else." Although he stood 6'2" and weighed a solid 185 pounds, he somehow never was able to generate any speed on a baseball field, which, over the years, made him the butt of many jokes in the Yankee clubhouse. One story that is frequently told about Dickey's lack of speed has Yankee pitcher Red Ruffing saying to coach Art Fletcher, "You know, Art, Babe Ruth is slowing down a lot. Why not make a catcher out of him? Then he won't have to run." The comment was made for Bill Dickey's benefit, and the Yankee catcher, not known for his humor, quickly responded. "Why not make a pitcher out of him? Then he won't have to think."

But Dickey was no joke behind the plate or with a bat in his hands. He pitched and caught for the Little Rock College team in 1925 and also played semipro baseball for Hot Springs. It was there that he was discovered by Lena Blackburne, the manager of the Little Rock Southern Association team, who signed him to a professional contract after the school semester ended. As Blackburne noted in *Great Catchers of the Major Leagues*, "He was a pretty crude catcher when I first saw him. I remember the day I saw him play for the Hot Springs team. I went there to look over a third baseman, but signed Dickey instead even though he threw a ball against the right field fence trying to pick a man off first. I could see that he had a strong arm." Dickey was sent down the Muskogee of the Western Association in 1926 to work on his catching technique, and he was quickly tested by the league's runners, who challenged his arm whenever they had the opportunity. But the young receiver was more than up to the task, compiling 58 assists in 61 games. After hitting .283 in Muskogee, he was brought back up to Little Rock midway through the season and finished the year sensationally, slugging the ball at a torrid .391 clip with 18 extra-base hits, including five home runs, in 21 games. After two more years learning the tricks of the trade in the bushes, his contract was purchased by the New York Yankees for $15,000 in 1928.

Bill Dickey quickly became a star on a team of stars under manager Joe McCarthy. In his first full year as the Yankee catcher, Dickey hit a resounding .324 in 130 games, with 30 doubles, 10 home runs, and 65 RBIs, and he led the league's catchers in assists with 95. It was the first of a record-breaking thirteen seasons that Dickey caught 100 or more games. The big left-handed hitter punished the ball at a .339 pace the next year and followed it up with a .327 season in 1931. He also led the league in putouts and fielding average that year. Bill Dickey became an expert at jerking balls down the right field foul line in Yankee Stadium, slamming 135 of his 202 career home runs in his home park. He helped the team that would be known as the Bronx Bombers win eight American League pennants and seven world championships between 1932 and 1943, including four in a row between 1936 and 1939. Those four years were Dickey's finest. Batting in the fifth slot behind DiMaggio and Gehrig, he put together seasons of .362 with 22 home runs and 107 RBIs, .332 with 29 homers and 133 RBIs, .313 with 27 homers and 115 RBIs, and .302 with 24 homers and 105 RBIs, while leading the league in putouts three times and fielding average twice.

In World Series play, he hit just .255 in 38 games, with five home runs and 24 runs batted in, but he was considered to be a dangerous clutch hitter by opposing pitchers. One of them said he would rather pitch to Joe DiMaggio or Lou Gehrig than Dickey. Behind the plate, he was outstanding, gunning down 11 of 17 runners attempting to steal for a 65 percent kill rate, and making just two errors for a .992 fielding average.

From 1939 until the emergence of Roy Campanella in Brooklyn in 1948, Bill Dickey had no equal as a major league catcher. Over the course of his 17-year career, Bill Dickey batted .313, the second highest career batting average for a catcher in modern baseball history, behind Mickey Cochrane. Playing in 1789 games, he pounded out 1969 base hits, with 343 doubles, 71 triples, and 202 home runs. His 1209 RBIs are exceeded only by Bench, Berra, Fisk, and Carter. He led the league in fielding a total of five times, putouts six times, and assists twice. And he threw out 41 of 93 prospective base stealers for every 154 games played, a 44 percent caught-stealing rate, four percent better than the league average. He was voted to the American League All-Star team six times between 1932 and 1941.

Bill Dickey's career ended prematurely in 1944 when he enlisted in the United States Navy during World War II. By the time he returned to baseball two years later, he was an old man of 39 whose immense skills were a thing of the past. The plaudits for Bill Dickey's talents from fellow players, sportswriters, managers, and baseball historians, would fill a volume. Paul Derringer was quoted in Jack Zanger's book as saying Bill Dickey was the best player on the New York Yankees "because of the way he handles the pitchers and because of the way he leads the team.... He's something more than a great hitter. He's a great thinker, and mechanically, he's just about a perfect catcher." Paul Richards, when asked who was the better catcher, Bill Dickey or Mickey Cochrane said, "I'd have to pick Dickey. He didn't have the fire that Cochrane did. Cochrane had a lot of flair, and he was a great catcher and a good hitter. But he didn't have the arm that Dickey had, and he didn't have the power that Dickey had. So I would take Dickey over all the catchers I've known. He's number one." And sportswriter Dan Daniels paid the Yankee backstop the ultimate compliment. "Bill Dickey isn't just a catcher, he's a ballclub."

Rick Ferrell

The next great catcher on the scene was one-half of the famous pitcher-catcher brother combination of Rick and Wes Ferrell. Rick Ferrell was born on October 12, 1906, on a farm in Durham, N.C., one of seven brothers. As a youngster, he bought his first catcher's mitt for $1.50, but he was more infatuated with boxing than baseball as a profession and, after winning 17 of 18 professional fights, he was crowned the lightweight champion of North Carolina, according to the book *Baseball's Hall of Fame*. The book also quoted him as saying he became a catcher by accident. "When several brothers decide to become pitchers, somebody has to catch 'em, and I took the job." His decision paid off, as his catching skills brought him to the attention of the St. Louis Browns, who offered him a $1,000 bonus to sign with the Missouri team in 1926. He declined the offer, signing instead with the Detroit Tigers' farm club in Kinston, Virginia. The solidly built 5'10", 170-pound backstop played in the minors for three years, hitting a personal high of .333 while on loan from the Tigers to the St. Louis Cardinal farm team in Columbus of the American Association in 1928. Baseball commissioner Kenesaw Mountain Landis almost emptied the St. Louis Cardinals' farm system because of unethical practices after the season, making Ferrell a free agent. The 22-year-old backstop made the most of his opportunity and accepted a $25,000 bonus to join the Browns in 1929. After four years in St. Louis, including two .300 plus seasons and membership on the American League's first All-Star team in 1933 (he caught the entire game) he was traded to the Boston Red Sox, where he caught his brother, Wes, for three years. The younger Ferrell had his best major league season in 1935, pitching to his brother. He led the American League in victories with 25, in complete games with 31, and in innings pitched with 322. He also ripped the ball at a sizzling .347 pace, with seven home runs in 150 at-bats. Rick Ferrell did his part by catching 133 games and batting .301 with three home runs.

Rick Ferrell was an outstanding defensive catcher in the major leagues for 18 years.

Rick Ferrell was traded to the Washington Senators in 1937, spending four years in the nation's capital, catching four knuckleball pitchers, including Bobo Newsom. The unenviable job of fighting the unpredictable flight of the butterfly pitches caused his passed ball frequency to skyrocket. He finished one year with 21. Wild pitches were also common practice in D.C. in the late '30s, with the staff responsible for 47 errant throws in both 1937 and 1940. Over the course of his 18-year major league career, he led the American League in putouts twice, assists twice, and fielding average twice. The durable receiver caught more than 100 games a season eleven times, including nine in a row. At one time he held the American League record for most games by a catcher, 1805. He was also a reliable contact hitter, with a lifetime .281 batting average, including five years over .300. He averaged 34 doubles, four triples, three home runs, and 67 runs batted in for every 550 at-bats, and his on-base percentage of .378 was exceeded by only five of the top 50 catchers. He also drew 84 bases on balls a year while striking out just 25 times. Rick Ferrell's outstanding all-around play was rewarded in 1984 when the Veterans Committee elected him to the Baseball Hall of Fame.

Ernie Lombardi

Ernie Lombardi's career spanned from 1931 to 1947. He battled Gabby Hartnett for recognition as the National League's leading catcher until Hartnett slowed down after his 1938 heroics, after which Lombardi took over the top spot for the next seven years. Unlike Hartnett, Cochrane, and Dickey, who excelled both offensively and defensively, Lombardi was primarily an offensive backstop who earned his keep with his bat, although he did have some weapons behind the plate. As Billy Werber noted in his biography, *Memories of a Ballplayer,* "E.L. was a big, easygoing guy from the Bay Area, was a superb hitter and defensive catcher, exceptional in every area except foot speed. He remains the only catcher to win two batting titles.

"Ernie was six-foot-three and at least 230 pounds. Pitching to him was like throwing to a warehouse behind the plate. Our staff liked throwing to him. He knew the opposition's strengths and weaknesses and called a great game. He was a shrewd operator. Lombardi could throw better than anybody — anybody. When an opposing runner tried to steal third, I knew we had an out when I saw Ernie's arm drop because the ball would always arrive on target and light as a feather."

Donald Honig quoted Werber as adding, "He had enormous hands.

He could wrap his hands completely around a baseball so you couldn't see it. Twice I saw him do something I never saw another catcher do, or even try to do. Once it was with Vander Meer pitching, the other time I think it was Derringer. They threw balls outside that were going to be wild pitches. Lombardi couldn't get his glove across in time, so he just stuck out that big hand and plucked the ball right out of the air as easily as you'd pick an apple off a tree."

Lombardi was born Ernest Natali Lombardi in Oakland, California on April 6, 1908, but he was better known as "Schnozz" because of his Jimmy Durante-sized proboscis. He began his professional baseball career with his hometown Oakland Oaks in the strong Pacific Coast League in 1926 as an 18-year-old catcher. He spent the next four years in the minor leagues, batting .398, .377, .366, and .370, bringing about his sale to the Brooklyn Dodgers. Lombardi caught about half the Dodgers games in his rookie season of 1931 and hit a respectable .297, but the Dodger brass thought the clumsy backstop's talents were suspect, particularly his lack of foot speed, his unusual batting grip, and his throwing technique. To begin with, he was one of the slowest runners in the league, and infielders played him back on the grass, daring him to beat out an infield hit. At the plate, he used a golfer's interlocking grip, which seemed to detract from his power. And behind the plate, he threw the ball sidearm like an infielder, rather than with the over-the-top snap throw used by most of the world-class catchers. Doubting he would ever make it as a major league catcher, the Dodgers traded him to Cincinnati during the off season. Brooklyn's loss was Cincinnati's gain.

Ernie Lombardi enjoyed a ten-year Hall of Fame career in Ohio, batting over .300 seven times with one batting title. In 1938, he caught 129 games, led the league in batting with an average of .342, cracked 19 homers and drove in 95 teammates. He also led the league in fielding with an average of .985. His outstanding all-around play, which kept the Reds in contention until late in the season, earned him the National League's Most Valuable Player Award. In 1940, he batted .319 in 109 games, with 14 homers and 74 RBIs, and led the league in fielding with an average of .989. And two years later, as a member of the Boston Braves, he won another batting title, hitting .330 in 105 games.

During his career, he played in two World Series with Cincinnati, losing to the New York Yankees in four straight in 1939 and defeating the Detroit Tigers in seven games in 1940. He hit just .235 in six games in the two Series, but his reputation as a defensive backstop intimidated opposing base runners to the extent that no one attempted to steal a base against him. In the '39 Series, an incident occurred that became a humiliating major league legend like Bill Buckner's muff of a ground ball and Fred Merkle's base-running blunder that cost the New York Giants a pennant in 1908. In the tenth inning of Game 4, with the score tied at four apiece, a single by Joe DiMaggio sent Frank Crosetti racing across the plate with the tie-breaking run. When Cincinnati right fielder Ival Goodman bobbled the ball, Charlie Keller broke for the plate, the ball and Keller arriving home at the same time. The collision between Lombardi, who was blocking the plate, and Keller reverberated around the park, with the Reds' catcher sent sprawling in the dirt. DiMaggio, seeing Lombardi lying stunned and motionless on the ground, also raced home with an insurance run. The incident has gone down in baseball lore as the Lombardi Swoon.

When he retired in 1947 after a noteworthy 17-year career, he had a lifetime .306 batting average, one of only five retired catchers in the study to post a .300 plus career average. Mickey Cochrane at .320 has the highest career batting average for a catcher, followed by Bill Dickey at .313 and Babe Phelps and Bubbles Hargrave at .310 each. Mike Piazza and Ivan Rodriguez also have .300 averages, but their careers are still active. Lombardi accumulated 1792 base hits, 190 home runs and 990 runs batted in in 5855 at-bats. He was elected to the Baseball Hall of Fame by the Veterans Committee in 1986.

Babe Phelps

Ernest Gordon Phelps was tagged with the unflattering nickname of the "Grounded Blimp" because of his fear of flying. The 6'2" 225-pound left-handed slugger was also known as Babe after his lookalike, Babe Ruth. Phelps was born in Odenton, Maryland, on April 19, 1908. And like Ruth, he could always hit. He led his minor leagues in batting his first three years, hitting .376 with Hagerstown in the Blue Ridge League in 1930, .408 with Youngstown in the Mid Atlantic League the following year, and .373 with Youngstown in the Central League in '32. After a short trial with the Chicago Cubs in 1934, Phelps was claimed on waivers by the Brooklyn Dodgers, where he enjoyed a successful seven-year career.

After batting a solid .364 in 47 games for the Dodgers in 1935, Phelps unloaded the next year, pummeling opposing pitchers to the tune of .367 in 115 games, good enough for him to win the National League batting championship. He batted .313 in 1937 and .308 the following year. On May 31, 1937, he had his biggest day in baseball, blasting five base hits in six at-bats, as the Dodgers ended Carl Hubbell's 24-game winning streak, rout-ing him and the New York Giants, 10–3. Babe Phelps's major league career came to an ignominious end on February 14, 1941, when his team left Brooklyn for Havana, Cuba, for spring training. The bulky backstop accompanied the team to Miami, Florida, by train, but refused to board the boat for Cuba, choosing to go home instead. He did spend one final year in the majors, after being traded to Pittsburgh in 1942. He batted .284 that year, then hung up the mitt for good.

During his career, Babe Phelps batted a solid .310, with 834 base hits in 2550 at-bats. He averaged 37 doubles, five triples, 12 home runs, and 90 runs batted in for every 550 at-bats. His defense however, was subpar, as he trailed his peers in most categories, including fielding average, caught-stealing percentage, assists, and range factor.

Harry Danning

Harry Danning was a hard-nosed catcher for the New York Giants from 1933 to 1942. The 31-year-old catcher enlisted in the U.S. Army in

Harry "The Horse" Danning played on three National League pennant winners with the New York Giants. *Courtesy Harring Danning.*

1943 and served his country honorably during World War II, but on his return home, his arthritic knees forced him into retirement. He was a minor league coach for the Hollywood Stars of the Pacific Coast League for several years before moving to Valparaiso, Indiana.

Danning was born in Los Angeles, California, on September 6, 1911 and began his professional baseball career with Bridgeport in the Eastern League in 1931. He moved up to Buffalo of the International League in 1932, working under the legendary Ray Schalk. Refining his skills under the tutelage of Schalk proved to be a valuable benefit to young Danning, who went on to carve out a reputation of his own as one of baseball's greatest defensive catchers. He was taught how to move his feet properly to catch outside pitches, then get back in position and be ready to throw, how to dig low pitches out of the dirt, how to catch knuckleballs, and how to make snap throws from behind his ear. The solidly built 6'1", 190-pound backstop made his major league debut with Bill Terry's Giants in 1933, but he had to bide his time in New York for four years because Gus Mancuso had the number one catching slot nailed down during the first half of the decade. By 1937, Mancuso was beginning to fade, and Danning stepped in as the main man. For the next six years, until he left for military service, he was the Giants' regular catcher. And he was one of the best. He appeared in two World Series, both against the hated Yankees, and he was named to four All-Star teams. One of Danning's biggest thrills in baseball was driving in a run with a single off Bob Feller in the 1940 All-Star game, won by the National League 4–0. He was the top catcher in the National League between 1937 and 1942, leading the league's catchers in most defensive categories. He was a take-charge backstop who was exceptional at handling his pitching staff and calling a game. He averaged five percentage points above the league fielding average, had a strong throwing arm that shot down 47 percent of all would-be base stealers, and possessed quick reflexes that gave him exceptional range. Danning was nicknamed "Harry the Horse" by broadcaster Ted Husing, who pulled it out of a Damon Runyon story. Danning said he got the nickname because he either looked like a horse or worked like one, he wasn't sure which.

Harry the Horse was not just a defensive backstop, however. The big right-handed batter also contributed to his team's success with the lumber, hitting over .300 three times in his ten-year career, with a high of .313 in 1939. He also contributed 16 home runs and 74 RBIs to the pot that year while catching 135 games. The following year, he hit .300 with 13 homers and 91 runs batted in. On June 15, 1940, he hit for the cycle in the Polo Grounds against the Pittsburgh Pirates. His home run was a tremendous inside-the-park shot to dead center field that traveled more than 460 feet on the fly. Danning was not a dead pull hitter, but could hit the ball to all fields. Although he was a line drive hitter who usually hit the ball on the ground, he did take advantage of the Polo Grounds' short foul lines by hitting three times as many home runs at home as he did on the road. His lifetime numbers include a solid .285 batting average with 847 base hits in 2971 at-bats.

Ken O'Dea

The last world class-catcher of the 1920–40 period was Ken O'Dea, who debuted in 1935. Even though baseball was well into the lively-ball

era at that time, O'Dea was not a potent offensive force in the mold of Hartnett, Cochrane, or Dickey, but he combined an outstanding defensive presence with a steady bat to enjoy a twelve-year career in the Big Show. The
native of Lima, New York, had everything required for a sterling career —
everything but luck. His timing was all bad. He was always in the wrong
place at the wrong time. Initially he showed great promise, rapping the ball
at a .333 clip for Keokuk in his professional debut in 1932. However, as
he climbed the ladder through AA and AAA ball, his batting average stabilized in the .265 range, but that, coupled with his superior defense, was
enough for the Chicago Cubs to bring him up to the National League.

Standing six feet tall and weighing 180 pounds, the left-handed
swinger found himself serving as backup catcher to Gabby Hartnet. When
Hartnett was injured, O'Dea stepped in and did a formidable job, putting
together seasons of .307 in 1936 and .307 the following year. Still he could
not break into the starting lineup. He was finally traded to the New York
Giants in 1939, but once again his timing was bad. He sat on the bench
most days watching Harry Danning carry the catching load. In 1942,
he moved on to the St. Louis Cardinals and found 27-year-old Walker
Cooper just settling in as the regular backstop. When Cooper enlisted
in the U.S. Navy three years later, O'Dea finally broke into the starting
lineup, catching 100 games, the only season in his career when he reached
that magic number. He took advantage of his opportunity to lead the league
in fielding with a percentage of .995, but the next year he was traded
to the Boston Braves so the Redbirds could make room for a 20-year-
old phenom named Joe Garagiola. The 33-year-old O'Dea retired after
the season ended.

Poor timing and just plain bad luck restricted Ken O'Dea's career to
one of serving as backup catcher to three other world-class catchers,
although he was probably the equal of both Danning and Cooper as an
all-around backstop. In addition to providing relief for the first-string
catcher, O'Dea was also his team's number one left-handed pinch hitter,
and in 1941 he led the National League with 42 pinch-hit appearances. He
did appear in five World Series during his 12 years in the majors and helped
the St. Louis Cardinals capture two world championships, in 1942 and
1944. Playing in 10 Series games, O'Dea batted .462 with six hits in 13 at-
bats with one home run and six runs batted in.

His career totals included 560 base hits in 2195 at-bats, for a .255 batting average in 832 games played. Defensively, Ken O'Dea was an excellent receiver with a strong throwing arm. He compiled a .983 career fielding
percentage, which was four points better than the league average. And his
50 percent caught-stealing rate was exceeded only by Campanella, Hart-

nett, and Westrum in modern baseball history. O'Dea was not the greatest catcher in the annals of major league baseball, but he was probably in the top 35 or 40. With a little luck he might have had a long career as a first-string catcher and might have left some notable defensive marks for other catchers to chase.

♦ 4 ♦

BASEBALL'S GOLDEN
AGE—1940 TO 1960

The game of baseball entered a new dimension after 1940. World War
II took center stage between 1941 and 1945, decimating professional baseball rosters and almost shutting the game down completely. President
Franklin Delano Roosevelt, however, came to the rescue of the sport, plead-
ing with baseball owners to maintain the continuity of the leagues for the
morale of the country. Roosevelt felt the people on the home front needed
a diversion from the horrors of war in order to keep their spirits up. For
four years the baseball world carried on as best it could. The minor leagues
were reduced from almost sixty leagues prior to the war to just a handful
during the first half of the decade. With most able-bodied men away fighting for their country, the major league rosters were full of retreads like Babe
Herman and Jimmie Foxx, mediocre minor leaguers, and players who had
handicaps, like one-armed Pete Gray. In 1946, the players returned from
military service to resume their careers, but it was a new game they were
returning to, primarily because of one important social adjustment — integration. Jackie Robinson, a veteran of the Negro Leagues, was signed by
Branch Rickey of the Brooklyn Dodgers to play for their Montreal farm
team. One year later, Robinson was a member of the Dodgers, and over
the next twelve years more than 100 Negro League veterans entered the
majors. These included such great players as Willie Mays, Hank Aaron,
and Ernie Banks. There were also many outstanding catchers, like Roy
Campanella and Elston Howard. Sadly, Josh Gibson, the Negro Leagues'
greatest catcher and perhaps the greatest catcher of all time, black or white,
died in 1945, just weeks after Jackie Robinson signed with Montreal. The
period from 1947 to 1960 has been called the Golden Age of Baseball, partly
because of the integration of the game that substantially increased the
quality of play in the professional leagues, and partly because, after 1960,

expansion became the law of the land, once again lowering the quality of play to previous levels or lower.

Ray Mueller

The first catcher of note between 1940 and 1960 was Ray Mueller, who was born in Pittsburg, Kansas, on March 8, 1912. Mueller was a husky 5'9", 175-pound, right-handed hitter who began his professional career with Harrisburg in the New York–Penn League in 1932. He struggled through two mediocre seasons with the bat in Harrisburg before breaking out with a .325 batting average in 1934. His performance brought him to the attention of the Boston Braves, who signed him to a major league contract for the following season, but after homering off Carl Hubbell in his first major league at-bat, he suffered through two years of futility at the plate, buying him a return ticket to the minors. Once again, Mueller responded to the challenge and hit a resounding .306 with 14 homers in 75 games with Knoxville in the Southern League. After two more years in Boston and a year in Pittsburgh, with his erratic bat, Mueller found himself back in the bush leagues, playing for Rochester in the International League and Sacramento in the Pacific Coast League for the next three years.

World War II rescued the thirty-year-old Mueller from the scrap heap and gave him yet another chance in the majors. In 1943 he was in a Cincinnati uniform and proceeded to catch a record 233 consecutive games, including all 155 games in 1944. He also hit a respectable .286 in '44 with 10 home runs and 73 RBIs. His durability earned him the nickname "Iron Man," a title that interested the U.S. government, and he was inducted into the armed forces in 1945. He returned to baseball following his discharge in '46 and played 114 games, hitting .254 and leading the league's catchers in fielding with a percentage of .994. The 34-year-old catcher's career started to wind down after that. He played five more years, but never caught more than 88 games in a season. His major league career totaled 14 years and 985 games. He batted .252 with 202 extra-base hits and 373 runs batted in. But Mueller's strength was defense. He was one of the top defensive catchers ever to play the game. His .988 career fielding average was a whopping eight points higher than the league average. And his 50 percent caught-stealing rate was a full six points above the league average. He was death on low balls, allowed only five passed balls for every 154 games played, and was one of the leaders in preventing wild pitches. If he could only have hit with more authority, he might have been one of the greatest all-around catchers of all time.

Birdie Tebbetts

Birdie Tebbetts was born George Robert Tebbetts in Burlington, Vermont on November 10, 1912. He was a tall, lanky kid with a high-pitched, squeaky voice, who acquired the appropriate nickname of Birdie while attending Providence College. After graduation, the cum laude scholar shunned the business world and entered professional baseball as a catcher. He spent three years in the minor leagues, two of them with Beaumont in the Texas League, before being called up to the Detroit Tigers in 1936. He stayed in the Big Show for 14 years. His career would have been longer if not for the three years he lost to military service in World War II. According to Al Hirshberg, "This heavyset six-footer starred behind the plate by sheer determination and brainpower. He couldn't run but never failed to be in the right places. He couldn't hit but ended up with a respectable lifetime batting average of .270. He was a peace-loving man, but he never ran away from a fight, and he instigated more than one. Tebbetts was also one of the game's greatest needlers. His acid tongue got him into plenty of trouble, but this never bothered him. He used his voice as a weapon to infuriate opposing ballplayers, for he knew that infuriated ballplayers make mistakes and mistakes lose games."

Birdie Tebbetts spent nine years in a Detroit uniform, giving Tigers fans some of the best backstopping they had ever seen. He directed his pitching staff with confidence and with authority. He knew which pitchers to cajole and which ones to terrorize. He prided himself in being on the same wavelength as his pitcher, so his calls were seldom waved off. And he kept his teammates on their toes with his constant needling. He committed more than the normal number of errors, but that was because he had a quick trigger on his throwing arm and was usually among the league leaders in catcher assists. He was regarded as the best catcher in the American League in the late '40s.

Tebbetts had considerable success in Detroit, but after the war his star waned, and the fans constantly berated him. Eventually, after hitting just .094 in 20 games in 1947, he was traded to the Boston Red Sox, where he was rejuvenated. Since his home was in nearby Nashua, New Hampshire, Boston was an ideal fit for him. And he enjoyed his finest years in a Red Sox uniform. The Sox of the late '40s and early '50s were considered to be among the finest teams ever to represent Beantown, but they always seemed to collapse at the end of each season under the relentless pressure from their pursuers, usually the New York Yankees. In 1948, they lost the American League pennant in a one-game playoff to the Cleveland Indians, and the following year they blew a one-game lead in the last two games of the season against the Yankees, in New York.

Tebbetts put together seasons of .299, .280, .270, and .310 in Boston in addition to giving them outstanding field leadership. He was 38 years old when he batted a career-high .310, but his constant complaints about the highly paid prima donnas on the team earned him a trade to Cleveland during the 1950–51 off season. After two years with the Indians, Tebbetts retired from active duty and became the manager of Cleveland's Indianapolis farm club. He went on to manage in the major leagues for 11 years, compiling a record of 748–705. On the playing field, he caught 1108 games in 14 years, with 1000 base hits and a .270 batting average.

Buddy Rosar

Buddy Rosar was another backstop in the mold of Ray Mueller, a top defensive catcher with a leaky bat. The 5'10", 170-pound backstop was born Warren Rosar in Buffalo, New York, on July 3, 1915. When he was 18 years old, he left the frozen winter's of western New York to seek his fortune with Wheeling, West Virginia, in the Mid Atlantic League. He hit a promising .293 with Wheeling; then, after missing the entire '35 season, he rapped the ball at a .347 clip with 26 homers and 97 RBIs for Norfolk in the Piedmont League in 1936 and followed it up with a mark of .344 with Binghamton in the New York–Penn League, although his home run production fell off to three in 427 at-bats. The strong-armed catcher continued to work his way up the minor league ladder, batting .332 with Newark in the top-rated International League in 1937, then surging to a stratospheric .387 the following year with 15 home runs and 79 runs batted in in just 323 at-bats. His future looked unlimited when the mighty world champion New York Yankees called him up for the '39 season.

Life in New York was exciting for young Rosar, backing up the great Bill Dickey and being part of an organization that was almost always in the pennant race. In fact, during his four years in New York, his team won three American League pennants and two world championships. Rosar's Series participation was limited to three games with one hit in one at-bat. His regular-season averages ranged from .276 to .298 during his first three years, playing in from 43 to 73 games, but when his average dipped to .230 in 1942, the 27-year-old backstop was traded to Cleveland in the off season. He spent two years with the Indians, followed by five years with the Philadelphia Athletics and two years with the Boston Red Sox, before retiring after the 1951 season, at the age of 36.

Buddy Rosar's career lasted 13 years and was highly successful. He was usually among the leaders in fielding percentage and led the American League in that category four times. And he led in assists three times. In 1946, he posted a perfect 1.000 fielding percentage, running up 121 consecutive errorless games. He extended his streak to 147 games the next year, setting a league record that was later broken by Yogi Berra. His career fielding percentage of .992 was 10 points higher than the league average, the widest spread between an individual catcher and the league in baseball history. Rosar also had one of the best caught-stealing records in major league history, tossing out 48 percent of runners who challenged his arm. His defensive strengths earned him selection to five American League All-Star teams between 1942 and 1948.

Buddy Rosar, like Ray Mueller, could have been one the best all-around catchers in the annals of major league baseball if he had had a stronger bat. His career batting average of .261 was adequate and would have been even better if he hadn't had several .210–.230 years interspersed with his other season averages. He never hit .300, but he was above .282 five times. His biggest problem at the plate was his lack of extra-base production. The outstanding power he displayed in the minors disappeared once he reached the Big Show. His extra-base totals of 35 doubles, six triples, and 18 home runs for every 550 at-bats in the minors dwindled to 25-3-3 in the major leagues. Still, Warren "Buddy" Rosar will go down in baseball history as one of the strongest defensive catchers ever to play the game.

Walker Cooper

Walker Cooper was one of the first primarily offensive catchers of the twentieth century, after Ernie Lombardi. That is not to say he was a bad defensive backstop; he was good, better than the average catcher of his day. Teammate Enos Slaughter said he was one of the best defensive catchers in the game, but unfortunately for him, his defensive strengths were in the intangible area of handling pitchers, calling a game, and blocking the plate, factors that could not be measured in this study. William Walker Cooper was born in Atherton, Missouri on January 8, 1915, the youngest of five boys in the family. Four of the boys gave professional baseball a shot, but only Walker and his older brother Mort reached the major leagues. Walker Cooper signed with the St. Louis Cardinals after high school and received his baptism of fire with the Rogers Cardinals in the Arkansas State League in 1935, where he hit a sizzling .359 with 14 home runs and 79 RBIs in 334 at-bats. His progress through the bushes was slow and steady, as was the practice of the times. Most players spent five or more years learning their trade in the minors before they were promoted to the big club. Walker's way stops included Springfield, Sacramento, Mobile, Houston, Asheville, and Columbus, and he improved both his hitting and his fielding year after year. In 1940, after hitting a solid .302 with Columbus in the American Association, he finished the year in St. Louis, joining his brother Mort, who was just completing his second full season with the Cardinals. Walker gradually took over the regular catching job from 35-year-old Gus Mancuso, who was traded to the New York Giants the following year.

Walker blossomed as an outstanding all-around catcher in 1942 and sparked his team to three consecutive National League pennants. He batted .281, .318, and .317 between 1942 and 1944 and guided his brother Mort to records of 22–7, 21–8, and 22–7. The Cardinals beat the New York Yankees four games to one in the '42 Series, with Walker contributing to the victory both offensively and defensively. In the ninth inning of the fifth and deciding game of the Series, Cooper led off with a single and carried home the eventual world championship run. Later in the inning, he picked Yankee second baseman Joe Gordon off second base to cement a 4–2 Redbirds victory. The big backstop hit .286 with four RBIs for the victorious Cardinals, while his counterpart, Bill Dickey, hit .263 with no runs batted in. The next year, Walker hit .294 in the Series, but St. Louis fell to New York in five games. They bounced back in 1944 to knock off the crosstown rival Browns in six games. Walker hit .318 and Mort tossed a shutout at the Brownies in Game 5, winning 2–0. The 1944 Series essentially ended the team of Cooper and Cooper. Walker spent most of the next year in the U.S. Navy and was sold to the New York Giants for $175,000 in January 1946.

The big Missouri farm boy played in the Big Apple for parts of four seasons and was part of the famous 1947 New York powerhouse team that clubbed a record 221 home runs in 155 games, becoming the first major league team to hit 200 or more homers in a season. Walker was a big part of the Giant outburst, hitting .305 with 35 home runs and 122 runs batted in. Despite the pyrotechnics, the Giants could do no better than a 81–73 record, good for a fourth-place finish, 13 games behind the pennant-winning Brooklyn Dodgers. Pitching and defense were once again the keys to victory, and the Giant pitchers finished next to last in ERA and the team led the league in errors. Cooper stayed with New York until midway through the 1949 season, then began a nomadic existence, playing for six teams over the next eight years, before retiring in 1957, completing a highly successful 18-year career.

Walker Cooper was big and tough, hardened by his life on the farm, and he guarded home plate as thought his life depended on it. By the time he reached the major leagues, he stood 6'3" and packed 210 pounds of muscle on his huge frame. Former teammate Ewell Blackwell once called him one of the strongest men he ever met. But his size didn't protect him from injury. According to Al Hirshberg, he "took a bad physical beating. In 1941, his rookie season at St. Louis, he broke his shoulder in a collision at the plate with Dick Mauney of the Phils. In the 1943 All-Star game at Philadelphia, he was knocked out by George Case of the Washington Senators in another clash at the plate. In 1947, while with the Giants, he was knocked cold by Enos Saughter, a former Cardinal teammate. And in 1948, a collision with Bobby Bragan of the Brooklyn Dodgers necessitated the knee operation that all but ended his career with the Giants."

In spite of the injuries, Cooper still caught more than 100 games per season seven times. And he was an eight-time All-Star between 1942 and 1950. His career record shows 1223 games caught, with 1341 base hits in 4702 at-bats, with 240 doubles, 40 triples, and 173 home runs. Overall he averaged 28 doubles, five triples, 20 home runs, and 95 RBIs for every 550 at-bats. His career slugging average of .464 may be in the top ten of world-class catchers, all-time. His defense was significantly above average, but as noted earlier, a large part of his defensive strength was in areas that could not be measured. He is one of baseball's greatest catchers, but he will probably not receive the recognition he deserves because of the deficiencies in the measuring system.

Yogi Berra

One of baseball's legendary catchers first saw the light of day on The Hill the Italian section of St. Louis, on May 12, 1925. He was christened Lawrence Peter Berra by his parents, Pietro and Paulina. When Berra was about twelve years old, he acquired a new nickname. One of his buddies dubbed him Yogi after a Hindu fakir in a movie they attended. Both the fakir and Berra often sat with their legs crossed and their arms folded, with a sour look on their faces. After graduation from high school, Yogi signed a professional baseball contract with the New York Yankees and was sent down to Norfolk of the Class B Piedmont League for seasoning. The new catcher for the Tars, a stocky kid who stood only 5'8" tall and weighed about 180 pounds, was not what you would call graceful behind the plate, but he was a terror with the bat. He was also a wild swinger who had no idea where the strike zone was. Once the pitcher threw the ball, Yogi was ready to hit it, whether it was off his shoe-tops or over his head. It was all the same to him, and somehow he always made contact and more often than not got a hit. The 18-year-old backstop hit a respectable .253 with the Tars, with 17 doubles, eight triples, and seven home runs in 376 at-bats. On defense, he led the league with 480 putouts and 16 errors. He didn't get a chance to experience a sophomore season in Norfolk because he was drafted into the United States Navy, where he spent the next two years.

Yogi Berra resumed his baseball career in 1946 with the Newark Bears of the tough International League, where he quickly became the first-string catcher. He played in 77 games for the Bears, slugging 15 home

Yogi Berra was an outstanding catcher who starred offensively and defensively. *Courtesy New York Yankees.*

runs in 277 at-bats and hitting .314. He was brought up to the parent club at the end of the season, batting .368 in seven games. The next year he became a permanent member of the New York Yankees, sharing catching duties with Aaron Robinson and Sherm Lollar. He earned his keep by compiling a .280 batting average in 83 games, with 15 doubles, three triples, and 11 home runs. His defense, however, left something to be desired, as he had considerable difficulty handling low pitches and his throwing was atrocious. Between Berra and Robinson, they threw out only 34 percent of runners attempting to steal, well below the league average. And the World Series was even worse. The Brooklyn Dodgers, led by Jackie Robinson, ran wild on the bases against the harried rookie, swiping five bases in six attempts and, according to most sources, "stealing everything but his chest protector." After catching three of the first four games of the Series and being humiliated by the swift Brooklyn runners, Berra sat out Game 5, then played right field in Games 6 and 7, as the Yankees captured the title with a 5–2 win in the finale. Fortunately for the Yankees, Yogi was not one to brood over mistakes or game failures. He was resilient and always upbeat. And sportswriters were mesmerized by his zany malapropisms, swarming around his locker like bees to honey, waiting for his latest colorful observation. Some of his comments have been quoted for more than fifty years, like his response to the question, "What time is it?" Yogi asked quite seriously, "You mean now?"

Nineteen forty-eight was a mirror image of 1947 for the kid from St. Louis. His bat hummed to the tune of .305, with 14 homers and 98 RBIs in 125 games, including 71 as a catcher. His adventures behind the plate continued, however, and his erratic throws and wrestling matches with low pitches kept manager Bucky Harris on the edge of his seat all summer. The following spring, with Casey Stengel now directing the team, former Yankees great Bill Dickey was brought in to teach Berra the fine points of catching a baseball. After working with Yogi for several days, Dickey gave Stengel his assessment of the situation, according to the *Cult Encyclopedia*. "I'd say Berra has the makings of a good catcher; I won't say great but certainly a good one." Dickey's statement was one of the understatements of the century. Yogi proved to be an excellent student and quickly picked up the nuances of moving behind the plate. And under Dickey's tutelage, he became one of the most outstanding throwers in the league. Years later, in typical Berranese, Yogi insisted, "Bill Dickey learned me all his experience."

Berra came out firing in 1949, catching 109 games, the first of nine consecutive seasons he would catch more than 100 games. By 1950 he was one of the top catchers in the American League, gunning down an astonishing 53 percent of the runners who challenged his arm, and upping his fielding average to a lofty .989. He led the league in putouts with 777 and assists with 64. He also sparkled at the plate, hammering the ball at .322 clip with 28 homers, 116 runs scored, and 124 runs batted in, in 151 games. The clumsy, ungainly backstop was on his way to becoming one of the legends of the game. In fact, Bill Dickey, reassessing his opinion of Berra's defensive skills, said in later

Bill Dickey helped transform Yogi Berra form the ugly duckling of catchers into the American League's premier receiver.

years, "Berra became one of the great catchers of all time." And his value wasn't merely in his bat and his throwing arm. He had quick reflexes that enabled him to run down balls other catchers could just look at. He was also adept at backing up bases and blocking the plate. In fact he became just the twentieth catcher in the twentieth century to pull off an unassisted double play, scooping up a bunt, tagging the batter who was still in the batter's box, and nailing the runner from third sliding home. And he became a dedicated student of batters' weaknesses and strengths. His manager, Casey Stengel, was quoted in *The Ballplayers* as saying, "He springs on a bunt like it was another dollar. To me, he's a great man. I'm lucky to have him and so are my pitchers. Yogi was a master at calling pitches and handling a pitching staff. He treated every Yankee pitcher differently; some he goaded and some he babied, depending on their temperament."

Yogi Berra followed his breakout season with a dozen more years of outstanding offensive and defensive contributions to the New York Yankee powerhouse. For the next eight years, he averaged between 22 and 30 home runs a year, driving in more than 100 runs four times and catching at least 121 games. Between 1957 and 1959 the husky Yankee backstop set a new major league record by catching 148 consecutive games and accepting 950 chances without an error. In 1958, he became one of only five major league catchers ever to field 1.000 in a season. Yogi's efforts helped the Yankees capture 14 American League pennants between 1947 and 1963, winning ten world championships along the way. Berra batted a hard .274 in the Series, with 12 home runs in 259 at-bats. He holds the record for most Series played, most games (75), and most at-bats. He was also a formidable force behind the plate, fielding .988 and keeping base runners honest. After his embarrassment at the hands of the Dodgers in 1947, and his schooling under Dickey, his caught-stealing success rate jumped up from 13 percent to 47 percent, and his total assists increased from six in 12 games to 30 in 51 games.

Berra had a career that few players can boast of. He played 18 years in all, batting .285 with 358 home runs in 7555 at-bats. Over the years, he became proficient at pulling balls down the right field foul line in Yankee Stadium, a la Bill Dickey. He probably could have hit many more home runs than the 358 that were credited to him if he only had Dickey's discipline. But Yogi was a notorious bad-ball hitter who refused to let the pitcher walk him. He often golfed low pitches into the cozy right field seats and drove high outside pitches into the left center field gap for extra bases. He was the American League MVP three times, in 1951, '54, and '55, and he was voted to the All-Star team four times. He led the league in putouts eight times, assists three times, double plays six times, and fielding average twice. His 49 percent caught-stealing rate was one of the top rates of all time, his fielding average was two points higher than the league average, and his seven passed balls allowed per year were fewer than such legendary defensive backstops as Cochrane, Hartnett, and Bench. Yogi was enshrined in the National Baseball Hall of Fame in Cooperstown, New York, in 1972.

Wes Westrum

Wes Westrum was born in Clearbrook, Minnesota on November 28, 1922. The 17-year-old catcher signed with the New York Giants in 1940 and spent his rookie season with Crookston of the Northern League in 1940, where he hit a respectable .275 in 56 games. Six years later, including three years of military service, Westrum made his major league debut on September 17, 1947, but it took a while for him to make New York his permanent home. He bounced back and forth between the Big Apple and the minor leagues for two years before settling in as the Giants' first-string catcher in 1950. During one of his sojourns to the International League, he hammered five grand slams for the Jersey City Giants in just 51 games while hitting a lofty .308. The New York Giants' hopes that their young receiver had finally come of age with the bat didn't materialize, however, as his high-water mark in the major leagues would be .243. The tall, rugged backstop was an outstanding AAA hitter, but he was over his head in the Big Show. But he did have above-average power, and he was a patient hitter capable of drawing many bases on balls, so he was able to protect his job in the short term. He caught more than 100 games in each of the next four years, but never hit above .236. In 1951, he hit only .219, but he put 20 balls into orbit and drove in 70 runs. He also coaxed 104 bases on balls from opposing pitchers in 124 games, giving him an outstanding .400 on-base percentage.

In spite of his low batting average, Wes Westrum had some big days with the bat in the major leagues, with June 24, 1950, probably his most memorable. The Giants crushed the Cincinnati Reds by a score of 12–2 on that day, with winning pitcher Sheldon Jones benefiting from seven New York home runs. Three of the homers came off the bat of Westrum, who drove in four runs and scored five in the rout. During the amazing 1951 pennant race, when the New York Giants battled back from a 13½-game Dodger lead in July to win the National League pennant in spectacular fashion on Bobby Thomson's famous "Shot Heard 'Round the World" in the bottom of the ninth inning of the last playoff game, Westrum made a number of important contributions to the victory parade. He ripped four base hits against the Philadelphia Phillies on June 17 to spark an 8–5 Giants win. In July, his grand slam paced New York to a 14–4 rout of St. Louis. He slammed a two-run homer off Ralph Branca in a 3–1 Giants victory, moving Leo Durocher's troops to within 10½ games of the top. Eleven days later, he hit a game-winning homer off Walt Dubiel of the Cubs, narrowing the gap to six games. His grand slam on September 11 paced New York to a 10–5 win over the Cardinals.

The Giants captured two National League pennants during Westrum's time with the team, losing the World Series to the New York Yankees four games to two in 1951, then sweeping the Cleveland Indians four straight in the Series notable for Willie Mays's sensational back-to-the-plate catch off Vic Wertz. Westrum caught every game of both series, going seven for 28, with one double, three runs batted in, and five bases on balls. His batting average was only .250, but his on-base percentage was an excellent .382. Defensively he intimidated the other team's base runners. He threw out the only runner who dared test his powerful arm, and he had one other assist and 52 putouts while being charged with just one error.

Wes Westrum played for the New York Giants for 11 years, during which time he was selected for two All-Star games, in 1952 and '53. He hit a paltry .217 during his career, but he still contributed to the offense by slamming 23 home runs for every 550 at-bats, with 75 RBIs. And his 117 bases on balls for every 550 at-bats gave him an excellent on-base percentage of .357, 26 points above the league average. He was a better than average defensive catcher, catching over 100 games four times and leading the league in games caught, assists, double plays, and fielding average once each. His .999 fielding average in 1950 set a new National League record for the highest single-season fielding average. Charles Johnson eventually broke the mark by fielding 1.000 in 1997. He had an above average career fielding percentage, and his 51 percent caught-stealing percentage was a full 10 percent above the league average, a differential exceeded only by Campanella, Hartnett, and Rodriguez. He was average in handling low pitches and in assists other than caught-stealing assists. His speed, however, was below average, which detracted from his game, both offensively and defensively.

Sherman Lollar

John Sherman Lollar was born in Durham, Arkansas, on August 23, 1924. When he was 19 years old, he signed a professional baseball contract with the Cleveland Indians and was sent to their AAA farm club in Baltimore of the International League. The 6', 180-pound right-handed batter exploded offensively two years later when he led the IL in batting with an average of .364 while hitting 34 home runs, driving in 111 runs and scoring 104 himself. In 1946, after spending the early part of the season in Cleveland, where he hit .242 in 28 games, he was sent back down to Baltimore, but couldn't get untracked and finished the season hitting just .234 in 67 games. He was traded to the New York Yankees over the winter, and after spending most of the year with their Newark farm team, where he hit .280, he was called up to New York just in time for the World Series against the Brooklyn Dodgers. He was rushed into two games of the Series after the Dodgers ran wild against Yogi Berra, and he banged out three base hits in four at-bats for a nifty .750 batting average. On defense, he played errorless ball and threw out one of the three runners who tried to steal on him.

Once Yogi Berra settled in behind the plate on a regular basis, Lollar became expendable, and he was traded to the St. Louis Browns in 1949. He spent three years with the hapless Browns, but hit a respectable .266 and showed flashes of power by hammering 29 home runs in 990 at-bats. He also led the league in fielding in 1951 with an average of .995. Fortunately for Lollar, the Chicago White Sox were gearing up to make a run at the New York Yankees and Cleveland Indians in the American League, and they needed a reliable catcher, so Lollar moved from St. Louis to Chicago on November 26, 1951. Frank Lane, the general manager of the White Sox, said, "It was the best trade I ever made. Sherm turned out to be one of the best catchers in the American League." The pride of Durham was definitely one of the league's standout catchers, both offensively and defensively. He was a good hitter with extra-base power, and his patience at the plate coaxed enough walks out of opposing pitchers to give him a good .357 on-base average. Lollar played for the White Sox for twelve years, catching more than 100 games a season eight times, and captured five more fielding average titles. He also intimidated base runners with his strong right arm. In 1954, he gunned down the last 18 runners who dared run on him. Over one five-year period, from 1955 through 1959, Lollar batted a solid .270 while averaging 20 home runs and 96 RBIs for every 550 at-bats. He caught 590 games during that time, going over the 100-game mark four times.

Sherm Lollar's most memorable season was 1959, when manager Al Lopez lit a fire under White Sox runners, sending them scampering around the bases like a bunch of startled fawns. The Go-Go Sox stole 113 bases that year, led by little Luis Aparicio, who swiped 56. Lollar led the team in home runs with 22 and in runs batted in with 84. Chicago beat out the Cleveland Indians by five games and faced the Los Angeles Dodgers in the World Series. In the opening game of the Series, in Comiskey Park, Early Wynn handcuffed Walter Alston's cohorts, whipping them by an 11–0 count. The Go-Go Sox should have gone home then. The Dodgers kept the White Sox batters in check over the next five games and limited the rabbits to just two stolen bases while pilfering five of their own. Larry Sherry was the hero of the Series for the Dodgers, appearing in four games, winning two and saving two. Lollar hit just .227, but he had one home run and drove in five runs in six games. On defense, he fielded flawlessly, but was victimized by Dodger runners five times in six attempts.

Lollar retired in 1963 after 18 years in the major leagues. Over that time, he played in 1752 games, catching 1571 of them. He compiled 1415 base hits in 5351 at-bats, good for a .264 batting average. His hits included 244 doubles, 155 home runs, and 808 runs batted in. He caught more than 100 games in a season nine times. He led the American League in fielding average five times, on his way to a .992 career average, an average exceeded by only four other catchers in the history of baseball: Elston Howard, Jim Sundberg, and Bill Freehan, who had fielding averages of .993, and Charles Johnson, who leads all catchers with a career fielding average of .994. Johnson, of course, is still active, so his average may change before he retires. Lollar allowed only five passed balls for every 154 games played, the lowest total of any world-class backstop. He was also one of the best at preventing wild pitches thanks to his quick reflexes. And his 43 percent caught-stealing success rate was one of the best in baseball.

Roy Campanella

Roy Campanella was one of baseball's most outstanding catchers. He could do it all, offensively and defensively. At the plate, he hammered the ball at a .276 clip, averaging 32 home runs

Roy Campanella, a nine-year Negro League veteran brought a spectacular all-around game to the major leagues.

and 112 runs batted in, for every 550 at-bats. Both totals were records for a catcher until the arrival of Mike Piazza. Campy was a dangerous .300 hitter when he was healthy, but he often played hurt, which affected his hitting but not his fielding. The stocky 5'8", 200-pound backstop was a career .292 hitter until he suffered a chipped bone in his wrist and played hurt most of the year, falling to a career-low .207 batting average. He bounced back to hit .318 in 1955, but the next year, he injured a nerve in his thumb, which prevented him from gripping a bat properly. The injury lingered through Campanella's last two years in the majors, causing his batting average to fall to .219 and .242. Then, on January 27, 1958, his major league career ended in tragedy. He lost control of his car on an icy Long Island road and crashed head-on into a tree, nearly severing his spinal column and leaving him paralyzed from the chest down. He spent the last 35 years of his life in a wheelchair, broken in body but not in spirit. The affable, good-natured backstop continued to work for the Dodgers, coaching their catchers in spring training and giving inspirational speeches around the country.

Roy Campanella was born in an integrated section of Philadelphia called Nicetown, on November 19, 1911, to a black mother and an Italian father. He was a natural athlete, with exceptional speed, outstanding agility, and excellent hand-eye coordination. When he was 16 years old, he joined the Baltimore Elite Giants of the Negro National League and came under the tutelage of Biz Mackey, considered by many people to be the greatest all-around catcher in Negro league history and definitely its greatest defensive catcher. Mackey instructed his young protégé in the fine art of catching, such as the correct way to block low pitches, how to shift his body for outside pitches, how to back up bases, how to catch pop-ups, and how to make snap throws to the bases without getting out of his crouch. Campanella was an excellent student and quickly became one of the best defensive catchers in the league. After a nine-year career in the Negro leagues, the husky backstop was signed by Branch Rickey, the general manager of the Brooklyn Dodgers, to a minor league contract. Two years later, Campanella was recalled to the big club, where he assumed the duties as the first-string catcher of Brooklyn's National League franchise. His major league debut was electrifying. Playing against the hated New York Giants, all Campanella did was rake Giant pitching for nine hits in 13 at-bats in three games, for a .692 average, with a double, a triple, and two home runs.

From 1949 through 1957, Campanella dominated the catching position in the National League. And Brooklyn dominated the league, winning five pennants and one world championship in nine years. In '49, they held off the St. Louis Cardinals to capture the pennant by a single game before falling to the New York Yankees four games to one in the Series. One of the few Series highlights for Leo Durocher's crew was the defensive play of Roy Campanella. In Game 4, Yankee shortstop Phil Rizzuto was caught in a rundown between third base and home. After making the tag on the Rizzuto, Campy fired the ball to Robinson at second to nab Henrich, who had rounded the bag. Eight innings later, Campanella picked Rizzuto off third, causing Phil to remark, "I was never picked off third base in my career, and Campanella made it look easy." In *The Artful Dodgers*, Tom Meany noted, "More than one observer has likened Campanella's quickness behind the plate to that of a cat. He can pounce on bunts placed far out in front of the plate and he gets his throws away with no lost motion. He not only has a rifle arm but an accurate one." He was always ready to throw off his mask and run down a pop fly, make a throw to a base, or outrun the batter to first base. Mickey Cochrane told Dick Young how he admired Campanella's "remarkable agility, his powerful throwing arm, and the disdainful confidence with which he pegged to any base at any time, never fearful of throwing the ball away."

In 1950, Campanella had a banner season. He hit .281 with 31 home runs and 89 runs batted in in 126 games. He also led the league in putouts and assists and tossed out 32 of 48 runners attempting to steal for a 67 percent success rate against a league average of just 43 percent. The Dodger catcher was never caught by surprise by a runner trying to steal, because he expected the runner to steal on every pitch and was always in a position to throw. Campy also contributed some offensive fireworks to his big season. On August 26, he hit three home runs off Ken Raffensberger of the Cincinnati Reds during a 7–5 Dodger victory. All three homers disappeared over the left field fence at Crosley Field, with the last one clearing the roof of a laundry located beyond the fence.

The next year, the husky catcher had an MVP season, hitting a career-high .325 with 33 homers and 108 RBIs while catching 143 games. He once again led the league in putouts and assists and nabbed 30 of 45 would-be thieves. On September 3, the Dodger backstop ripped six consecutive hits, including two homers, in a doubleheader sweep of the Boston Braves. On the 23rd, he had four hits, including a homer, in a 6–3 win over the Phils. In 1953, the stocky right-handed slugger batted .312 with 41 homers and a league-leading 142 runs batted in, and walked away with his second Most Valuable Player trophy. He also led the National League in fielding with an average of .989, and at one point in the season, he went 52 consecutive games without allowing a stolen base, a streak that had begun on September 5 the previous year. Campy's performance once again paced the Dodgers to the

National League pennant. After an off season the next year due to a chipped bone in his left hand, he bounced back in '55 and attacked the ball with a vengeance, hammering out a .318 batting average with 32 homers and 107 RBIs. His 672 putouts led the league, but his caught-stealing percentage fell off to 48 percent, still good enough to lead the league and five points above the league average. His third MVP season helped the Dodgers turn the National League pennant race into a shambles, with their 10–2 victory over the Milwaukee Braves on September 8 setting a record for the earliest pennant clinching in league history. This time, after five failures, the Big Blue Machine finally got revenge on their Yankee nemesis, winning the World Series on Johnny Podres's brilliant 2–0 shutout in Game 7. Campanella scored the first run of the game after ripping a double into the left field corner.

Most catchers are honored for either their offensive strengths or their defensive strengths, but when people talk about Roy Campanella, they talk about both his powerful bat and his powerful throwing arm with equal enthusiasm. His 32 home runs for every 550 at-bats were the highest home run average of any catcher in baseball history until Mike Piazza entered the league. Overall, Campanella played 1215 games over a ten-year career, with 1161 base hits in 4202 at-bats, with 242 home runs and 856 runs batted in. On defense, he caught 100 or more games in each of his nine full seasons in the major leagues, from 1949 through 1957. He led the league in games played four times, in putouts six times, in assists once, in fielding average twice, in double plays twice, and in caught-stealing percentage nine times. He left the game with a reputation for having the strongest throwing arm the game had ever seen. But if it wasn't the strongest, it was at least the quickest and the most accurate. His career 58 percent caught-stealing percentage is a full five percentage points higher than the number two man, Gabby Hartnett. In addition to his regular-season averages, Campy played in 32 World Series games, all against the New York Yankees, with four homers, 12 RBIs, and a .237 batting average. He fielded .996 with just one error in 32 games, and he threw out 11 of 21 attempted steals, for a 52 percent caught-stealing rate. The eight-time All-Star also set a record for the most consecutive innings caught in All-Star game competition, catching 50 consecutive innings for the National League beginning in 1949 and continuing to 1954. Included in the record was a 14-inning stint behind the plate in 1950.

Del Crandall

Del Crandall was an outstanding defensive major league catcher for 16 years, from 1949 to 1966, playing all but three of those years with the

Boston/Milwaukee Braves. Crandall was born Delmar Wesley Crandall in Ontario, Canada. on March 5, 1930. He became interested in baseball at an early age, and by the age of ten, being chubby and not naturally gifted athletically, he became a catcher. By the time he reached high school, he had filled out into a sleek 6'1", 195-pound All-Star catcher, and major league scouts were beginning to take notice of his many skills. Eventually, the strawberry blonde backstop signed with the Boston Braves and was sent to their

Del Crandall, a defensive specialist, also carried some pop in his bat. *Courtesy Jay Sanford.*

farm team in Leavenworth, Kansas, in the Western Association. Although he was only 18 years old, he became the outstanding catcher in the league, batting .304 with 15 homers and 84 RBIs in 123 games. Promoted to Milwaukee of the strong American Association at the end of the year, he hit just .083 in five games. He started 1949 with Evansville in the Triple I League, but was called up to the Boston Braves after slugging the ball at a .351 pace in 38 games in Indiana. The California youngster made his major league debut on June 17, 1949. He played in 67 games for Boston that year, catching 63 of them, and hit .263. According to Al Hirshberg, he "had all the tools to be a star. He was fast, smart, a pepperpot and a throwing marvel. He could rifle the ball to any base and wasn't bashful about doing it." The sophomore jinx caught up with Crandall in 1950, however, and he slumped to .220 before being called to military service.

He spent the next two years in the army, most of it in Japan, where he was still able to play a lot of baseball. He returned to the Braves in 1953, but found himself now playing in Milwaukee instead of Boston since the franchise had moved during the off season. Del Crandall, now more mature and focused, hit a solid .272 with 15 homers and 51 RBIs in 382 at-bats. His enthusiasm and intensity quickly made him one of the town's favorite players. He also became one of the top catchers in the National League, behind Campanella. Defensively, Crandall could do it all. He had a rifle for an arm and intimidated base runners with his quick release. He gunned down almost 50 percent of the runners who dared challenge him. And his fearlessness in throwing the ball to any base at any time kept most runners glued to their posts. Over an eight-year period, from 1953 through 1960, he caught over 100 games a year each year and led the league in total assists six times.

Del Crandall's batting average fell off to the .236–.242 range the next three years, but he hit with power, slamming 63 home runs and driving in 174 runs in 1214 at-bats, an average of 29 home runs and 79 RBIs for every 550 at-bats. In 1957, the Milwaukee Braves captured the National League pennant, beating the St. Louis Cardinals by eight games. Crandall batted .253 with 15 homers and 46 RBIs in 383 at-bats. Hank Aaron was in his prime in '57, and he batted .322 and led the league in home runs with 44, runs batted in with 132, and runs scored with 118. The Braves went on to whip the New York Yankees in the World Series four games to three. Lou Burdette blanked the Yankees 5–0 in the finale, and Del Crandall led the Milwaukee attack with a single and a home run. He batted just .211 for the Series, but he was outstanding on defense, playing errorless ball and throwing out three of four runners who tried to steal on him. In 1958 the Braves won the National League pennant again, this time beating the Pittsburgh Pirates by eight games. The big blonde backstop hit .272 with 18 homers and 63 RBIs in 427 at-bats. He was behind the plate in 131 games and led the National League in fielding with an average of .990. The World Series was not as much fun for the Braves in '58. They lost to the New York Yankees, four games to three. Crandall hit .240 with a homer and three RBIs. He fielded flawlessly again and threw out one of the two runners who tested his strong right throwing arm.

He played another five years with the Braves before finishing his career with the San Francisco Giants and Cleveland Indians. Del Crandall played in 1573 games in 16 years, with 1276 base hits in 5026 at-bats, for a .254 average. His hits included 179 home runs and 657 runs batted in, which would average 20 homers and 73 RBIs for every 550 at-bats. He was not a high-average hitter, but he was a very dangerous man in the clutch, as attested to by his RBIs. But his forte was defense, and he was one of the best defensive catchers ever to play the game. He caught over 100 games a year eight times, led the league in games played five times, in putouts three times, total assists six times, double plays twice, and fielding average four times. He was also one of the best at throwing out would-be base thieves. His 46 percent caught-stealing rate was six percentage points above the league average. Additionally, he allowed only six passed balls for every 154 games played, one of the top marks for world-class catchers. His outstanding contributions to his team was recognized by his selection to eight National League All-Star teams.

Smoky Burgess

Legend has it that Forrest Harrill Burgess entered this world with a bat in his hand. Certainly the stocky backstop was a very dangerous individual with the lumber. He first saw the light of day in Caroleen, N.C., on February 6, 1927, and soon inherited his father's nickname of "Smoky." He began his professional baseball career at the age of 17 with Lockport in the Pony League, where he hit a rousing .325 with 32 RBIs in 54 games. He played 12 games with Portsmouth in the Piedmont League in 1945 before being called into military service. He spent most of the next two years in the army, but returned to play one game for the Los Angeles Angels of the Pacific Coast League at the end of the 1946 season. The next year Smoky Burgess's bat was on fire, as he pummeled Tri-State League pitching to the tune of .387. And he continued to terrorize pitchers the next year, batting .386 for Nashville to lead the Southern Association in that category. He also slammed 22 home runs and drove in 104 runners for the Vols. After playing 19 games for Los Angeles in 1949, the beefy catcher was called up to the Chicago Cubs, where he hit .268 in 46 games. The next year, he batted .327 for Springfield in 88 games and once again was called up by the Cubs. He finished out the year in the Windy City, batting a modest .251 in 94 games.

He was now in the big time to stay, but not with the Cubs. He was traded to Cincinnati, then on to the Philadelphia Phillies over the winter. He had a successful first year in Philadelphia, playing in 110 games and punching out a creditable .296 average. The next year the left-handed swinger hit .292 and led the National League in fielding with an average of .993. In 1954 he had a career season, hitting a monstrous .368 in 108 games. His on-base percentage of .437 was second best in the National League behind Richie Ashburn's .442, and his slugging average of .510 was also among the league leaders. In spite of his success, he was shuttled off to Cincinnati shortly after the next season got under way, and he had another fine year with the bat, hitting .306 and exhibiting surprising power. After having hit just 18 home runs in his first 1324 at-bats, he unloaded 20 homers in 421 at-bats with the Reds. He also drove in 77 markers, an equivalent of 26 homers and 101 RBIs for every 550 at-bats. Included in his big season was a nine-RBI day against the Pittsburgh Pirates on July 29. Three of his four hits that day were home runs, one a grand slam. Smoky trailed off a bit the next year, hitting .275 with 12 homers. Never again would he hit more than 14 homers in a season.

Over the years, Burgess proved himself to be an adequate, if not outstanding, catcher. He was durable, catching more than 100 games in a season eight times. He was above average in fielding, leading the league in 1960 and '61, and he was solid in blocking low pitches and in blocking the plate. On the flip side, he was slow and had a weak throwing arm. But it was his bat that was his main weapon. He went on to bat over .300 twice more over the next 12 years, and continued to maintain outstanding on-base-percentages and slugging averages. Other highlights in Smoky Burgess's career included a 1956 home run off Chicago's "Sam" Jones, which gave the Reds a new National League single-season home run record of 221. In that game, he was sent up to the plate to pinch hit by manager Chuck Dressen with the order, "Make it a home run or nothing." Two years later, he hit a game-winning, three-run homer in the bottom of the ninth inning against the Chicago Cubs, completing the comeback from an 8–2 Cubs lead and giving the Reds a 10–8 victory. In 1962, his two-run homer in the tenth inning sank the Giants 6–4. On the receiving end, he caught a three-pitcher no-hitter in 1956, and three years later, he caught Harvey Haddix's 12-inning perfect game against the Milwaukee Braves.

As he got older he became one of the major leagues' most dangerous pinch hitters. He wound up his career in 1967 after playing three years with the Chicago White Sox, where he was primarily a pinch hitter. He appeared in 243 games with the Sox, 236 of them as an emergency batter. Overall, he hit .286 as a pinch hitter, with 145 pinch hits in 507 at-bats, including ten pinch-hit homers. He held the major league record for pinch hits for twelve years until Manny Mota broke it in 1979. The 5'8", 187-pounder was an excellent offensive catcher who hit for average and had above-average power. He had a sizzling minor league career batting average of .360. His major league average of .295 was the seventh highest of the 50 world-class catchers in the study whose careers have ended, his on-base percentage of .364 was the tenth highest, and his slugging percentage of .446 was the 13th highest. During his 18-year major league career, Smoky Burgess accumulated 1318 base hits in 4471 at-bats, averaging 15 home runs and 83 RBIs for every 550 at-bats. He was in the upper echelon of offensive catchers, but unfortunately his defensive weaknesses hurt his overall rating. In many areas he was adequate, as noted above, but his lack of speed and weak throwing arm penalized him. He led the league in fielding average three times, but he had a below-average range factor, and he threw out only 34 percent of the runners who attempted to steal against him, compared to a league average of 40 percent. It was the worst differential of all catchers in the study.

Gus Triandos

Gus Triandos was born in San Francisco, California, on July 30, 1930. He began his ascent to major league stardom in 1948 with Twin Falls in the Pioneer League, where he stung the ball at a .323 clip, with 18 home runs and 85 runs batted in, in just 92 games. The big 6'3", 223-pound backstop, who was called "Big, powerful, strong-armed, and slow-footed" by *The Ballplayers*, continued his way up the minor league ladder between 1949 and 1953, with two years out for military service, rattling the fences in every league in which he played. He hit a sizzling .435 with 10 homers and 42 RBIs in just 28 games with Twin Falls in '49 before moving on to Norfolk in the Piedmont League, where he smashed 16 homers in 86 games. He batted .363 with Amsterdam in the Canadian-American League in 1950, and .296 with 18 homers with Kansas City in the American Association in 1954 after returning from his tour of duty in the army.

Traded from the New York Yankees to the Baltimore Orioles in 1954, he embarked on a successful 13-year major league career. In his rookie season, he hit a tough .277 with 12 homers and 65 RBIs in 140 games, while fielding .989. The next year, he hit .279 with 21 homers and 88 RBIs in 131 games, but those two years were his high-water marks for batting average as he settled into the .250 range for the remainder of his major league career. His power numbers were still peaking, however. He slammed 30 home runs with 79 runs batted in in 1958 and banged out 25 more, with 73 RBIs, the next year. He spent eight years with Baltimore before being traded to Detroit in 1963, retiring two years later. The most exciting day of Triandos's career was June 21, 1964, when he caught Jim Bunning's perfect game against the New York Mets. It was the first perfect game in the National League in 84 years.

Gus Triandos played in 1206 games during his career, catching in 992 of them. He batted only .244 but averaged 24 home runs and 86 RBIs for every 550 at-bats. He fielded .987 and shot down 41 percent of all the runners who challenged his strong right arm.

Ed Bailey

Lonas Edgar Bailey, Jr., a native of Strawberry Plains, Tennessee, joined the Cincinnati Reds in 1953 at the age of 22, after just two years in the minor leagues plus two years in military service. He broke in as a backup to veterans Andy Seminick and Smoky Burgess for three years before assuming control of the backstopping duties himself in 1956. For the next five years he caught more than 98 games a year, giving manager Birdie Tebbets strong defensive play in addition to a powerful bat. He had a career year in his first full season in 1956, scorching the ball to the tune of .300 while clubbing 28 home runs and driving in 75 teammates. He hit 20 homers the next year; then fell off to the 11–17 range the next five years before hammering 21 homers in 1963.

In 1962, playing with the San Francisco Giants, Bailey split the back-stopping duties with rookie Tom Haller, batting .238 with 13 homers and 51 RBIs in 107 games. He caught two games as Alvin Dark's team edged the Los Angeles Dodgers in a three-game playoff for the National League pennant before falling before the New York Yankees in the World Series. Bailey went four for seven in the playoffs, good for a .571 average, but was held to a .071 average by Whitey Ford and company in the series.

Ed Bailey had several big days with the bat during his career. On June 24, 1956, he hit three home runs in a 10–6 win over the Brooklyn Dodgers. On August 10 of that year, the big left-handed slugger delivered a grand slam homer in an 8–1 victory over the Milwaukee Braves. Four years later, on April 16, 1960, he ripped five base hits, including a homer, in an 11–3 romp over the Pittsburgh Pirates. One month later, his ninth-inning grand slam powered the Reds over the Braves, 9–5. And in a game in 1965, he knocked in eight runs. When he retired the following year, the 6'2", 205-pound backstop left the game with a .256 career batting average, while averaging 24 doubles, 20 home runs, 70 bases on balls, and 69 RBIs for every 550 at-bats. Although he was known as an offensive catcher, Bailey handled his defensive responsibilities with the best of them. He had a fielding average of .986, tossed out 39 percent of all the runners who attempted to steal on him, allowed only seven passed balls for every 154 games, and racked up 65 total assists a season.

♦ 5 ♦

JOHNNY BENCH AND THE MODERN CATCHER— 1960 TO 1980

The period from 1960 to 1980 was a time of rapid change in the grand old game. The changes included expansion, the dissolution of the reserve clause, the birth of the free swinger, and the introduction of the designated hitter. Major League Baseball expanded from the 16 teams that had constituted the roster since 1901 to 26 teams by 1977. The American League expanded first, adding the Washington Senators and the Los Angeles Angels in 1961, and the National League followed suit the next year with the introduction of the Houston Colt .45s and the New York Mets. Casey Stengel was lured out of retirement to manage the expansion team in New York, and he echoed the sentiments of the other expansion team managers regarding the talent they inherited, as reported by Jonathon Light. "I got one catcher that can throw but can't catch, and one that can catch but can't throw, and one who can hit but can't do either." Casey's Mets set a record for futility in their first season, winning only 40 of 160 games and finishing 60 ½ games behind the pennant-winning San Francisco Giants and a full 18 games behind the ninth-place Cubs. The major leagues jumped up from 20 to 24 teams in 1969, and up again to 26 teams in 1977. The dissolution of the reserve clause in 1975 also brought about a significant change in the face of the game. Pitchers Andy Messersmith and Dave McNally played the season without a contract, then challenged baseball's reserve clause that had held players to one team during their entire career, unless they were traded. The players won, and the effects of that decision have been skyrocketing salaries for the players and frequent changes of teams by players when they become eligible for free agency after six years' major league service. The designated hitter was adopted by the American

League in 1973. The new rule, which allowed a hitter to bat for the pitcher, was never adopted by the National League because they believed it would take away much of the strategy of the game. And a new player philosophy also began to permeate the game of baseball during the '70's. Players began to believe they could make more money by hitting more home runs, that home runs were the ultimate achievement, and that strikeouts were unimportant. That mindset has led to a generation of free swingers, players who swing from their heels on every pitch and who ignore strikeout totals and lower batting averages.

Earl Battey

Earl Jesse Battey, Jr., was born in Los Angeles, California, on January 5, 1935. When he reached the age of 18, he left home to try his hand at professional baseball, signing a contract with Colorado Springs in the Western League. He played just 26 games his first year and hit a lowly .158, but by the time the next year rolled around, he had come of age, and he starred for Waterloo in the Three-I League, catching 129 games and hitting .292 with 11 home runs. Another big season with Charleston in the American Association brought him a look-see with the Chicago White Sox, where he hit .286 in seven games. He spent the next year with Toronto in the International League and got into four games with the White Sox in September. In 1957, he split his time between Los Angeles in the Pacific Coast League and Chicago, where he backed up Sherm Lollar. Unable to dislodge Lollar, he was traded to the Washington Senators in 1960, where he settled in as the regular catcher, a job he held for the next seven years.

Earl Battey batted .270 with 16 home runs a year during his 13-year career. *Courtesy Jay Sanford.*

In his rookie season with the Senators, Earl Battey caught 137 games and hit .270 with 15 homers and 60 RBIs. He also won the first of his three straight Gold Gloves as the league's best defensive catcher. In 1961, playing with the transplanted Senators in Minnesota, he hit .302 with 24 doubles and 17 homers. It was the only time in his career, he reached the .300 mark. The following year was a big year in the career of the rugged 6'1", 205-pound backstop. He rapped the ball at a .280 clip in 148 games. On defense, he fielded .991 and was credited with throwing out 24 runners attempting to steal and picking another 13 men off base. As a result, he was selected for the American League All-Star team, and won another Gold Glove. As satisfying as 1962 was, Earl Battey went one step further in '63. Having arguably his best overall season with the bat, he hit .285 with 17 doubles, 26 home runs, and 84 runs batted in in 508 at-bats. He also collected another All-Star selection and another Gold Glove.

But the best was yet to come. In 1965, the Twins beat the Chicago White Sox by eight games to win the American League pennant. Shortstop Zoilo Versalles was the spark plug of the team, hitting .273 and leading the league in runs scored (126), doubles (45), triples (12), and total bases (308). He also smashed 19 home runs, drove in 77 runners, and stole 27 bases. Earl Battey, who was the top vote getter on the American League All-Star squad, was also a major contributor to the pennant chase, catching 131 games and hitting a tough .297, with 60 runs batted in. Mudcat Grant (21–7) and Jim Kaat (18–14) led the pitching brigade. In the World Series against the Los Angeles Dodgers, the Twins went down to defeat in Game 7 when Sandy Koufax tossed a 2–0, three-hitter at them. Battey was just three for 25 in the Series, but gunned down five of the eleven men who tried to steal. He also played the last four games with a sprained neck after running into the dugout railing while chasing a foul ball.

His age and his injuries began to catch up with him in 1967. He played in 115 games, the fewest games he had played in seven years, and he hit a modest .255 with 30 RBIs. In 1967, he played in just 48 games, batting a miniscule .165, and he called it quits after the season ended. He was 32. Like most catchers, Earl Battey often played with injuries. During his career, he had more mangled fingers than he dared count. He had bad knees and suffered from a goiter that periodically flared up and ballooned his weight to 60 pounds above normal. Twice he suffered broken cheekbones from errant pitches, and he had the sprained neck, compliments of Dodger Stadium. On viewing the position of catcher, he once noted, "To be a catcher, you have to be big, and you've got to be dumb, and I qualify on both counts." He did qualify as big, but Battey certainly wasn't dumb. He was an intelligent catcher and a tough one, who never backed off from a collision and who was a block of granite to opposing base runners trying to score. In 13 major league seasons, he batted .270 with 969 base hits in 3586 at-bats, with 104 home runs and 449 RBIs, averaging 16 homers and 69 RBIs per 550 at-bats. He caught 1087 games in the majors, with a high of 147 games in 1962. He had seven years in which he caught more than 100 games. His career fielding average of .990 was one point above the league average, and his caught-stealing rate of 40 percent was four percent above the league average. He was a four-time All-Star and a three-time Gold Glove winner. And a great guy to boot.

Elston Howard

Elston Howard was born in St. Louis, Missouri on February 23, 1929, the only child of Wayman Hill, a high school principal, and Emmaline Howard, a professional dietician. His impressive ancestry included George Washington Carver, the great botanist and educator. Elston was an outstanding athlete in high school, playing football, track, basketball, and baseball. Although he was offered numerous college scholarships, he was lured to the game of baseball by a $500 bonus offered to him by the Kansas City Monarchs of the Negro American League. The 19-year-old outfielder-first baseman-catcher hit .283 as a rookie, gradually improving his average to .319 by 1950, when he was purchased by the New York Yankees. He finished the year with Muskegon in the Central League, where he played outfield and hit .283 with nine homers in 184 at-bats. After spending the 1951 and '52 seasons in the U. S. Army, most of it in Japan, he joined the Kansas City Blues of the American Association in 1953 and proceeded to hit .280 with 10 home runs and 70 runs batted in. New York Yankees manager Casey Stengel was impressed with Howard's batting skills, but he thought the youngster was too

Elston Howard was another in the long line of great Yankee catchers. *Courtesy of New York Yankees.*

slow to be a major league outfielder, so he changed Howard's position to catcher and brought Bill Dickey in to accelerate his development. The following year, Elston Howard had a breakout season with Toronto of the International League, where he stroked the ball at a .330 pace, hammered 21 doubles and 22 home runs, led the league in triples with 16, and knocked in 109 runs. His feats in Canada earned him the league's Most Valuable Player award.

That was good enough for the Yankees. They had seen all they needed to see, and they brought him up to the big club in 1955, where he backed up Yogi Berra and played left field. He was the first black to play for the Yankees, who were one of the last teams to integrate. He came to New York with a reputation as a fine defensive catcher with few weaknesses and a strong contact hitter who rarely struck out, who hit the ball hard and often. During Howard's first five years in the American League, he played 306 games in the outfield, 177 games behind the plate, and 57 games at first base. He compiled a batting average of .279 during that time, with 16 homers and 82 runs batted in for every 550 at-bats. Beginning in 1960, the Negro league graduate took over the reins as the regular catcher and Yogi Berra replaced him in left field.

In 1961, as the Yankees' regular catcher, Elston Howard enjoyed an outstanding season, hitting a career-high .348 with 21 homers and 77 RBIs in 129 games, but his exploits were overshadowed by the exciting Roger Maris-Mickey Mantle home run race. The following year, although his average fell off to .279, he hit 21 homers and drove in 91 teammates. In 1963, he once again provided significant offensive support to his team by hitting .287 with a career-high 28 homers and 85 RBIs in 135 games, and he was duly rewarded with the American League's Most Valuable Player award. New York was embarrassed by the Los Angeles Dodgers, who swept them four straight in the World Series and held them to a grand total of four runs. Howard was the only Yankee to solve the deliveries of Koufax, Drysdale, and company, pounding out five of the Yankees' 22 base hits while batting .333.

Howard batted .313 in 1964; then his career began to wind down. He retired four years later at the age of 39, ending a memorable 14 years during which he accumulated 1471 base hits in 5363 at-bats, for a .274 average. He averaged 17 home runs and 78 RBIs for every 550 at-bats. His offensive contributions suffered because half his games were played in Yankee Stadium, a field that punished right-handed hitters like Howard and Joe DiMaggio. The 6'2" 200-pounder was an outstanding defensive catcher who had a career fielding average of .993, which is tied with Bill Freehan and Jim Sundberg for the highest career fielding average in major league history. He also excelled in throwing out prospective base stealers, in preventing passed balls, and in general catching know-how. As Jonathon Light noted, "Yogi Berra played farther behind the hitter than the other prominent Yankee catcher of the 1950s and 1960s, Elston Howard. Because Howard could catch the ball before it dropped out of the strike zone, he was credited by Yankee pitchers with getting more low strike calls." During his career, Howard appeared in five All-Star games and in an unprecedented ten World Series, which rewarded him with four World Championship rings.

John Roseboro

John Roseboro was born in Ashland, Ohio, on May 13, 1933. He entered organized baseball at the bottom of the ladder, with Sheboygan of the Class D Wisconsin State League in 1952, playing under the legendary Joe Hauser, the all-time minor league home run king. Hauser had hit 63 home runs for Baltimore of the International League in 1930 and 69 home runs with Minneapolis three years later. Roseboro batted a league-high .365 for Sheboygan, but his 68 games did not qualify him for the batting title. After helping Hauser's team to a pennant, the 6', 190-pound backstop moved up the minor league ladder, finally landing in Brooklyn as the backup to Roy Campanella in 1957. The 25-year-old receiver became the Dodgers' regular catcher after Campy was crippled in a car accident during the off season. He joined forces with the powerful Los Angeles Dodger pitching staff of Koufax, Drysdale, Podres, Osteen, and Perranoski to help guide the Dodgers to four National League pennants and three world championships between 1959 and 1966. He set several catching records along the way, including a new major league record of 848 putouts in 1959 (which he broke two years later), as well as a National League record of 902 total chances. He also kept opposing base runners honest with his accurate throws, allowing only seventeen stolen bases for the year. During his career, Roseboro led the league in total chances five times, putouts four times and double plays once.

John Roseboro was more than a defensive stalwart however. He was also a dangerous clutch hitter whose big hits contradicted his modest batting average. In the 1959 National League playoff against the Milwaukee Braves, he won the first game with a tie-breaking, sixth-inning home run, giving Larry Sherry a 3–2 victory. Four years later, in the World Series against the New York Yankees, the left-handed batter smashed a first-inning, three-run homer into the upper right field deck in Yankee Stadium off Whitey Ford to spark the Dodgers and Sandy Koufax to a 5–2 victory in Game 1, setting the stage for a four-game sweep. And in 1965, against the Minnesota Twins, Roseboro hit a two-run single in the fourth inning against Camilo Pascual to break open a scoreless tie and give Claude Osteen all the runs he needed in a 4–0 shutout. The victory brought the Dodgers back from a two-games-to-none deficit and put them on the road to an eventual seven-game triumph.

The pride of Ashland was the center of one of the ugliest incidents ever witnessed in a major league park on the night of August 22, 1965. In a game against the San Francisco Giants in Candlestick Park, he was attacked with a bat by Giants pitcher Juan Marichal, who thought the Dodger catcher's return throws to the pitcher were coming too close to his head. The clubbing did not seriously injure Roseboro, but it triggered a 14-minute free-for-all that emptied both benches and led to the ejection of Marichal, whose subsequent nine-game suspension proved costly to the Giants. They blew a five-game lead with only two weeks left in the season, giving L.A. the title by two games.

John Roseboro's major league career spanned 14 years, 11 of them with the Dodgers. He played in 1585 games, with 1206 hits, 338 extra-base hits, and a .249 batting average. Blessed with better-than-average speed, the big catcher stole 67 bases in his career, including 11 in 1958 and 12 in 1961. Roseboro was an outstanding defensive catcher, winning six Gold Gloves between 1961 and 1966. He caught over 100 games 12 successive years and was one of the best game callers in the business. In a sport that requires dedication, concentration, and maximum effort, John Roseboro was a winner.

Joe Torre

Most baseball fans today think of Joe Torre as the successful skipper of the New York Yankees, whose teams won six American League pennants and four world championships between 1996 and 2003. But long before the Brooklyn native won the hearts of New York City's fickle fans, he was an outstanding major league baseball player who won All-Star status at three different positions. He came by his baseball talents naturally, following his older brothers, Rocco and Frank, to the ballpark and learning the game from the ground up. His brother Frank went on to play in the major leagues for seven years in the late '50s and early '60s. Joe was a powerful hitter as a kid, but major league scouts were discouraged by the boy's girth. He tipped the scales at a hefty 240 pounds by the time he was

15 years old. He was the star hitter for St. Francis Prep School and was offered several college scholarships, but he leaned toward a career in baseball. Although he had played first base and third base most of his early years, he was considered to be too fat for those positions, and he was converted to a catcher by the manager of the local sandlot team. The change turned out to be a good move. Torre took to the new position like a duck to water, and the extra physical exertion associated with catching melted off some of his weight. Gradually his weight stabilized around the 210-pound mark, giving the 6'1" backstop a rock-solid fame.

Once Joe Torre streamlined his body, the major league scouts came back for another look, and the Milwaukee Braves, who had earlier signed his brother Frank, nabbed the youngster for a bonus of $26,000. The 20-year-old right-handed hitter began his professional baseball career with Eau Claire in the Northern League, and he proved to be too strong for the competition there, stroking the ball at a .344 clip and capturing the batting title. He also chipped in with 23 doubles, 16 home runs, and 74 runs batted in in 369 at-bats. He was on the fast track to the major leagues, and after playing just two months with Louisville in the American Association in 1961, he was promoted to the Braves to back up the 31-year-old veteran, Del Crandall, whose eleven-year major league career was beginning to take its toll on his body. Crandall came down with a mysterious shoulder ailment that would limit his playing time to just 15 games, so Joe Torre took over the catching chores, playing in 113 games and hitting a respectable .278 with 10 homers. And his work ethic and baseball savvy brought plaudits from his pitchers. Warren Spahn, the venerable southpaw ace of the Braves who already had eleven 20-victory seasons under his belt, was duly impressed with his young batterymate, as reported by Jack Zanger. "From the first day, you knew this was an exceptional kid. He catches for the pitcher — not for himself. He's not afraid to call for the change-up or the screwball with runners on. Some catchers like the fastball all the time so they can defend themselves against the base runners. Joe knows the object of the game is to get the hitter out."

Torre became the Braves' first-string catcher in 1963 when Crandall was traded to San Francisco, and he repaid his manager's confidence in him by slamming 20 home runs and driving in 109 runs while scorching opposing pitchers to the tune of .321. He also led the league in fielding with an average of .995, and he was selected for the National League All-Star team, the first of his eight All-Star games. Over the next four years, he was arguably the best all-around catcher in the National League, averaging 25 home runs, 84 runs batted in, and hitting .290. And in 1968 he once again led the league catchers in fielding with a .996 average. Joe Torre, who had missed almost a month of the season with an injury, was beginning to feel the effects of 19 years of squatting behind the plate, so when he was traded to the St. Louis Cardinals for Orlando Cepeda in March of 1969, he moved to first base for one year, alternated between catcher and first base in 1970, then spent the next seven years as either a first or third baseman. He had some outstanding seasons in St. Louis. He won the National League Most Valuable Player award in 1971 after capturing the batting title with a stratospheric .363 batting average, while leading the league in base hits with 230 and RBIs with 137. He also led all third basemen in games played (161) and putouts (136). Two years later, he had his best day in baseball, hitting for the cycle in a 15–4 romp over the Pittsburgh Pirates. And the following year, he led all first basemen in assists with 102 and double plays with 144. Joe was traded to the New York Mets in 1975, and after three years in the Big Apple he called it quits, capping an outstanding 18-year major league adventure.

Joe Torre played 2209 games in the majors, 903 of them behind the plate, 787 at first base, and 515 of them at third base. He was selected to eight All-Star teams, four as a catcher, three as a third baseman, and one as a first baseman. He compiled a hefty .297 batting average, with 2342 base hits in 7874 at-bats, including 344 doubles, 59 triples, 252 home runs, and 1185 runs batted in. He was a steady if not spectacular defensive catcher, who was above average in fielding, caught-stealing percentage, blocking the plate, and pitch calling.

Tom Haller

Tom Haller was one of the finest catchers ever to wear a Giants uniform. He was solid on defense and exceptional on offense, banging out 19 home runs for every 550 at-bats. He played 12 years in the big show, seven of them with the Giants, and helped the orange and black capture the National League pennant in 1962, when he hit 18 home runs and drove in 55 runs in 272 at-bats. In the losing World Series against the New York Yankees, the left-handed hitter batted .286 and hit a big two-run homer in the second inning of Game 4, sparking the Giants to a 7–3 victory.

Thomas Frank Haller was born in Lockport, Illinois, on June 23, 1937. After a notable college career as quarterback for the Fighting Illini of the University of Illinois, he began his professional baseball career with Phoenix in the highly rated Pacific Coast League in 1958, hitting .228 with 16 home runs and 54 RBIs in 105 games. Three years later, he was in San Francisco backing up the veteran Ed Bailey. In 1964, the 33-year-old Bailey was traded to the Milwaukee Braves and Haller took over the back-stopping reins for manager Al Dark's club. In his baptism of fire, he caught all 23 innings of a game against the New York Mets on May 23. He caught more than 100 games for the Giants for the next four years, hitting in the .250 range and slamming 14 to 27 homers a year. He was traded to the Los Angeles Dodgers in 1968 and set the National League record for double plays with 23. He retired four years later at the age of 35.

During his 12-year career, Tom Haller had 1011 base hits in 3935 at-bats, for a .257 batting average. He averaged 21 doubles, four triples, 19 home runs, 67 bases on balls, and 70 RBIs for every 550 at-bats. Behind the plate, he showed an excellent .992 fielding average, four points higher than the league average.

Bill Freehan

William Ashley Freehan was born into a middle-class family in Detroit, Michigan, on November 29, 1941. His major interests as a child were sports, any sport — baseball, football, or basketball. He played them

Bill Freehan, an outstanding all-around catcher, is tied for the highest career fielding average for a catcher at .993. *Courtesy Jay Sanford.*

all and played them all well. And since he was always big for his age, he often played against older boys, which accelerated his development. The family moved to St. Petersburg, Florida, when Bill was fourteen, and he attended Bishop Barry High School, where he starred in both baseball and football. After graduation, he accepted an athletic scholarship to the University of Michigan, catching on the baseball team and playing end on the football team. As a 19-year-old sophomore, he hit a lusty .500, attracting major league scouts in droves. The offers were too much for the youngster to ignore, and he concluded his collegiate career after just two years, signing a $100,000 bonus contract with the Detroit Tigers, after they assured him he would be in the major leagues within two years.

The Tigers' predictions were accurate, and the muscular 6'2", 205-pound receiver got his first taste of the major leagues after his first season in professional baseball. He was not yet 20 years old. He began his career with Duluth-Superior in the Northern League in 1961, but was promoted to Knoxville in the Sally League after rattling the Northern League fences to the tune of .343 in 30 games. He hit a solid .289 with Knoxville, then rapped four hits in ten at-bats for Detroit in late September. The next year, he caught for Denver in the American Association, batting .283 with nine homers and 58 RBIs in 113 games. That combined with his spectacular defense led to his promotion to the big club in 1963. It was the beginning of a brilliant major league career that lasted fifteen years. Freehan entered the major leagues with a reputation as a graceful, well coordinated receiver. He called an excellent game, was outstanding at blocking low pitches, and was quick to pounce on bunts or back up a base.

In his rookie season, splitting his time between catcher and first base, he fielded flawlessly, committing only two errors in 73 games, although major league pitching was still ahead of him, holding him to a .243 batting average. But in 1964, 22-year-old Bill Freehan came of age. He caught 141 games, the first of nine consecutive years in which he caught 100 or more games. Once again he had no peers behind the plate as he committed only seven errors, good enough for a .993 fielding percentage. And he finally came to life on offense, banging the ball at a .300 clip with 18 homers and 80 runs batted in. It was the only time in his career that Freehan hit .300, but he continued to display long-ball power, smashing as many as 25 home runs and driving in as many as 84 runs in a single season. Over the years, he had several exciting moments on the field. On June 15, 1965, he made a record-tying 19 putouts in a game. Three years later, on August 16, 1968, he tied a major league record he would rather not have shared. In a game against the Boston Red Sox, Freehan, who was notorious for crowding the plate, was hit by a pitch in three consecutive at-bats, on his way to tying the single-season record of 24. He had a much more enjoyable day on August 9, 1971. He lofted three home runs over Fenway Park's famous Green Monster, but it wasn't enough to bring his team a victory. The Tigers lost to the Sox 12–11. His most satisfying season was 1968, when the Detroit Tigers, led by Denny McLain's amazing 31–6 season, the last 30-win season in the major leagues, won 103 games to capture the American League pennant by a hefty 12 games over Baltimore. Their opponents in the World Series were the defending world champion St. Louis Cardinals, led by Bob Gibson. But this was the Tigers' year, and they nipped the

Redbirds in seven games on the strength of Mickey Lolich's 4–1 win over Gibson in the finale. Bill Freehan doubled in Detroit's third run in their big seventh-inning uprising that broke open a scoreless pitching duel between the two aces. The Cardinals ran on Freehan whenever they could, swiping eleven bases, but he gunned down five of them, which discouraged them from testing his arm in the last two games, both Tiger victories.

When Bill Freehan retired in 1976, he had caught 1581 games, banging out 1591 base hits in 6073 at-bats with 241 doubles, 200 home runs, and 758 runs batted in, an average of 18 homers and 69 RBI s for every 550 at-bats. The fearless right-handed batter was hit by pitches 114 times in his career. On defense, he led the league in games played four times, putouts six times, double plays once, and fielding average three times. His career fielding average of .993 is tied with Elston Howard and Jim Sundberg as the best ever. He caught more than 100 games a season ten times, won five Gold Gloves, and was selected to play in eleven All-Star games, including ten in a row from 1964 to 1973.

Manny Sanguillen

Manuel DeJesus Sanguillen was born in Colon, Panama, on March 21, 1944. He was signed to a free agent contract by the Pittsburgh Pirates in 1964 and began his professional baseball career with Batavia in the New York-Penn League. He made his major league debut with the Pirates on July 23, 1967, becoming just the 15th player of Panamanian descent to play in the major leagues. Baseball.com had this to say. "Speedy for a catcher, free-swinging Manny Sanguillen had great hitting ability, a strong arm, and a cat-like quality behind the plate. The bad-ball hitting Sanguillen was a good contact hitter, but rarely walked. He was durable, catching more than 100 games in seven of his first eight full seasons with the Pirates."

Sanguillen stroked the ball at a .303 pace in 1969, .325 in 1970, and .319 in '71. On May 8, 1969, the 6', 193-pound right-handed hitter smashed a single, double, and triple in the Bucs' 7–1 win over the San Diego Padres. On October 9, 1972, he homered to drive in the winning run in a 3–2 victory over the Cincinnati Reds. He also excelled behind the plate during this time. He led the league in assists with 72 and double plays with 12 in 1971. And he shot down 106 out of 230 prospective base stealers over the three-year period, a 46 percent success rate.

The Pittsburgh Pirates won the National League Eastern Division title four times in five years between 1970 and 1974, finishing third in 1973, two and a half games behind the New York Mets. The Bucs lost the NLCS in '70, '72, and '74, but defeated the San Francisco Giants three games to one in the 1971 NLCS and went on to meet the Baltimore Orioles in the World Series. The pride of the Steel City prevailed in the Fall Classic four games to three, taking the finale 2–1 behind the four-hit pitching of Steve Blass. Sanguillen played flawlessly in the field and pounded Oriole pitching for 11 base hits and a .379 batting average.

Manny Sanguillen completed his 13-year major league career in 1980, having played 1448 games with 1500 base hits in 5062 at-bats, for a .296 batting average. He averaged 24 doubles, six triples, nine home runs, and 64 RBIs for every 550 at-bats. He was also among the top receivers on defense, particularly regarding his arm. He outgunned his peers in stolen base attempts and in picking men off base.

Johnny Bench

Johnny Lee Bench was one of the catching fraternity's most outspoken self-promoters, a man who created an almost mythical image of himself. Although, in all likelihood, he was the greatest catcher of the last 40 years, whether or not he was the greatest catcher of all time remains to be seen. Many of today's younger fans, who never saw Berra, Campanella, Dickey, Cochrane, or Hartnett, but who constantly heard Bench proclaim he could throw out any base runner alive, consider him to be the best ever. That theory will be addressed later in this book.

Bench came out of Oklahoma City, Oklahoma, in 1965 to begin a memorable 19-year professional baseball career. After a three-year internship in the minor leagues, Johnny Lee Bench caught 154 games for the Big Red Machine in his rookie season, hitting .275 with 15 home runs and 82 runs batted in. And he led the league with 942 putouts and 102 assists. His demeanor, however, occasionally drew the ire of his teammates. He was flashy, cocky, and brash. He notified his teammates early in the year that he was going to win the National League Rookie of the Year award, and then he went out and won it. He took control of the game on the field from day one, insisting on calling the pitches and on positioning the infielders. Some pitchers called him "The Little General," and one pitcher said Bench treated him like a two-year-old. Veteran infielders like Leo Cardenas, Tommy Helms, and Pete Rose resented the rookie's dictatorial attitude.

Bench was a durable workaholic who caught 100 or more games his first 13 years with Cincinnati, tying the major league record set by Bill Dickey. On August 3, 1969, he pounded out five hits to pace Cincinnati to a 19–17 win over Philadelphia. A year later, on July 26, he took Steve Carlton of the St. Louis Cardinals deep on three consecutive at-bats in a 12–5 Redlegs victory. He repeated the feat against Carlton on May 9, 1973, as the Reds prevailed 9–7, and on May 29, 1980, he made it a trifecta, slamming three homers off Randy Jones of San Diego in a 5–3 Cincinnati victory. In 1970, the Binger Banger had a career season, hitting a career-high .293 while leading the league in home runs with 45 and RBIs with 148. His remarkable achievements were rewarded with the National League's Most Valuable Player Award. The Reds rode Bench's long ball barrage to a division title, winning the west by 14½ games. They went on to sweep the Pittsburgh Pirates in the NLCS, but were eventually derailed by the Baltimore Orioles, who shut them down in the World Series, winning it in five games. During the off season, the Oklahoma native made a concerted effort to promote himself as the greatest catcher in baseball history. He accompanied Bob Hope on a tour to visit and entertain the troops in Vietnam. He made a number of guest appearances on TV shows, played in the Bob Hope celebrity golf tournament, and acted in an episode of *Mission: Impossible*. When people began comparing him with another outstanding catcher, Thurman Munson, Bench boasted, "When people think of catchers, they think of me first."

The Reds finished fifth in the six-team Western Division in 1971, but the next year they were back in control. Johnny Bench once again led the league in home runs with 40, including seven in a five-game span in late May. He also showed the way in runs batted in with 125, as the Reds whipped the Los Angeles Dodgers by 10½ games in the West, then nipped the Pirates three games to two in the NLCS. Once again, however, their magic failed them in the World Series, and they fell to the American League champions, this time the Oakland Athletics. Bench was involved in one of the most memorable incidents in that Series, but it was one he would rather forget. In the third game, he stepped to the plate with runners on second and third and one man out. Gene Tenace motioned for an intentional walk after the count reached three and two, and Johnny Bench watched helplessly as Vida Blue slipped a slider over the outside corner for strike three.

Between 1970 and 1981, Cincinnati won seven division titles, four National League pennants and two world championships. They defeated the Boston Red Sox in the 1975 World Series, four games to three, and they beat the New York Yankees in the 1976 Fall Classic, four-zip. Injuries and the strain of catching finally caught up with Johnny Bench in 1981, and he was moved to the infield, at either first or third base, during his last three years in the majors. He was physically and mentally exhausted from 14 years of catching, noting that he was more tired after catching one game than he was after playing a week at first base.

During his career, Johnny Bench was considered baseball's reigning guru. He popularized the one-handed catching style that was pioneered by Randy Hundley, and that permeated the game during the last three decades of the twentieth century. Although Bench was able to use the hinged mitt successfully, a generation of young catchers who emulated Bench's style, but didn't have his skills, suffered through major problems with their defense, including more passed balls, more wild pitches, and more stolen bases. As Thomas S. Owens noted, "The newer gloves promote one-handed catching. Catchers seldom shift and move for balls out of the strike zone or in the dirt. Instead, they paw at the pitch or backhand the ball, creating more passed balls." Owens went on to quote Dodgers general manager Branch Rickey as saying, "The catcher is never a shortstop on ground pitches, and it is almost criminal for a catcher to try to handle such pitches only with his glove."

When Bench retired in 1983, he left a batch of records and honors behind. He held the major league record for most career home runs by a catcher (327). He holds National League records for the most consecutive years catching 100 or more games (13), the most home runs in five consecutive games (seven), and the most doubles by a catcher in a season (40). He won two Most Valuable Player trophies (1970 and 1972), was named to fourteen National League All-Star teams, and won fourteen Gold Gloves for his defensive genius. He played in 2158 games in 17 years, 1742 of them as a catcher, compiling a .267 batting average with 2048 base hits in 7658 at-bats, including 381 doubles, 24 triples, 389 home runs, and 1376 runs batted in. On defense, he was outstanding in most phases of the game, including preventing passed balls and wild pitches, backing up bases, and blocking the plate. He was the game's preeminent gun behind the plate, but he himself overstated his performance. In his autobiography, he said, "...my record for throwing out base stealers was better than 50 percent, compared to an average of 25 to 30 percent among other catchers." In fact, he tossed out 43 percent of all runners who attempted to steal on him, seven percent above the league average, outstanding but not the mythical record he publicized.

Ted Simmons

Ted Simmons was one of the game's most talented switch-hitters. Three times during his illustrious career he hit home runs from both sides of the plate in the same game. He was a decent, although not outstanding, defensive catcher, but his primary enjoyment in life was hitting a baseball, something he did with consistency and with power. Ted Lyle Simmons first saw the light of day in Highland Park, Michigan, on August 9, 1949. The rugged 5'11", 195-pound receiver began his professional baseball career at the age of 17, with the Sarasota Cardinals in the Gulf Coast League. After punishing the ball at a .350 clip in six games, he was promoted to Cedar Rapids in the Midwest League, where he played 47 games and batted a respectable .269 with four homers in 171 at-bats. The next year, the 18-year-old phenom led the California League in hitting with an average of .331 and in RBIs with 117. He also chipped in with 28 homers in 493 at-bats. That performance earned him a trip to St. Louis, where he appeared in two games at the end of the season. In 1969, with Tulsa in the American Association, he hit .317 in 129 games, with 16 homers and 88 RBIs. He returned to Tulsa to start the 1970 season, but was recalled to the Cardinals after punishing American Association pitchers for a .373 average in 15 games. He played 82 games with St. Louis, batting .243 with three homers. The next year he had a breakout season, batting .304 with seven homers and 77 RBIs in 133 games, with a .989 fielding average. He would catch more than 100 games for the next ten consecutive seasons. In 1972 he hit .303 and upped his power numbers to 16 homers and 96 RBIs in 152 games, with a .991 fielding average.

Ted Simmons was a long-ball threat from both sides of the plate, as he demonstrated on three occasions. On April 17, 1975, he hit home runs from both sides of the plate in a 14–7 loss to the New York Mets. Four years later, he duplicated

Ted Simmons, one of the game's best hitting catchers, pounded out 2472 base hits during a memorable 21-year career. *Courtesy Jay Sanford.*

the feat, hitting homers both right- and left-handed in a 9–7 win over the Los Angeles Dodgers. And he did it one more time, on May 2, 1982 when, as a member of the Milwaukee Brewers, he powered his team to an 11–4 win over the Minnesota Twins by hitting two three-run homers.

The man known as "Simba" because of his long hair played with the Cardinals through the 1980 season, and although the team challenged for the pennant several years, they couldn't grab the brass ring. Over the winter of 1980, he was traded to the Milwaukee Brewers. While a Cardinal, he hit a solid .298 with 17 homers and 89 RBIs for every 550 at-bats. In 1982, he paced the Milwaukee Brewers to the pennant by one game over Baltimore, rapping the ball at a .269 clip with 23 homers and 97 RBIs. He also led the league with a .995 fielding percentage. In the American League Championship Series, the Brewers came back from a two-game deficit to beat the California Angels 4–3 in the fifth and deciding contest. They saw the other side of the sword in the World Series when the St. Louis Cardinals fought back from a three-games-to-two deficit to take Games 6 and 7, keeping Milwaukee from the champagne celebration reserved for world champions. Unfortunately, after such a dominating regular season, Ted Simmons was not much help to his team in the postseason, batting a feeble .167 in the ALCS and .174 in the Series, with a total of two home runs and four runs batted in, in twelve games. Whitey Herzog's Redbirds also victimized him seven times in nine attempts on the bases.

Ted Simmons played with the Brewers for five years, then played three years with the Atlanta Braves before hanging up his mitt for the last time in 1988. During a notable 21-year career, he played in 2456 games, catching 1771 of them. He also played occasionally in the outfield and at first or third base. He accumulated 2472 base hits, a major league record for catchers, in 8680 at-bats, for a .285 batting average. He hit above .300 seven times, hit 20 or more home runs six times, and drove in more than 100 runs three times. He averaged 31 doubles, three triples, 16 home runs, and 88 runs batted in, for every 550 at-bats. His 483 career doubles are 46 all-time, and his 182 National League home runs are a league record for a switch-hitter. If he had been stronger defensively, he would have been among the legendary catchers in baseball history. He called a good game, and he was an above-average fielder who led the league in putouts and assists twice each and fielding average once. But he had a weak throwing arm, and he had trouble handling low pitches. He appeared in eight All-Star games, six times for the National League and twice for the American League.

Thurman Munson

New York Yankee pitcher Sparky Lyle was asked if Thurman Munson was moody, to which he replied, "No. Thurman's not moody. Moody people have good days. Thurman's just mean." He was also called gruff, grumpy, cocky, surly, and combative. He may have been all of those things at one time or another, but if so, it was probably due to his innate shyness. He was a very private person who had difficulty relating to people, but he was admired and respected by teammates and opponents alike. He was considered to be a strong competitor and an exceptional field leader. Whitey Herzog said it best, in Christopher Devine's excellent biography of the Yankee catcher. "He could throw, he could hit, he was aggressive, took charge of the game the way a catcher should. I haven't seen many catchers who do the job offensively and defensively as he could." Off the field, Thurman Munson was a loving husband and a devoted family man.

Thurman Lee Munson was born in Akron, Ohio, on June 7, 1947, to Darrell and Ruth Munson. The family moved to Randolph when Thurman was four years old, and he grew up in "the sticks," with no neighbors and only his brother Duane to play with. The two boys were taught the game of baseball by their father, a reported "hard-nosed competitor." Darrell pushed Thurman to the limit, giving him a strong work ethic that stayed with him throughout his life. By the time Thurman was old enough to play organized sports, the family was living in Canton, and he attended Worley Grade School and Lehman High School in that city, where he excelled in baseball, football, and basketball, captaining all three sports in his senior year. The tall, lean youngster played shortstop on the baseball team, but he also pitched and caught a few games. He was selected to the All-Ohio team in his senior year after hitting a rousing .581. He attended Kent State University on a baseball scholarship, where he filled out his 5'11"frame by adding 20 pounds of muscle to 195, and became a full time catcher. He was an All-American in his senior year after hitting .413 and was drafted by the New York Yankees in the first round. The Yankees gave him a $100,000 signing bonus and shipped him off to Binghamton in the Eastern League at a salary of $500 a month. The 21-year-old backstop didn't waste much time in the minor leagues, hitting .301 for Binghamton in 1968 and a sizzling .363 for Syracuse in the top-rated International League the next year before being called up to New York in August of that year.

Thurman Munson had a sensational rookie season in New York, batting .302 in 132 games, with six homers and 53 runs batted in. Defensively, he led the league in games played (126), innings (1093), and assists (80).

He also fielded .989, one point higher than the league average, and he threw out 52 percent of the runners who attempted to steal. His all-around performance earned him the American League Rookie of the Year award. As a sophomore, he batted .251 with 10 homers and 42 RBIs in 125 games. He also led the league in fielding with an average of .998, committing only one error. And he gunned down an amazing 61 percent of all runners who challenged his arm. The Yankee receiver continued to hit with consistency throughout the '70s, but he was not a long-ball threat except for 1973, when he hit 20 home runs, and 1976 and '77, when he hit 17 and 18 respectively. He was a dangerous run producer, however, driving in 102, 105, and 100 runs from 1975 through 1977, while hitting .318, .302, and .308. His defense began to suffer in the mid–70s when his body suffered a constant battering from baseballs and from opposing players. In 1974 he injured his thumb in spring training when the New York Mets' Dave Schneck's bat crashed into his right thumb on his backswing, causing damage to his medial nerve. The injury hampered Munson all year, forcing him to change his throwing delivery. Enemy base runners took advantage of his disability and stole 62 percent of the bases they attempted. He also led the league with 22 errors and saw his fielding average plummet to .974. The unnatural throwing motion eventually caused bursitis in his shoulder.

The New York Yankees were a mediocre team during Munson's first six years in the league, but by 1975 they had assembled a competitive group of athletes. One year later, they captured their first pennant in twelve years, winning the East Division by 10½ games over Baltimore, then beating the Kansas City Royals in the ALCS. They met their match in the World Series, however, as the Big Red Machine, led by Pete Rose and Johnny Bench, pummeled the Bronx Bombers in four straight. Thurman Munson was one of the few Yankees to solve Cincinnati pitching, tattoing the ball at a .529 clip. His National League counterpart edged him by three points, batting .532. The next year, with Reggie Jackson on board, New York once again edged Baltimore for the East Division crown, knocked off the Royals again, three games to two, and took the Los Angeles Dodgers to task in the World Series, four games to two. Munson hit .320 with two doubles, a homer, and three RBIs. The next year, it was more of the same. In fact, it was almost a repeat of 1977. They beat Boston, Kansas City, and Los Angeles, and Munson hit .320 again, with seven RBIs in six games. In all, in 16 World Series games, Thurman Munson batted .373 with five doubles, one home run, and 12 runs batted in. Behind the plate, he fielded a perfect 1.000 and tossed out 12 of 26 base runners for a 46 percent success rate. In the ALCS, he was almost as good, hitting .339 with four doubles, two homers, and ten RBIs. His caught-stealing percentage was 43 percent on a 12-for-28 performance, which was significantly affected by a dislocated shoulder suffered late in the season.

He was having another fine season in 1979 when his life was snuffed out in a small plane accident on August 2. He was 32 years old. He left a wife and three children and the memories of a brilliant career. The durable New York Yankee catcher caught more than 100 games a season his first nine full seasons in the majors, often playing with injuries that would bench most players. He accumulated 1558 base hits in 5344 at-bats for a .292 batting average. He hit 24 doubles, three triples, 12 home runs, and drove in 72 runs for every 550 at-bats. In addition to his substantial offensive contributions, he was also an excellent defensive catcher, once stating, "I like hitting, but defense is more important because it affects so many people and has a huge impact on the game." He was an outstanding handler of pitchers. He was aggressive behind the plate, he had the quickest release in the American League, and he was not afraid to throw to any base at any time. That approach resulted in a high number of assists for Munson, but also led to many errors. He had a sensational caught-stealing rate of 52 percent for his first five years in the league, before shoulder problems reduced his effectiveness. His career caught-stealing rate of 44 percent was still seven points above the league average, one of the highest differentials of all time. He was honored as the American League's Most Valuable Player in 1976, was a seven-time American League All-Star, and was the recipient of three Gold Gloves.

Gene Tenace

Gene Tenace is one of the most underrated catchers in baseball history. Although his career batting average was one of the lowest in this study, his 123 bases on balls for every 550 at-bats gave him an outstanding on-base percentage and his 25 homers and 84 runs batted in produced a slugging percentage 40 points above the league average. Tenace, born Fiore Gino Tennaci in Russelton, Pennsylvania, on October 10, 1946, began his professional baseball career as an outfielder with Shelby in the Western Carolina League in 1965. The 18-year-old right-handed hitter was overmatched in his rookie season, hitting just .183, but his plate discipline was already obvious as he drew 13 walks in 32 games. The next year, with Leesburg in the Florida State League, splitting his time between the outfield, first base, third base, and pitching, he hit a modest .211 in 91 games. Gradually his hitting improved as he worked his way up the minor league ladder, and by the time he reached AA and AAA ball, he had his average up to .319 and .282 respectively. And his power numbers were particularly impressive. He slammed 20 homers for Birmingham in the Southern League in 1969 in just 276 at-bats. The next year, with Iowa in the American Association, he put 16 balls into orbit in 319 at-bats.

He made his debut with the Oakland Athletics on May 29, 1969, hitting .158 in 16 games, then hit .305 in a second call-up in 1970, ripping seven homers in 105 at-bats. That performance made him a full-time major leaguer, although he was relegated to the bench as a backup to Dave Duncan. His batting average, which fell off to .274 and .225 in '71 and '72, was disappointing, but it was no worse than Duncan's, and he was a better defensive catcher than Duncan. By the time the season ended, with the A's capturing the American League West by five and a half games over the Chicago White Sox, Tenace had been named the A's regular catcher. In the ALCS, they beat the Detroit Tigers three games to two, with Tenace's only hit of the series driving in the pennant-winning run in his team's 2–1 victory in the finale. Oakland completed their amazing season by whipping the Cincinnati Reds in seven games in the World Series, for the first of their three straight world championships. And Gene Tenace enjoyed a magnificent Series, walking off with the Most Valuable Player trophy for his .348 hitting with four homers and nine runs batted in in seven games. His four home runs tied a World Series record at the time. He started Oakland on the world championship trail by smashing two home runs and driving in all the runs in the opening game 3–2 victory. In the process, he became the first player in World Series history to homer in his first two Series at-bats. His bat was quiet in Games 2 and 3, which the two teams split, but in Game 4 he homered in the fifth inning to give his team a 1–0 lead. Then he singled and scored the game-winning run in the bottom of the ninth. He hit his fourth home run of the Series in Game 5, a three-run shot in the second inning, giving his team a temporary 3–1 lead, but they eventually lost the game 5–4. He had a single in Game 6, won by the Big Red Machine, 8–1. And in the finale, he singled in the first run of the game in the first inning, then singled to drive in the tie-breaking run in the sixth inning as the A's prevailed 3–2 for their first world championship.

The Oakland Athletics repeated as American League champions in both 1973 and 1974, winning the world championship both times. In 1973, Gene Tenace slammed 24 home runs and drove in 84 runs in 160 games as the A's nosed out the Kansas City Royals by six games in the AL West, then went on to beat the Baltimore Orioles in five games in the ALCS and the New York Mets in seven games in the World Series. Gene Tenace batted only .158 for the Series, but he drew 11 bases on balls in seven games for a .467 on-base percentage. The next year, they took the West by five games over Texas, beat Baltimore three games to one in the ALCS, and took the measure of the Los Angeles Dodgers four games to one in the Fall Classic. Tenace hit .222, but drew three walks in five games for a .417 OBP. The 6', 190-pound slugger caught more than 100 games a season between 1973 and 1975, but shoulder injuries forced him to play more games at first base than catcher in 1976. He left Oakland after that season as a free agent and was eventually signed by the San Diego Padres, where he played four years. He was traded to the St. Louis Cardinals after the 1980 season and finished his career with Pittsburgh in 1983.

Gene Tenace enjoyed a 15-year major league career, catching 892 of the 1555 games in which he appeared while hitting .241. His 1060 base hits included 179 doubles and 201 home runs, giving him an average of 22 doubles, three triples, 25 home runs, 84 RBIs, and 123 bases on balls, for every 550 at-bats. His .391 on-base percentage and .429 slugging average make him one of the top offensive catchers in baseball history. He led the league in bases on balls twice, with 110 in 1974 and 125 in 1977, and he drew more than 100 walks in four other seasons. His plate patience also resulted in his being hit by pitches 91 times in his career, including a league-leading 13 in 1977. Although he is now being recognized for his offensive contributions to his teams, he was also a steady, dependable, defensive catcher. His .986 fielding average was two points above the league average, and his caught-stealing percentage was also above average. He led the league with a .998 fielding average in 1979.

Joe Ferguson

Joseph Vance Ferguson was born in San Francisco, California, on September 19, 1946. He was signed by the Los Angeles Dodgers in 1972 and shipped off to Tri-City in the Northwest league to begin his professional baseball training. After just two years in the bushes, the 6'2", 215-pound right-handed hitter started commuting between AAA Albuquerque and the parent Dodgers, finally settling in with the big club in 1973, playing in 136 games and hitting .263 with 25 homers and 88 RBIs. Although the Dodgers also had another world-class backstop on the team in the person of Steve Yeager, Ferguson was the more experienced of the two and handled most of the catching duties. He set a major league record by committing only three errors in his first full season, while leading the league in fielding average and double plays. Yeager and Ferguson alternated behind the plate the next two years, until Yeager, the stronger defensive catcher of the two, won the regular backstopping job, with Ferguson going to left field to keep his powerful bat in the lineup.

Ferguson was traded to St. Louis in 1976, then moved on to Houston the following year. He returned to Los Angeles in 1978, where he once again shared catching duties with Yeager. The California native had more than his share of injuries during his 14-year career. In 1975, his season ended on July 1 when he was involved in a free-for-all against San Diego that sent him to the hospital with a broken arm. He carried a metal plate in that arm for three years. After the 1979 season, he had surgery to remove a bone spur from his right elbow, and in 1980 he suffered a back injury that limited his playing time to 77 games. Although he hit just .238 in '80, he enjoyed the most memorable game of his career that year. On October 3, with the Dodgers trailing the Houston Astros by three games with just three games left in the season, they tried desperately to overtake their division foes. In the first game of a three-game season-ending series between the two teams, Ferguson supplied the punch the Dodgers needed. After Tommy Lasorda's cohorts tied the game in the bottom of the ninth inning, Ferguson put one of Frank LaCorte's fastballs into orbit in the bottom of the tenth to win the game. The Dodgers went on to sweep the series, but they couldn't sustain the momentum, losing the one-game playoff.

Joe Ferguson retired in 1983 after helping the Dodgers win two National League pennants, in 1974 and 1978. He batted .240 during his career, with 719 base hits in 3001 at-bats. The big catcher averaged 22 doubles, two triples, 22 home runs, 82 bases on balls, and 82 runs batted in, for every 550 at-bats. Defensively, he led the league in fielding average, double plays, and runners caught stealing, once each.

Darrell Porter

Darrell Ray Porter was born in Joplin, Missouri, on January 17, 1952. The big, rugged teenager was drafted by the Milwaukee Brewers out of high school and began his baseball career with Clinton in the Midwest League in 1970, hitting just .200 in 62 games, with four home runs. The following year, he hit .271 with 24 homers and 70 runs batted in, in 101 games for Danville in the same league, earning him a late-season promotion to the two-year-old expansion Brewers, winners of just 65 of 163 games in 1970. He got into 22 games for the Brewers, batting .214. The next year, the 6', 193-pound catcher backed up Ellie Rodriguez, spending most of his time, watching the action from the bench. He played in only 18 games, with seven base hits in 56 at-bats. By 1973, he was ready to assume full control of the Brewer pitching staff, and Rodriguez was on his way to California. Porter caught 90 games in '73 and hit a respectable .254 with 16 homers and 67 RBIs in 350 at-bats. On June 17, he had his biggest day with the bat, hitting a grand slam in a 15–5 rout of the Chicago White Sox. He also tossed out 34 of 77 runners who attempted to steal, an intimidating 44 percent success rate.

After three more seasons in Milwaukee, with his batting average bouncing between .208 and .241, he was traded to the Kansas City Royals in a five-player deal. The left-handed swinger had his most productive years with the bat in K.C., hitting .271 with 61 homers and 301 RBIs in 1895 at-bats, an average of 18 homers and 87 RBIs for every 550 at-bats. In 1979, he had a career season, batting .291 with 23 doubles, 10 triples, 20 home runs, 101 runs scored, 121 bases on balls, and 112 runs batted in, in 157 games, He also had highs in on-base percentage and slugging percentage with marks of .421 and .484 respectively. And he was outstanding on defense, gunning down 47 percent of prospective base stealers. In 1980, the Royals won the American League Western Division by a whopping 14 games over the Oakland Athletics and swept the New York Yankees three straight in the championship series to set up a World Series encounter with the Philadelphia Phillies. After dropping the first two games in the Fall Classic, the Royals fought back to take the next two, before losing in six games. Porter batted .143 but threw out two of the five men who tested his arm. The next year, the big catcher was on the move again, signing a free agent contract with the St. Louis Cardinals. He played five years in St. Louis, helping them capture two National League pennants and one world championship. In 1982, he rapped the ball at a torrid .556 pace in the NLCS and was named the series MVP. He also played a key role in the World Series, batting .286 and excelling defensively. His two-run double in the sixth inning of Game 2 of the World Series drove in the tying runs in a 5–4 Cardinal win. And his two-out single in the eighth inning of Game 7 drove in the fifth run in a 6–3 St. Louis victory. All told, in three World Series, he batted .211, fielded flawlessly, and threw out seven of 16 base runners for a 44 percent success rate.

Darrell Porter retired from the game after the 1987 season, having played 1782 games over a 17-year career. He caught 1506 games, including nine seasons of catching 100 or more games. He was considered to be a good handler of pitchers, and had one of the best throwing arms in baseball, with a 38 percent success rate, two percent above the league average. In his early years, he threw out well in excess of 40 percent of runners trying to steal, but as so often happens, the wear and tear on his body eventually took its toll on his throwing. As a batter, he hit just .247, but he was dangerous in the clutch, as evidenced by his 19 homers and 82 RBIs for every 550 at-bats. His .409 slugging average was 21 points higher than the league average. And his patience at the plate paid off with 90 bases on balls a year, giving him an excellent .354 on-base percentage. All things considered, Darrell Porter has to be regarded as one of the top all-around catchers in baseball history.

♦ 6 ♦

PIAZZA AND THE BIG
SLUGGERS—1980 TO 2005

The era from 1980 into the twenty-first century brought about another philosophical change in the responsibilities of the catcher. Where catchers from 1920 to 1980 were required to combine strong defense with a powerful bat, the emphasis after 1980 was primarily on power. Catchers were recruited for their expertise in wielding a bat, often at the expense of defense. The caught-stealing figures reflected this change as the league averages dropped from 40–45 percent from 1920 to 1960, to 35–40 percent between 1960 and 1980, down to approximately 30 percent from 2000 through 2003. Thomas Owens said that today's catchers don't work at the art of catching. They are too busy practicing hitting. Harry Danning noted, "In our day, catchers ran the game. They called the pitches, moved the fielders, and kept the base runners honest. Today's players aren't catchers. They're receivers. They just catch the ball. They're always looking into the dugout for a sign." That observation may be correct in general, but there were still several world-class catchers who ran the game like the old-timers, combining both a powerful offense and an exceptional defense.

Carlton Fisk

The first of these old-time throwbacks was born in the little town of Bellows Falls, Vermont, on December 26, 1947, the best Christmas present his mother ever received. As a catcher on a kid's baseball team, the chubby youngster was called "Pudgy," later reduced to just Pudge. The nickname stuck. Carlton "Pudge" Fisk attended the University of New Hampshire, where he dreamed about being a power forward for the Boston Celtics, but he was sidetracked when the Boston Red Sox drafted him in the first round of the 1967 baseball draft. The 20-year-old receiver received his baptism by fire with Waterloo in the Midwest League in 1968 after spending the summer of '67 in military service. He tattooed the ball at a healthy .338 pace with 12 home runs and 34 runs batted in in 62 games for Waterloo. The next year, as a member of the Pittsfield Red Sox of the Eastern League, he slumped to a mediocre .243 average. But he rebounded to hit .299 with Pawtucket and .263 with Louisville the next two years, earning a spot as the regular catcher for Boston in 1972.

The big backstop, who had melted away the blubber of his younger days, was now a muscular 220 pounds, well distributed over his 6'2" frame. He caught 131 games for the Sox in '72 and suffered with the rest of the team when they were nipped at the wire by the Detroit Tigers, losing the American League pennant by a scant half-game. Still, Fisk covered himself with glory in the pennant race, batting .293 with 22 homers and 61 RBIs in 457 at-bats. His .538 slugging average, combined with his sterling defensive performance, brought him a unanimous selection as the American League's Rookie of the Year. The next few years were trying ones for the pride of Bellows Falls. After catching another 131 games in 1973, a series of injuries to his knee, his groin, and his arm reduced his playing time to just 52 games in '74 and 79 games the following year. But Fisk came back strong after breaking his arm in spring training in '75, slugging the ball at a solid .331 clip down the stretch, to help the BoSox beat Baltimore for the division flag, then hitting .417 as the Sox swept the Oakland Athletics three straight in the ALCS. The 1975 World Series against the Cincinnati Reds has gone down as one of the greatest World Series ever played, and Carlton Fisk played a major role in the drama. His game-winning, 12th-inning home run off the left field foul pole is replayed every October. But the Big Red Machine took Game 7, 4–3, to capture the world championship.

Carlton Fisk played another five years in Boston, giving his team outstanding offense and a steady defense. He was generally regarded as one of the top two American League catchers of the seventies, along with Thurman Munson. The competition, in fact, was often heated between the two receivers, particularly on Munson's part. Thurman felt Fisk was overrated, and he resented Pudge's popularity. His pent-up feelings finally surfaced on August 1, 1973, when the Yankees visited Fenway Park in the heat of the pennant race. The score was tied at 2–2 in the top of the ninth, with Munson on third and Felipe Alou on first, when Gene Michaels, attempting to squeeze the run home, missed the pitch, leaving Munson out to dry. Thurman continued home and hit Fisk head-on. Both men hit the ground in a heap, with Fisk still holding the ball. A shoving match followed, but the two players were separated before any real damage could be done. Fisk left the Red Sox as a free agent in 1981, signing a contract with the Chicago White Sox, where he finished out his career. In his first game against his old team on April 10, Pudge ripped a three-run homer to pace his new team to a 5–3 victory. The following year, on May 16, the big backstop hit for the cycle against Kansas City, becoming the only American League catcher to hit for the cycle in the twentieth century. The cycle contained his only triple of the year. In 1985, he belted two three-run homers to spark his team to a 12–1 rout of the Texas Rangers. On September 5, 1987, he reached a milestone when he clubbed the 300th homer of his career. Two years later, on July 17, he chalked up his 2000th major league hit, in a 7–3 win over the New York Yankees.

More milestones followed for the ageless backstop. On October 3, 1991, he slammed two home runs against the Minnesota Twins, one of them a grand slam, becoming, at age 43, the oldest player ever to hit two home runs in the same game and the oldest player to hit a grand slam. Two years later, on June 24, he broke Bob Boone's games-caught record by catching his 2226th game. He retired from the game four days later, leaving a career record that will be difficult to match. Carlton Fisk was one of the major leagues' top catchers for 24 years. He was one of the game's most durable players, catching more than 100 games in a season twelve times and establishing a major league record by catching a total of 2226 games during his career. He was an eleven-time All-Star, the 1972 American League Rookie of the Year and a Gold Glove winner. He was also the All-Time leader in career home runs by a catcher with 351 until Mike Piazza broke his record in 2004. Fisk had a career batting average of .269 with 2356 base hits in 8756 at-bats. He hit 421 doubles, 47 triples, and 376 home runs, with 1330 runs batted in, averaging 26 doubles, 3 triples, 24 home runs, and 84 RBIs for every 550 at-bats. His .457 slugging average was 58 points above the league average. The big catcher had above-average speed, which served him well on the bases and in the field. His 127 career stolen bases, an average of eight stolen bases for every 154 games, were by far the highest total of the 50 catchers in this study. On defense, he was outstanding at blocking the plate, at calling a game, and as a field leader. His career fielding average of .988 was two points above the league average. He was one of the best at preventing passed balls, and his pitching staff had the lowest wild-pitch totals of all the catchers studied. His only weakness was his throwing arm, which was successful only 33 percent of the time in nailing would-be base stealers, three percent below the league average. In spite of that minor deficiency, *Baseball Digest* rated him as the best all-around catcher of the 1980s, beating out such renowned backstops as Bob Boone, Lance Parrish, and Gary Carter. They gave him the highest marks for offense and leadership and second highest for game calling and for defense. Nash and Zullo reported that Fisk was one of the best catchers at rattling a batter. Dave Winfield said, "Fisk is always talking to batters, crying about his aches and pains or his bad swing. I don't want to hear any of that. Catchers like that are just looking for ways to get me out because they know I'll do some damage." Fisk was also one of the best at stealing strikes. He showed very little movement when he caught a pitch, making it seem to be in the strike zone when it wasn't. And he was one of the top catchers at working an umpire, complaining about pitches called balls, hoping to get the umpire to call the next one a strike. Carlton "Pudge" Fisk will definitely go down as one of the most exceptional all-around catchers in the annals of major league baseball.

Jim Sundberg

James Howard Sundberg was born in Galesburg, Illinois, on May 18, 1951. After graduation from the University of Iowa, the 22-year-old catcher was drafted by the Texas Rangers and was sent to the farm team in Pittsfield, Massachusetts in the AA Eastern League, where he hit .298 in 88 games. That performance earned him a promotion to Texas as the team's first-string catcher, replacing Ken Suarez. The rugged six-footer got off the mark quickly in the Lone Star state, catching 132 games, batting .247, and demonstrating his defensive genius by committing only eight errors in 132 games, by throwing out 39 percent of the players who tried to run on him, by permitting just six passed balls, and by leading the league in double plays with 15. He proved to be a fearless receiver who had a cannon for an arm and who would throw to any base at any time, keeping the opposition solidly anchored to their bases. It took Sundberg two more years to get his bat

Jim Sundberg was a defensive genius for the Texas Rangers from 1972 to 1983. *Courtesy Texas Rangers.*

working, but when he did get untracked, he put together five notable seasons, batting between .273 and .291, at the same time providing remarkable defensive prowess behind the plate. He led the league in fielding twice, with averages of .997 and .995. He showed the way in putouts and assists three times each and topped the league in double plays twice. And his powerful throwing arm kept the league's rabbits in check.

Although Sundberg was not noted for his offensive contributions, he had several memorable days with the bat. In 1978, on his way to a .278 season, he put together a 22-game hitting streak where he pounded the ball at a .395 clip. On May 14, 1983 the right-handed hitter ripped five base hits in one game, and the next year, he hit two home runs in a game, a feat he repeated two years later.

Sundberg had an exceptional 43 percent caught-stealing rate during his first eleven years in the major leagues, but by 1985, the abuse his body took began to show, and his caught-stealing percentage fell off considerably. From 1985 through the end of his career in 1989, his rate was at the league average of 34 percent. Still, his career success rate of 40 percent was six percent above the league average, one of the highest differentials in baseball history. When he retired in 1989, he was generally recognized as one of the greatest defensive catchers in the annals of the game. His offense, however, was another matter. He had a few good seasons with the bat, but he was more often bogged down in the sub-.250 range. His 16-year career credited him with a .248 batting average based on 1493 base hits in 6021 at-bats. He averaged 22 doubles, three triples, nine home runs, and 57 runs batted in, for every 550 at-bats, with a .327 on-base percentage and a .348 slugging average. On defense, he caught more than 100 games in a season twelve times. He led the league in games played five times, in putouts six times, assists six times, double plays four times, and fielding percentage six times. He had the major league record for the highest single-season fielding average for 150-plus games, at .995. And he was tied with Elston Howard and Bill Freehan for the highest major league career fielding average, .993. He is number four all-time in career games caught with 1927 and number six in career putouts with 9767. He was a six-time Gold Glove winner, emblematic of the best defensive catcher in the league.

Gary Carter

Carter was an incessant chatterbox who, according to some batters, didn't know when to shut up. More than once an irritated batter stepped out of the batter's box to complain about Carter's antics. One time' however, Carter was outguessed, by a pitcher no less, according to *Baseball Confidential*. George Frazier, a pitcher with the Chicago Cubs, reportedly said to Carter, "Tell your pitcher just to throw three straight down the middle. I'm gonna take three and then go sit down. "He agreed and the first pitch was right down the middle," Frazier continued. "I hit a line drive up the middle for a base hit. Carter was cussing me all the way up the first base line." Carter was also considered to be an expert at conning an umpire into calling a pitch a strike. He was smooth at catching a ball and making it look like it hit the corner of the plate. One player claimed that Carter got his pitcher at least six undeserved strikes during a game. Carter is also near the top of the list of catchers who complain to the umpire, hoping to influence the ump's decision on future pitches. One pitcher was quoted in *Baseball Confidential* as saying, "Carter will

Gary Carter, another defensive magician, paced the New York Mets to their World Series victory over the Boston Red Sox in 1986. *Courtesy Montreal Expos.*

whine on every pitch that's called a ball, and he does it so often that the umpire will finally call the same pitch a strike. The umps respect Carter, so if he whines about a pitch, then the ump thinks it must be a strike." Be that as it may, Gary Carter was one of the greatest defensive catchers in the annals of major league baseball.

He was born Gary Edmund Carter in Culver City, California, on April 8, 1954. An all-around athlete in high school and the captain of the baseball, football, and basketball teams, he was also a member of the National Honor Society, dispelling the stereotype that all athletes are somewhat dimwitted. His plan to attend UCLA in 1972 quickly evaporated when he was drafted by the Montreal Expos in the free agent draft. The 18-year-old former outfielder spent three years in the Montreal farm system, learning how to catch, before moving up to the Expos in 1975. He showed some promise with the bat in his rookie season, hitting .270 with 17 homers and

78 RBIs in 144 games, and was voted the National League's Rookie of the Year by the *Sporting News*. The next year, the sophomore jinx struck, and he missed the first 60 games after colliding with the outfield wall in spring training. That effectively ended his outfield career, and he took over the catching duties from the light-hitting Barry Foote when he returned to action. Beginning in 1977, the gung-ho Carter caught 100 or more games for twelve consecutive seasons and was generally recognized as the best defensive catcher in the National League. He was outstanding in all phases of the defensive game. As noted in *The Ballplayers*, he was "the most popular catcher of the 1970s and early '80s after Johnny Bench retired. [He was] known for his ebullience, durability, clutch hitting (10 career grand slams), and skill at handling pitchers and balls in the dirt."

Gary Carter had an excellent season in 1980, batting .264 with 29 home runs and 101 runs batted in, as the Expos battled the Philadelphia Phillies for the National League pennant. And he saved his best for last, ripping the ball at a .360 clip in September, with 22 RBIs, but Montreal fell one game short when Mike Schmidt's 11th-inning home run beat them 6–4. The next year, it was déjà vu all over again. In a season when he won All-Star game MVP honors on the strength of two home runs, the Los Angeles Dodgers came on to capture the National League pennant by edging the Expos 2–1 in the fifth game of the NLCS on Rick Monday's ninth-inning home run. Carter, however, was brilliant in postseason play, slugging the ball at a .421 clip in the division series and ripping Dodger pitching to the tune of .437 in the championship series. He went on to have several more big seasons in Montreal, leading the league in putouts, assists, and games played in 1982 while hitting .293 with 29 homers and 97 RBIs. He led the league in assists, double plays, and fielding percentage the next year and batted .294 with 27 homers and 106 runs batted in in 1984.

On December 10, Carter was traded to the New York Mets for four players in a payroll-cutting move. He had two big years for the Mets before time caught up with him. In 1985, he had a big season with the bat, hitting .281 with a career-high 32 homers and 100 runs batted in. The next year, as the Mets rolled to the National League pennant, the outspoken backstop hit .255 with 24 homers and 105 RBIs. He hit a solid .276 in the World Series against the Boston Red Sox, with two home runs and nine runs batted in. In the famous Bill Buckner game, his two-out single in the bottom of the tenth inning ignited a three-run Met rally that culminated in a thrilling 6–5 victory. The Mets completed the comeback the next day, winning the world championship with an 8–5 win. Gary Carter's career began to decline after that year, and he retired in 1992, completing an exciting 19 years.

The 6'2" right-handed hitter proved to be a dangerous man with a bat in his hands during his playing days, slamming 20 or more home runs nine times and driving in 100 or more runs four times. His .262 career batting average, based on 2092 base hits in 7971 at-bats, included 371 doubles and 324 home runs, a figure exceeded by only three catchers in baseball history. Behind the plate, the converted outfielder was nothing short of sensational. He led the league in games played six times, in putouts eight times, in assists five times, in double plays four times, in runners caught stealing three times, and in fielding percentage twice. He was an eleven-time All-Star during his career, winning two All-Star MVPs, and he was the recipient of three Gold Gloves. He is number three all-time in games caught with a National League record 2056, number seven in total chances per game with 6.38, number nine in putouts per game with 5.74, number one all-time in career putouts, with 11785, number ten in career fielding average with .991, and number eight in double plays with 149.

Lance Parrish

Lance Parrish was another of the superb defensive catchers who flourished during the 1980s, along with Carter, Sundberg, and Boone. *Baseball Confidential* rated Lance Parrish as one of the best catchers of his era at blocking the plate. Sparky Anderson paid Parrish the ultimate compliment, saying, "If you try to run into Lance, you're just going to get yourself hurt." An opposing player seconded that opinion. "Lance just stands right in there and takes everything you have to give him." Parrish was not only a wall of granite around home plate; he was also a slick-fielding receiver with a powerful throwing arm and excellent range.

Lance Michael Parrish was born in Clairton, Pennsylvania, on June 15, 1956. He was drafted by the Detroit Tigers after graduating from high school in 1974 and made his professional baseball debut as a third baseman with Bristol in the Appalachian League, batting just .213 but showing exceptional power for an 18-year-old, with 11 home runs in 253 at-bats. The Tigers, who already had a marvelous third baseman in Aurelio Rodriguez, were looking for someone to replace the aging Bill Freehan behind the plate, so they converted Parrish into a catcher. It proved to be a stroke of genius, as Parrish responded to the challenge, took to the mask and mitt with enthusiasm, and developed into one of the top catchers in baseball. His batting average hovered around the .220 mark for two years, before he broke out with Evansville in the American Association in 1977, hitting a solid .279 with 25 home runs and 90 runs batted in, in 115 games.

That earned him a promotion to the big club at the end of the season, and he never again returned to the bush leagues.

Bill Freehan retired in 1976 and Milt May assumed the catching duties the following year, backed up by the husky kid from Pennsylvania. Standing 6'3" tall and tipping the scales at a muscular 220 pounds, Parrish refined his skills under the direction of manager Ralph Houk, watched May closely from the bench, and played sporadically. He played in just 85 games in 1978, hitting only .219 but shining on defense with a .987 fielding average and a sensational 44 percent caught-stealing rate. The big thrill in his rookie season was a 16th-inning, game-winning home run against the Seattle Mariners on May 16. In 1979, he assumed command of the catching position, beginning a long, successful career that saw him catch 100 or more games eleven times. His batting averages bounced around between .215 and .286 depending on how battered and bruised his body was, but he always showed above-average power, hitting between 10 and 33 home runs a year and up to 114 runs batted in over a 15-year period. On September 28, 1982, the big right-handed slugger pounded his 31st home run of the season, breaking the American League single-season home run record for a catcher. His defense was exceptional, including his game calling and leadership qualities. His only weakness was handling low pitches, which he never quite mastered. He led the league in passed balls in 1979 with 21 and followed that with a league-leading 17 the next year. He also led the league in passed balls in 1988 and 1991.

In 1984, he realized the dream of all major league players when he helped the Tigers reach the World Series. He slammed 33 home runs and drove in 98 runs during the regular season as Sparky Anderson's club ran away with the American League East title, winning 104 games to leave Toronto gasping for air, 15 games in arrears. They went on to sweep the Kansas City Royals three straight in the ALCS and moved on to the World Series against the National League–champion San Diego Padres. Anderson's fired-up crew disposed of the Padres in five games behind the two complete-game victories of Jack Morris and the slugging heroics of Kirk Gibson, who hit two homers and drove in five runs in the deciding game. Parrish, who hit .278 for the Series, also homered in the finale. And on defense, he tossed out three out of the five men who dared test his arm.

When he retired in 1994, Lance Parrish had compiled an exemplary record. He batted a respectable .252 with 1782 base hits in 7067 at-bats, including 305 doubles and 324 home runs. His offensive contributions included 24 doubles, two triples, 25 home runs, and 83 runs batted in, for every 550 at-bats. He had a low on-base percentage but an excellent .440 slugging average. And his defense was impeccable, with a .991 fielding average, five percentage points above the league average, a 39 percent caught-stealing success rate, also five points above the league average, and outstanding range. He was an eight-time All-Star and the recipient of three Gold Gloves.

Mike Scioscia

Michael Lorri Scioscia holds the record for most games played in a career by a Dodger catcher. The hard-nosed backstop appeared in 1395 games for Los Angeles between 1980 and 1992. The previous record holders were John Roseboro (1218) and, before him, Roy Campanella (1183). The 6'2", 220-pound athlete was the ideal man behind the plate, because he asked no quarter and gave none. He was the best plate-blocking catcher of his era, and some executives have called him the best of all time.

Mike Scioscia of Upper Darby, Pennsylvania, came up through the Dodger farm system, arriving in Los Angeles in 1980 after five years of minor league preparation. He suddenly found himself in a hot pennant race the following year and performed admirably down the stretch, giving first-string catcher Steve Yeager a much needed breather. He took over the reins as the number one catcher in 1982, and except for an injury-plagued '83 season, he bore the brunt of the long summer schedule until 1992. Scioscia was an outstanding defensive catcher. He had a strong arm, called an excellent game, and was like a wall of granite to base runners attempting to score. Surprisingly, the big catcher was not a power hitter, averaging under ten home runs a year. He did have a good eye at the plate, however, striking out only 36 times a year, and combining a .259 batting average with 80 bases on balls, to give him a respectable .353 on-base percentage. Scioscia's best year at the plate was 1985, when he hit .296 and drew 77 bases on balls, giving him an OBP of .409, second best in the National League.

During his career in Los Angeles, Mike Scioscia played on four division

Mike Scioscia was the heart and soul of the great Dodger teams of the 1980s. *Courtesy Jay Sanford.*

winners and two world championship teams. He was a member of the "Miracle Dodgers" of 1988, a rag-tag group of scrappers who were much maligned in the press, but who rose to mythical heights to defeat the highly favored New York Mets in the National League championship series, then took the measure of the mighty Oakland Athletics in five games in the World Series. Scioscia's most memorable day in baseball occurred in the League Championship Series. The New York Mets had defeated the Dodgers ten times in eleven meetings during the regular season and were odds-on favorites to polish them off quickly in the playoffs. The odds seemed to be accurate, as the New Yorkers took two of the first three games and were leading 4–2 after eight and a half innings in Game 4, with 18-game winner Doc Gooden on the mound. Gooden inexplicably issued a two-out walk to John Shelby. Then Mike Scioscia hit a dramatic two-run homer into the right field stands to deadlock the game at four runs apiece. Kirk Gibson won the game with a home run in the 12th, and L.A. went on to win the NLCS in seven games.

When Scioscia retired in 1992, he had compiled a .259 batting average with 1131 base-hits, including 278 extra-base hits, in 4373 at-bats. His defense was impeccable as he led the league in putouts three times, assists twice, and caught-stealing percentage twice. But the comments of the Los Angeles executives tell more about the mild-mannered backstop than mere cold statistics ever could. Executive vice president Fred Claire called Scioscia "the ultimate team player," and Tommy Lasorda added, "He is a tremendous young man, and he is one of the finest competitors that has ever worn a uniform."

Tony Pena

Antonio Francisco Pena was born in Monte Cristi in the Dominican Republic on June 4, 1957. He learned the game of baseball from his mother, who had been an outstanding softball player in her youth. By the time he was a teenager, he was being scouted by several major league teams. He was finally signed by the Pittsburgh Pirates when he was 18 and sent to Bradenton in the Gulf Coast League, where his unusual catching style and his exuberance stood out. Unlike other catchers, Pena crouched on one leg with the other leg straight out. His boyish enthusiasm quickly made him a clubhouse leader and the club's unofficial cheerleader. Pena hit just .209 in his rookie season, .224 and .238 with Charleston in the West Carolina League the next two years, and .230 with Shreveport in the Texas League the following year. He was already a polished receiver by that time, but his poor hitting was keeping him out of the major leagues. Finally, in 1979, the 22-year-old right-handed hitter solved the pitching puzzle, batting .313 with Buffalo in the Eastern League. Moving up to the tough Pacific Coast League with Portland, Pena continued to sizzle at the plate, hitting .327 with 77 RBIs in 124 games. He was brought up to the Pirates at the end of the season and impressed everyone with a .429 batting average in nine games. He was in the majors to stay.

As a rookie in 1981, Tony Pena caught 64 games, hitting a lofty .300 in 210 at-bats, and he quickly "became a fan favorite at Three Rivers Stadium for his aggressive base running and avante-garde one-leg crouch," according to Baseballlibrary.com. In 1982 he caught 137 games, the first of twelve successive seasons he would catch 100 or more games. The lean six-footer, who weighed in the neighborhood of 181 pounds, played a total of seven years in the Steel City, excelling both offensively and defensively. He demonstrated some unexpected power in his early years, hitting between 10 and 15 home runs a year from 1982 through 1986. He had his best overall season in 1983, hitting .301 with 15 homers and 70 RBIs in 151 games. And behind the plate, he fielded .992 with a 36 percent caught-stealing rate while leading the league in putouts.

Pittsburgh fans were shocked when their favorite player was traded to the St. Louis Cardinals in 1987 for Mike LaValliere, another slick-fielding backstop with a powerful throwing arm, and center fielder Andy Van Slyke. Both catchers went on to have several outstanding years with their new clubs, and Van Slyke sparked the Pirates to three consecutive National League East titles in the early 1990s. Tony Pena struggled through a tough year in 1987, hitting a barely visible .214 before he relented and started wearing glasses late in the season. The Redbirds won the National League East title that year without his help, but with his new "eyes" he came through in fine style in the postseason. He was eight for 21 for a .381 average against the San Francisco Giants in the NLCS, and he tripled and scored the only run of the game in the second inning of game six, as St. Louis won the series, four games to three. In the World Series against the Minnesota Twins, he batted .409 with four RBIs, but the Twins prevailed in seven games.

Pena moved on to Boston in 1990 and helped the Red Sox win the American League East title, hitting .263 while fielding .995 and leading the league's catchers in games played, putouts, and assists. Unfortunately, the Sox were swept four straight by the Oakland A's in the ALCS. Five years later, as a member of the Cleveland Indians, Pena was back in postseason play, as the Indians swept Boston in the division series and took the Seattle Mariners to task, four games to two, in the ALCS before dropping a four-games-to-two Fall Classic to the Atlanta Braves. The 38-year-old Pena did his part, hitting a collective .286 in eight postseason games. He retired two years later after a notable 18-year career, during which time he hit .260 with 1687 base hits in 6489 at-bats. On defense, the enthusiastic Dominican caught 1950 games over that period, the sixth highest total in major league history. He is number four in putouts with 11021 and number six in double plays with 153. He led the league in games played five times, putouts five times, assists twice, double plays four times, and fielding average twice. He was a five-time All-Star and the recipient of four Gold Gloves. One of the game's leading publications gave him the highest rating for his defensive skills, with high marks for his arm, his game calling, and his leadership. He was also noted for his exceptional range. And he was rated the top catcher at rattling batters by Nash and Zullo. His major weapon was just small talk, but he also had other weapons. Outfielder Herm Winningham complained about Pena's tactics. "I stepped into the batter's box and was waiting for the pitch when all of a sudden, he spit on my shoe. I took the pitch then stepped out of the box and told Tony, 'If you do that again, I'll beat you with this bat.' I didn't really mean it, but I had to say something back. Of course, he did what he set out to do. He broke my concentration."

Darren Daulton

Darren Arthur Dalton was a hard-nosed catcher for the Philadelphia Phillies from 1983 until 1997. Born in Arkansas City, Kansas, on January 3, 1962, the 6'2", 201-pound left-handed hitter joined the Helena club of the Pioneer League in 1980. After spending three years moving up the minor league ladder, the injury-prone receiver debuted with the Phillies on September 25, 1983. He was a capable defensive catcher and a promising long-ball hitter when he first came up. Unfortunately, Dalton's major league career was erratic, as he made eleven trips to the disabled list between 1984 and 1996, including four season-ending injuries. On June 2, 1986, he tore the ACL in his left knee, ending his season. When he returned to the wars, he was unable to crouch as low as he could before the injury. On May 6, 1991, he was involved in a car accident and suffered a broken eye socket. Three years later, on June 28, 1994, he broke his collarbone, putting him out of action for the rest of the season. In August 1995, he tore the ligaments in his right knee, and in April 1996, he went back on the disabled list, missing almost six months.

When he wasn't injured, he was the inspirational leader of the team and a dangerous hitter. In 1992, he batted .270 with 27 home runs, 88 bases on balls, and a league-leading 109 runs batted in. The next year, he hit a tough .257 with 24 homers, 117 bases on balls, and 105 runs batted in, to lead the Phillies to the National League Eastern Division title by three games over the Montreal Expos. In the NLCS, he batted .263 with a homer and three RBIs as Jim Fregosi's team knocked off the favored Atlanta Braves in six games. He hit .217 with two doubles, a homer and four RBIs in the Phils' six-game loss to the Toronto Blue Jays in the World Series.

Darren Daulton compiled a .245 batting average during his 14-year major league career, averaging 23 doubles, three triples, 19 home runs, an impressive 95 bases on balls, and 89 RBIs. His .357 on-base percentage and .427 slugging average put him in the upper echelon of offensive catchers. The two-time All-Star selection led the league in putouts, assists, and runners caught stealing, once each, and in double plays twice.

Mickey Tettleton

Mickey Lee Tettleton was born in Oklahoma City, Oklahoma, on September 16, 1960. He grew up to be one of the more underrated catchers in the major leagues, probably due to his low batting average. The handsome Okie stood 6'2"tall, weighed 200 pounds, and swung the bat with bad intentions from both sides of the plate. He was drafted out of Oklahoma State University by the Oakland Athletics in 1981 and sent to their farm team in Modesto, in the California League. He stayed on the coast for three years, alternating between catcher, first base, and the outfield and trying to learn to hit the curve ball. His batting average was a mediocre .246, .249, and .243 for his three-year stay, but he showed some power with a total of 20 home runs in 769 at-bats. In 1984, he hit just .231 for Albany in the Eastern League, but he was called up to Oakland late in the season and hit a respectable .263 in 33 games. It was his highest batting average in four years of pro ball.

Tettleton's early career was plagued by injuries. He spent four terms on the disabled list between 1982 and 1987, suffering from such things as a pinched nerve in his back, an infected foot, bad knees, and a strained groin. When he was healthy, the 27-year-old catcher gave the A's some fine all-around backstopping, but his inability to stay healthy brought about his release from the A's after the '87 season. He subsequently signed with the Baltimore Orioles, where he finally came of age as a world-class receiver. After platooning with Terry Kennedy for a year, he assumed the responsibility as the Orioles' first-string catcher in 1989, beginning a run of eight years where he played more than 100 games. He caught 100 or more games just twice in his career because of bad knees, but he also played some first base and served as the designated hitter on occasion to keep his bat in the lineup. Tettleton's offensive contributions were deceptive, because his low batting averages, which ranged from .223 to .263, were offset by his power and by his ability to draw bases on balls. Beginning in 1989, he put together eight outstanding years offensively. He hit 26 home runs that year, coupled with 73 bases on balls in 117 games, to give him an excellent on-base percentage of .369 and a sensational .509 slugging average. He hit 31 home runs in 1991 and 32 in '92, '93, and '95, with 110 runs batted in in '93. He drew more than 100 bases on balls five times over that period, including a league-leading 122 walks in 1992. His odd batting stance, however, also led to many strikeouts. He held the bat straight up next to his head, and, as reported in Baseballlibrary.com, "He was forced to commit to a pitch early and had trouble laying off change-ups and breaking balls." His strikeout totals, which reached as high as 139 in 1993, averaged 153 for every 550 at-bats, which is the seventh highest strikeout frequency in major league history.

Tettleton had two memorable days with the bat when he played with the Detroit Tigers. On June 22, 1991, he became the 17th player to hit a ball out of Tiger Stadium, in a 10–3 loss to the California Angels. Four days later, he repeated the feat, this time in an 8–7 win over the Milwaukee Brewers. The powerful switch-hitter also hit home runs from both sides of the plate on three occasions, on June 13, 1988, while playing for Baltimore, on May 7, 1993, with Detroit, and on April 8, 1995, with the Texas Rangers.

Mickey Tettleton played major league baseball for 14 seasons, averaging .241 with 25 doubles, two triples, 29 home runs, 112 bases on balls, and 86 RBIs for every 550 at-bats. His home run average, which is exceeded by only Mike Piazza and Roy Campanella in this study, is the 49th highest in baseball history, and his walk percentage is 12th. His on-base percentage of .369 is the eighth highest of the 50 catchers in this study, and his slugging average of .449 is the 13th highest. On defense, he led the league in runners caught stealing in 1991 and in fielding percentage with .996 in 1992, on his way to a fine career fielding average of .991, two percentage points higher than the league average. The two-time All-Star also liked to distract batters when he worked behind the plate. According to Nash and Zullo, he liked "to throw dirt on the shoes of batters he [knew] personally just to get a little rise out of them."

Chris Hoiles

Christopher Allen Hoiles was one of baseball's best-kept secrets during the 1990s. The big six-foot, 213-pound right-handed hitter was one of the major leagues' best catchers from 1991 through 1998, both offensively and defensively, but very few people outside baseball were aware of that fact.

Hoiles was born in Bowling Green, Ohio, on March 20, 1965. He was drafted by the Detroit Tigers in the 19th round of the free agent draft in 1986, but after three years in the Detroit farm system, he was traded to the Baltimore Orioles in a multiplayer deal in September 1988. After moving back and forth between Baltimore and their International League farm team in Rochester, N.Y. for two years, he settled in Baltimore to stay in 1991. In his first full season in the Big Time, Hoiles hit just .243, but he exhibited good power, banging 15 doubles and 11 home runs in 107 games. He also led the American League in fielding with a percentage of .998. The next year, he got off to an excellent start when disaster struck. He went down with an injury in mid–June and was lost to the team for two months. When he returned to the field on August 18, he made up for lost time, crashing 20 home runs in 310 at-bats and batting .274. And he excelled again behind the plate, fielding .994 with just three errors in 95 games. The next year, the 28-year-old receiver put together his best season in the major leagues, catching 110 games and committing only five errors for a .993 fielding percentage. In spite of the fact that he missed three weeks in August because of an injury, he pummeled opposing pitchers to the tune of .310, hitting 28 doubles, 29 home runs, and driving in 82 runs in 419 at-bats.

Chris Hoiles was the Orioles' regular catcher for five more years, during which time he led the league in fielding three times, including a perfect 1.000 fielding percentage in 1997. But injuries reduced his playing time considerably and slowed him down at the plate. His batting averages ranged from .247 to .262 over his last five years, but he maintained his power numbers, hitting 90 home runs and driving in 289 teammates in 1678 at-bats, an average of 29 homers and 95 RBIs for every 550 at-bats. And he had some memorable days with the bat, including May 17, 1996, when the Ohio native became only the fourth major league player to hit a game-ending grand slam as the Orioles edged the Seattle Mariners 14–13. Three months later, on August 15, he hit two home runs in an 18–5 slugfest against the Oakland Athletics. The next year, on May 8, 1997, Hoiles banged out two home runs and a double, good for six RBIs, as the Orioles ended Randy Johnson's 16-game winning streak with a 13–3 victory. On April 9, 1998, he participated in four double plays. And on August 14, he had another big day at the plate, becoming the ninth player and the first catcher to hit two grand slams in the same game, as Baltimore routed the Cleveland Indians, 15–3.

When Charles Johnson was traded to Baltimore in 1999, the oft-injured 34-year-old Hoiles, after suffering through spring training with a bad hip, gracefully retired. He left behind an enviable record, including one of the top fielding averages of all time, committing just 29 errors in 819 games behind the plate for a .994 average. The quick, agile backstop was also among the leaders in range factor, the fewest passed balls allowed and the fewest wild pitches made by his pitching staff. And his overall offensive numbers included 739 base hits in 2820 at-bats, for a .262 batting average. During his career he averaged 21 doubles, 27 home runs and 85 runs batted in for every 550 at-bats.

Ivan Rodriguez

Ivan Rodriguez was born in Vega Baja, Puerto Rico, on November 30, 1971. Major league scouts were first drawn to the young catcher, known as Pudge because of his chunky build, for his defensive skills, not his bat. He had excellent instincts behind the plate, as well as a cannon-like throwing arm. The 17-year-old receiver was signed by the Texas Rangers and sent to Gastonia in the South Atlantic League to refine his catching technique and to improve his hitting. In his first year of pro ball he batted .238 with seven homers in 112 games. The next year, with Charlotte in the Florida State League, he brought his batting average up to .287, and after spending the first half of 1991 with Tulsa in the pitching-tough Texas League, he was added to the Texas Rangers' roster, where he immediately stepped in as the number one man behind the plate. He was just 20 years old.

Rodriguez was a star from the first day. He hit .264 in 88 games after his recall, put opposing base runners on notice when he gunned down 34 of 70 runners who tried to steal, and chalked up an incredible 62 total assists. As he matured, his defense got even better. He tossed out a league-leading 57 runners on failed steal attempts in 1992, although he still had problems with pitches in the dirt, being charged with 10 passed balls. He batted .260 in 123 games, but still exhibited little power. By 1994, the 5'9" right-handed hitter had bulked up to a solid 205 pounds and was beginning to become dangerous with the bat. That year, he hit .298 in the strike-shortened season, with 16 home runs in 99 games. He also tightened up his defense, being charged with just three passed balls, while fielding .992 and tossing out 38 percent of runners attempting to steal, a good success rate for the average catcher, but low for him.

Pudge Rodriguez was entering his prime in 1995, batting .303, the first of nine times he would exceed the .300 mark through 2005. He hit .300 in 1996 and upped his home run total to 19, with 86 runs batted in and 116 runs scored, in 153 games. The next year, he hit .313 with 20 homers and 77 RBIs. In '98 he hit .321 with 21 homers, and in '99 he had a career season with the bat, ripping the ball at a .332 clip, with 35 homers, 113 RBIs, 116 runs scored, and an amazing 25 stolen bases, numbers that won him the American League's Most Valuable Player award. On defense, his caught-stealing success rate was 51 percent, an amazing 21 percent higher than the league average. Pudge was in a world of his own in taking out base runners. No catcher in either league could come close to his success rate. In fact, not since Johnny Bench posted a 57 percent success rate in 1972 had a catcher exhibited such an arm. And he was just

Pudge Rodriguez is one of the top-throwing catchers ever to put on the "tools of ignorance." *Courtesy Ivan "Pudge" Rodriguez Foundation.*

beginning. In 1997 he had a 57 percent success rate. In 1998 it was 56 percent, and in '99 it was 55 percent. He also led the league in total assists every year from 1995 through 1998. During his MVP season, Rodriguez had several memorable days at the plate, including June 25 when he hit two homers and drove in five runs as Texas routed Seattle, 14–4. And five weeks later, on August 1, he pounded out five hits, including a home run, in a 12–5 Rangers win over the Kansas City Royals.

As the twenty-first century got under way, Ivan Rodriguez's career peaked. He hit a personal high of .347, with 27 homers and 83 RBIs in 91 games, giving him a sensational .667 slugging average. And he led the American League in fielding with a .996 percentage, in double plays with 10, and in caught-stealing with a 49 percent success rate. The husky receiver enjoyed a two-homer game on April 3, 2000, before the largest crowd in Texas history, pacing the Rangers to a 10–4 victory over the

Chicago White Sox. Unfortunately, his season ended prematurely on July 24 when he broke his thumb on Mo Vaughn's bat while attempting to make a throw. His bat stayed hot through 2003, although he began to show signs of slowing down, both offensively and defensively, due to ten brutal years of wearing the so-called "tools of ignorance." His batting averages dipped slightly to .308, .314, and .297, and his home run totals fell to 25, 19, and 16 respectively. His caught-stealing rate, which peaked at 60 percent in 2001, plummeted to 37 percent and 33 percent the next two years.

During his career, Rodriguez has been on four division championship teams, three with Texas and one with the Florida Marlins. The Rangers lost all three division playoffs they appeared in, in 1996, 1998, and 1999. The Marlins, who were a wild card entry in the 2003 postseason playoffs, astounded the baseball world by capturing the world championship, defeating the proud New York Yankees in seven games. And Pudge was a major contributor to the victory. He hit a sizzling .353 in the Division Series, with a homer and six RBIs in four games, and he followed that up with a .321 average, two homers and ten RBIs in the NLCS. In the World Series, he hit .273 with two doubles, threw out two of four base runners attempting to steal, and fielded flawlessly.

The pride of Puerto Rico completed 15 years behind the plate in 2005, with an excellent .304 career batting average, the seventh highest career batting average for a catcher in baseball history, behind Bubbles Hargrave, Babe Phelps, Mickey Cochrane, Bill Dickey, Ernie Lombardi, and Mike Piazza. His 2190 base hits in 7198 at-bats include 445 doubles and 264 home runs, giving him an average of 34 doubles, three triples, 20 home runs, and 80 RBIs for every 550 at-bats. And his defense is flawless. He has exceptional range, is outstanding at preventing passed balls and wild pitches, and has the game's deadliest throwing arm. His caught-stealing rate of 48 percent is one of the best in baseball history and the highest since Yogi Berra hung up the pads more than 40 years ago. At this point in his career, he has been selected to 10 All-Star teams and has won ten Gold Gloves, tying him with Johnny Bench for the most Gold Gloves won by a catcher. He is unquestionably the best all-around catcher of his generation, a force to be reckoned with, either swinging a bat or wearing a glove.

Javy Lopez

Javy Lopez is another of the modern-era backstops who defy the popular philosophy of baseball management by combining a superb brand of powerful offense with strong defense. The popular native of Ponce, Puerto

Rico, completed his 14th season in the major leagues in 2005 and shows no signs of slowing down. Born on November 5, 1970, he began his baseball career with the Bradenton Braves in the Gulf Coast League in 1988, batting a wafer-thin .191. He spent another five years in the minor leagues, finally hitting his stride with a .321 batting average, 16 homers, and 60 RBIs with Greenville in the Southern League in 1992 and a .305 mark with 17 homers and 74 RBIs with Richmond in the International League the next year. His performances earned him late-season call-ups to the Atlanta Braves both years, and by 1994, he was ready to become a full-time major leaguer.

Lopez joined a team in the midst of a decade-long dynasty that saw them go from a cellar-dwelling club finishing 26 games behind the Cincinnati Reds in 1990 to a division winner in '91. Bobby Cox's team, with baseball's best pitching staff of Greg Maddux, Tom Glavine, and John Smoltz, captured their division title 11 times over a twelve-year period through 2003. And their new catcher played a big part in their success. In his rookie year, Javy Lopez was a mediocre .245 hitter, but he showed superior power with 13 home runs in 277 at-bats. And on defense, he made just three errors in 75 games. The next year, playing in 100 games, the tall, lanky receiver tattooed the ball at a .315 clip, with 14 homers and 51 RBIs, but he was just getting started. In the next two years he improved his power numbers to 23 homers both years, then exploded to 34 homers and 106 runs batted in, in 1998. Then, just when things were looking bright, the 6'3", 185-pound Lopez suffered a disappointing setback. In 1999, he was having one of his better seasons, hitting a personal high of .317, with 11 homers in 65 games, when disaster struck. He injured his knee in late July and spent the rest of the season on the bench. He bounced back to have an outstanding year in 2000, and after slumping somewhat in 2001 and 2002, he had a career year in 2003, batting .328 with 43 home runs and 109 RBIs. And he fielded .994 with five errors in 120 games and was charged with just six passed balls.

Javy Lopez's career has included trips to seven Division series, six National League Championship Series, and two World Series. Overall, he has hit .278 in the fifteen postseason series, with 10 home runs and 28 RBIs in 60 games. In 1996, he was the NLCS MVP after slugging the ball at a .542 clip with two homers and six RBIs, to lead his team to a seven-game victory over the St. Louis Cardinals. His proudest moment came in 1995 when the Braves defeated the Cleveland Indians, four games to two, to capture the world championship.

Javy Lopez elected free agency after the 2003 season and signed to play for the Baltimore Orioles. During his twelve-year career in Atlanta, he pounded out 1148 base hits in 4003 at-bats, for a .287 average. His hits included 190 doubles and 214 home runs, giving him an average of 26 doubles, two triples, 29 home runs, and 95 runs batted in for every 550 at-bats. Defensively, he has been one of the top catchers in the league, with a career fielding average of .992, including a league-leading .995 in 1996. He also has exceptional range, is perennially one of the league leaders in assists, and is especially tough blocking low balls and preventing wild pitches. Overall, the three-time All-Star is considered to be a superior all-around catcher, although not the equal of Ivan Rodriguez. His offense and defense are equally exceptional.

Mike Piazza

The secret to becoming a successful major league hitter is quite simple.

1. Get your father to build you a batting cage behind your house when you are 11 years old.

2. Take personal hitting instructions from Ted Williams when you're 16.

3. Get the Los Angeles Dodgers to draft you in the free agent draft.

Of course, it helps if you have talent.

Michael Joseph Piazza was born in Norristown, Pennsylvania, on September 4, 1968. His father, Vince, a baseball enthusiast, built his son a batting cage in the back yard of his house when the boy was eleven years old. Five years later, Ted Williams visited the Piazza household after meeting Vince at a baseball function. He spent several hours with young Mike, watching him bat and giving him some sage advice. And three years later, as an unheralded first baseman for Miami Dade North Community College, the 6'3", 197-pound slugger was drafted by the Los Angeles Dodgers in the 62nd round of the free agent draft as a favor by Dodgers manager and Piazza family friend Tommy Lasorda. When Piazza joined the Salem Dodgers in the Northwest League, he was immediately converted to a catcher since the parent club already had three first basemen, including Eric Karros.

Mike Piazza worked hard to learn the rudimentary skills needed to become a decent receiver, but his primary objective was to become a major league hitter. He advanced through the Dodgers' farm system over the next four years, honing his catching technique and perfecting his compact batting stroke. In 1992, after hitting a torrid .341 with the Albuquerque Dukes in the Pacific Coast League, and on his way to being voted the Minor League Player of the Year, he was rushed up to L.A. late in the season to replace Mike Scioscia, who was retiring at the end of the year. Mike got into 21 games for L.A., hitting .232 with one home run. The next year was the beginning of "Mike Piazza Time" in the National League. The big right-handed slugger terrorized opposing pitchers to the tune of .318, with 35 home runs, a record for rookie catchers, and 112 runs batted in. He was the first National League rookie to hit .300, with 30 homers and 100 runs batted in, since Wally Berger in 1930. The converted first baseman also performed adequately behind the plate, fielding .989, leading the league with 99 assists, and throwing out 35 percent of the runners who tested his arm. When the season ended, he was a unanimous choice as the National League's Rookie of the Year.

Piazza's bat sizzled over the next three years, with averages of .319, .346, and .336, and along the way he experienced some big days at the plate. On August 27, 1995, he pounded out two doubles and two home runs, with seven RBIs, to lead L.A. to a 9–1 win over the Philadelphia Phillies. The next year, on June 29, Piazza hit three homers and drove in six runs as the Dodgers nipped the Colorado Rockies in a Rocky Mountain slugfest, 13–10. Ten days later, he homered in the All-Star Game as the National League defeated the American League by a 6–0 count. Then, in 1997, the Norristown Bomber slugged his way into the record books with the greatest offensive season ever generated by a catcher. He ripped the ball at a .362 pace, with 201 base hits, 32 doubles, 40 home runs, 104 runs scored, and 124 runs batted in. The .362 batting average tied him with Bill Dickey for the highest batting average by a catcher who played in 100 or more games. The next year, he got off the mark quickly, hitting a grand slam against Arizona on April 9 to pace the Dodgers to a 7–2 victory, and following that up with another grand slam the next night, to power L.A. to a 7–2 win over the Houston Astros. On April 24, he hit his third grand slam of the month, tying a major league record. Then, incredibly, just three weeks later, the new Dodger owners traded their world-class receiver to Florida, who subsequently sent him to the New York Mets.

The new uniform apparently didn't discourage Mike. He continued his cannonading with the Mets, hitting .328 in 1998, with 32 homers and 111 RBIs. He followed that up with marks of .303, with 40 homers and 124 RBIs, and .324, with 38 homers and 113 RBIs the next two years. On April 14, 2000, Piazza chalked up five base hits, including a double and two home runs, in an 8–5 victory over the Pittsburgh Pirates. On June 30, his three-run homer in the bottom of the eighth inning sparked a nine-run Mets uprising that wiped out an 8–1 Atlanta lead, with the Mets winning 11–8.

He also had a 15–game streak in which he drove in at least one run, and later in the year, he had a 24-game hitting streak. New York went on to win a wild card berth in the 2000 postseason playoffs, and they made the most of it. First they beat the San Francisco Giants in the NLDS, three games to one. Then they defeated the St. Louis Cardinals in the NLCS, four games to one, to qualify to meet the New York Yankees in the World Series. But their luck ran out one series too soon. They fell to the Bronx Bombers in five games. Piazza, however, had a productive postseason for himself. After hitting just .214 in the Division Series, he hit a stratospheric .412 in the NLCS, with two doubles and two home runs. And he followed that up with a .273 average, with two homers and four RBIs, in the Fall Classic. The big catcher kept pounding the ball at a record pace in 2001, putting 36 balls into orbit, and followed that up with a 33-homer season in 2002, before losing half of the 2003 season to a painful groin injury.

The battering Piazza's body is taking has forced him to move out from behind the plate and become a first baseman periodically, a position that may become his permanent home in the near future. Piazza has played in 1703 games through 2005, and 1535 of them have been as a catcher. At the plate, the ten-time All-Star has accumulated 1929 base hits in 6203 at-bats for a .311 batting average. His 308 doubles, 397 home runs, and 1223 RBIs convert to 27 doubles, 35 home runs, and 108 RBIs for every 550 at-bats. His .388 on-base percentage is 55 points above the league average, and his .572 slugging average is 155 points higher than the league average. He may well be the greatest-hitting catcher in major league history. Unfortunately, his defense is spotty. He is an average fielder, has good range, is solid at blocking the plate, and does a workmanlike job digging balls out of the dirt and preventing passed balls and wild pitches. But he also has an erratic throwing arm that permits opposing runners to take liberties on the bases. He has yielded the most stolen bases of any National League catcher nine times in twelve years, being victimized an average of 132 times for every 154 games. And his intangibles, such as calling games and field leadership, are questionable.

Charles Johnson

Mike Piazza is unquestionably the most devastating offensive catcher of recent times, and Charles Johnson may be the most dominant defensive catcher of recent times. Charles Edward Johnson was born in Fort

Pierce, Florida, on July 20, 1971. He was drafted by the Florida Marlins in the first round of the 1992 amateur draft assigned to Kane County in the Midwest League. The 6'2", 215-pound right-handed hitter compiled a creditable .275 batting average in 1993, with 19 homers and 94 runs batted in in 135 games. Moving up to Portland in the Eastern League in '94, he led the league with 28 home runs while hitting .264. That was enough to convince Marlins management that their young backstop was ready for the big time, and he was brought up to Florida in September to get the feel of being a major leaguer.

In October, 1994, Florida's first-string catcher, the highly talented Benito Santiago, filed for free agency, leaving the catching job to the 23-year-old Johnson. But Charles was more than up to the task. After beginning the season slowly, with a barely visible .143 average on June 22 and on the brink of a demotion to the minors, he suddenly caught fire. He stroked the ball at a .337 pace the rest of the season, finishing with a respectable .251 batting average, with 11 homers and 39 RBIs in 97 games. While he struggled with his hitting, his defense was never in question. He became just the second rookie catcher to win a Gold Glove, thanks to an outstanding .992 fielding average, a sensational 43 percent caught-stealing rate, and a league-leading 63 assists. And all this in a season cut short by a hand injury. Johnson's 1996 season was another mixed bag. He lost a month to injury and saw his batting average plummet to .218, while his home runs and RBIs essentially duplicated his rookie season. But once again, his magic on defense brought him a Gold Glove. He led the league with a .995 fielding average, with just four errors in 120 games, pulled off a league-leading 12 double plays, and gunned down a phenomenal 48 percent of would-be base stealers.

Charles Johnson had a career year in 1997. The light-hitting backstop put up a .250 batting average, complete with 19 homers and 63 RBIs, in 124 games. On defense, he was almost perfect. He set a major league record by fielding 1.000, charged with just one passed ball. He also shot down 47 percent of the runners who challenged his arm and was involved in 17 double plays. His contributions were critical to the Marlins' successful National League season, as they clinched a wild card entry to the postseason playoffs after finishing nine games behind the Eastern Division champion Atlanta Braves. Behind the overpowering pitching of Livan Hernandez and Kevin Brown and the timely hitting of Craig Counsell, Gary Sheffield, and Johnson, the Florida Marlins swept the San Francisco Giants three straight in the NLDS and took the measure of the Atlanta Braves in six games in the NLCS. The team completed their magical season by edging the Cleveland Indians in seven games in the World Series. Johnson batted a hefty .357 in the Fall Classic, with a homer and three RBIs, and fielded 1.000 with a 38 percent caught-stealing percentage.

On March 31, 1998, Charles Johnson made a wild throw to first base in the first inning of the opening day game against the Chicago Cubs. It was his first error in 172 games, a major league record. Johnson atoned for his miscue in the bottom half of the inning by ripping a three-run homer, to pace the Marlins to an 11–6 victory. Less than two months later, Johnson was traded to the Los Angeles Dodgers, where his .218 batting average brought about a trade to the Mets, who traded him to the Orioles in the off season. The Florida native was traded again, to the Chicago White Sox, in midseason of 2000, but still put together a career year. He batted a personal high of .304, with 31 homers and 91 RBIs in 128 games, although he suffered a dropoff in defense, fielding .987 and cutting down just 38 percent of the would-be base stealers. Over the next three years, Charles Johnson had mixed results. He hit .259 in 2001, then hit just .217 the next year in an injury-riddled season. And in 2003 he slammed 20 homers and drove in 61 runs in 108 games, in spite of a .230 batting average. Defensively he was almost as good as ever. He fielded between .993 and .996 those three years and threw out from 40 percent to 42 percent of opposing base runners, still about 10 points above the league average.

The free-swinging receiver completed twelve years of major league service in 2005, with a .245 career batting average, based on 940 hits in 3836 games. His 211 doubles, 167 homers, and 570 RBIs, equate to 30 doubles, 24 home runs, and 82 RBIs for every 550 at-bats. His on-base percentage is not very good, but his power numbers always make him a dangerous man with a bat in his hand. And on defense, Charles Johnson has no equal. The two-time All-Star and possessor of four Gold Gloves has a .994 career fielding average, which will be the highest of all time if he can maintain that percentage throughout the rest of his career. And his 41 percent caught-stealing rate is one of the best in recent times, although not up to the level of Ivan Rodriguez.

Jorge Posada

Jorge Rafael Posada was born in Santurce, Puerto Rico, on August 17, 1971. The eighteen-year old catcher was drafted by the New York Yankees in the 1990 amateur draft and sent to Oneonta in the New York-Penn League the next spring. He batted .235 for Oneonta, then played for another five minor league teams between 1992 and 1996 before finally getting his chance with the parent club. According to Baseballlibrary.com, "The Yankees had to wait for three years for Jorge Posada to realize his potential. Over his first three seasons, Posada hit well only in streaks, suffered stretches in which he couldn't hold onto pitches that hit the center of his glove ... and battled confidence problems."

In 1997, Posada caught 60 games for the Yankees, hitting .260 with six homers and 25 RBIs. His fielding was acceptable, with a .992 fielding average, but his caught-stealing percentage was a sorry 20 percent. The next year he upped his batting average to .268 and chipped in with 17 homers and 63 RBIs in 111 games. On defense, he showed a significant improvement, with a .994 fielding average, only four errors, no passed balls, and a fine 40 percent caught-stealing success rate. After an off season in 1999, where he hit only .245 with 12 homers and 57 RBIs, his offense became his strong point over the next four years, with his batting average ranging from .268 to .287, his home runs ranging from 22 to 30, and his RBIs ranging from 86 to 101. His fielding average hovered around the league average, as did his caught-stealing rate.

During Posada's nine years in New York, the Yankees have been in the postseason eight times, with five trips to the World Series culminating in three world championships. The 6'2", 205-pound catcher has been a major factor in the team's success, but surprisingly, it has been primarily with the glove. His postseason batting average is a lukewarm .226 with seven homers and 25 RBIs in 72 games, but he has fielded at a .994 percentage with just three errors, at the same time being charged with only two passed balls and gunning down 37 percent of runners who attempted to steal. His caught-stealing rate in the World Series is a sizzling 64 percent.

Jorge Posada may be entering the prime of his major league career, and if he is, he may well be ranked with the elites of the catching profession before he retires. He has played eleven years in the major leagues, although two of those years were just end-of-season visits. The Santurce native has caught 100 or more games for seven consecutive years, after catching only 159 games total in his first two full seasons. Through nine years, the four-time All-Star has accumulated 1034 base hits in 3843 at-bats for a .269 batting average. His 235 doubles, 175 home runs, and 678 runs batted in give him an average of 34 doubles, 25 home runs, and 97 RBIs for every 550 at-bats. The switch-hitting backstop has a fine .378 on-base percentage and an excellent .474 slugging average, which at present is the tenth highest slugging average of all the catchers in this study. Defensively, he needs to step up his overall fielding, including cutting down his errors and his passed balls, while improving his caught-stealing percentage.

Jason Kendall

Jason Kendall was born in San Diego, California, on June 26, 1974. Baseballlibrary.com characterized the young catcher in the following manner: "Spirited, speedy Jason Kendall emerged in the late 1990s as one of the game's top catchers. A high school player, he relishes contact, and often ranks among the league leaders in hit-by-pitches. Kendall's aggressive style of play and amiable personality have made him a popular player among his teammates and Pirate fans alike." Kendall began his professional baseball career at the age of 18 with the Pirates in the Gulf Coast League. His impressive defensive performances plus his .300 batting averages brought him to Pittsburgh in 1996.

The 6', 180-pound backstop tattooed the ball at a .300 clip in his rookie season, earning him a spot on the National League All-Star team. On September 21, 1998, the fleet-footed Kendall stole his 26th base of the season, setting a new National League record for catchers. On May 3, 1999, he banged out five base hits in five at-bats, including two doubles, as the Pirates defeated the San Francisco Giants 9–8. The following year, on May 19, he hit for the cycle in a 13–1 rout of the St. Louis Cardinals. He homered in the first inning, singled in the second, doubled in the third, and tripled in the eighth. Kendall is still going strong in his tenth major league season. His career batting average is a solid .302. His .385 on-base percentage is one of the highest all-time for a catcher, the fourth best of the 50 catchers in this study. And his slugging average of .422 puts him in the top 40 percent in that category. His 148 stolen bases broke Carlton Fisk's record for a catcher. His totals include 26 stolen bases in 1998, 22 the following year, and 22 in 2000. In 2003, at the age of 29, the right-handed batter hit .325 with eight stolen bases while catching 146 games.

Part II

◆ ◆ ◆

A Statistical Analysis of Baseball's Greatest Catchers

7

SABERMETRICS—DEVISING A STATISTICAL SYSTEM FOR COMPARING CATCHERS

There have been dozens of outstanding catchers in the major leagues over the past 129 years. The catchers who are considered to be the class of the position have been profiled in the first six chapters of this book. Some outstanding catchers, unfortunately, were found to be ineligible for consideration as the best catcher of all time, for various reasons. Some of them performed at a time when the rules of the game were different, making it impossible to equate their statistics with those of players from the modern era. Other players were prevented from playing organized baseball because of the color of their skin, and they had to play out their careers in the Negro Leagues. For these Negro League players, their offensive statistics could be converted satisfactorily to a major league base point, but their defensive records were not available, so they had to be eliminated from consideration. And finally, at least one potential Hall of Fame candidate played in Japan, and his defensive statistics could not be converted satisfactorily to a major league base point, so he was also left on the outside looking in.

In the end, the 50 catchers deemed to be the best at their position were included in the study. The first item on the agenda was to determine what offensive and defensive statistics should be entered into the equation in order to properly compare the individuals. The offensive factors considered important in judging catchers included games played, at-bats, runs, hits, doubles, triples, home runs, runs batted in, bases on balls, stolen bases, sacrifice hits, double plays hit into, on-base percentage, and slugging average. The defensive factors deemed important included fielding average, caught-stealing performance, putouts, total assists, errors, assists minus caught-stealing assists, passed balls, wild pitches by the pitching staff, and range factor.

The next step was to locate or develop the necessary statistical formulas that would allow a valid comparison of one player to another. In reviewing baseball's statistical landscape, it was discovered that almost all the player ratings and all the All-Star team selections made by baseball historians, authors, magazines, newspapers, and even by Major League Baseball itself over the first eighty years of the twentieth century were nothing more than popularity contests. *Street and Smiths Baseball* magazine presented their "Dream Team" in 1990 based on a poll of baseball players, coaches, managers, executives, and media personnel. Nine years later, Major League Baseball announced its All-Century team, supposedly the greatest players to play the game over the preceding one hundred years, but being based on a poll of fans, most of whom had never even heard of players like Honus Wagner or Lefty Grove, the final team was composed primarily of modern day players like Nolan Ryan, Cal Ripken, Jr., and Johnny Bench. Once again, it was a popularity contest. There were essentially no player ratings made, or All-Star teams selected, up to about 1978 that were based on a statistical analysis of the players under consideration.

Occasionally, over the past 25 years, there have been some player ratings made based on a player's offensive statistics, such as his batting average, home runs, and runs batted in. One such exercise can be found in G. Scott Thomas's book, *Leveling the Field*, in which he proposed a system to evaluate position players utilizing the offensive basics, like run production, batting average, and slugging average. He also included a player's "summit season," an average of a player's five best years. In making his selections for the "greatest" players, he ignored a player's defensive contributions, because, as he said, "... selection processes for All-Star teams and the Hall of Fame seem to focus almost entirely on hitting." By Thomas's calculations, Johnny Bench emerged as the greatest catcher of the twentieth century. Unfortunately, his rules limited the selection process to players who played at least 1000 games at their position and had a minimum of 5000 at-bats, eliminating such worthy contenders as Gene Tenace, Joe Torre, Buddy Rosar, Mickey Tettleton, Ray Mueller, and, in particular, Roy Campanella. Recently, there have been several studies conducted by baseball historians to identify the greatest-hitting catcher in baseball history. Kevin Fullam of Stats, Inc., rated the best catchers in baseball history using OPS, the sum of a player's on-base percentage and his slugging average, as his criteria. OPS is a common criterion used by many baseball historians today to rate players, although there is some question as to whether or not the two criteria are a duplication of effort since they both

Left: Joe Torre was selected for the All-Star game at three positions during his career. *Courtesy Jay Sanford. Right:* Gene Tenace, one of the most underrated catchers in baseball history, was the Most Valuable Player in the 1972 World Series. *Courtesy Gene Tenace.*

include the player's singles. Fullam's ratings, not surprisingly, had Mike Piazza in the number one position, followed by Mickey Cochrane, Gabby Hartnett, Roy Campanella, and Yogi Berra, in that order. Johnny Bench could do no better than fourteenth place, which is a far cry from Thomas's rating. Another study, made by Jim McMartin, was based on runs generated (RG), which, as he described it, "estimates how many runs above or below the league average a hitter contributes to his team, where 0=the league average. Runs generated (RG) is useful for cross-era comparisons, 1920 to present." McMartin, according to Charles Rosciam, "was willing to sacrifice some degree of accuracy to gain a more user-friendly measure." The formula is:

$$RG = (.35)(\text{total bases} + \text{walks}) - (.25)(\text{at bats} - \text{hits})$$

Baseball's scientific analysis took a giant leap forward in the mid–1970s when Bill James and Pete Palmer arrived on the scene. James, called the "Sultan of Stats" by the Boston *Globe*, is a longtime baseball historian and statistician who published one the most popular baseball books of all time in 1985, *The Bill James Historical Baseball Abstract,* which sold thousands of copies worldwide. It has since been updated and improved. Palmer is another hard-working and longtime baseball statistician, now in his fourth decade of identifying and simplifying the baseball numbers. His credits include co-author of the original *Total Baseball,* statistician for the American League from 1976–1987, chair for SABR's Statistical Analysis Committee, and a contributor to *Retrosheet.* These two mathematical geniuses, working together and independently, brought the game of baseball and its analysis into the computer age, where every game and every facet of a game can be broken down into its smallest unit and analyzed under the proverbial microscope. Baseball had moved into the age of Sabermetrics, a term coined by Bill James to identify "the search for objective knowledge about baseball." It was also called "the mathematical and statistical analysis of baseball records." Sabermetrics included not only the modern, sophisticated formulas of James and Palmer, but also mathematical formulas for fielding average, batting average, and ERA that were developed as far back as the 1850s. Henry Chadwick, the "Father of Baseball," provided the first baseball box score in 1863 and identified each position by number, with the pitcher number one, the catcher number two, and so on. Other early Sabermetricians included F.C. Lane, George Lindsey, and Allan Roth, the longtime team statistician for the Brooklyn Dodgers. One of Bill James's contributions to statistical analysis was his runs created (RC) formula which measures the hitting contributions of players. The formula is:

$$RC = (H + BB + HBP - CS - GIDP)(TB + .26)(BB - IBB + HBP) + .52(SH + SF + SB), \text{ all divided by } AB + BB + HBP + SH + SF$$

Where:

H = Hits	TB = Total bases
BB = Bases on balls	IBB = Intentional bases on balls
HBP = Hit by pitches	SH = Sacrifice hits
CS = Caught stealing	SF = Sacrifice flies
GIDP = Grounded into double plays	SB = Stolen bases

Pete Palmer and John Thorn proposed another formula for measuring a player's offensive contributions, which they called batting runs (BR), which included such factors as singles, doubles, triples, home runs, at-bats, and out-on-base, in addition to some of the statistics noted above. The batting runs formula is:

$$BR = (.47)1B + (.78)2B + (1.09)3B + (1.4)HR + (.33)(BB + HB) + (.30)SB - (.60)CS - (.25)(AB - H) - .5(OOB).$$

Charles Rosciam compared the formulas of McMartin, James, and Palmer and Thorn for 12 Hall of Fame catchers, 18 notables (not HOF), and eight active catchers for a total of 38 catchers of his choice. He then standardized them to 500 at-bats and averaged the three formulas to arrive at his own catcher ratings. Once again, Mike Piazza gained the number one ranking.

Another offensive rating system was utilized by Don Zminda, of Stats, Inc., who proposed what he called a player's "Relativity Index," which measures how a player performs relative to the other players of his era. Zminda's Relativity Index, which was first introduced in the *Stats All-Time Baseball Source Book*, took the runs created, divided it by 27 outs, then divided that result by the league's RC/27 and multiplied that result by 100. The resulting offensive ratings, again adjusted for the 50 catchers in this study, show Mike Piazza at the top of the list.

Rob Neyer of ESPN proposed his own system for rating the greatest catchers of all time. He listed his top six picks, along with their offensive stats such as runs, RBIs, OBP, SLG, and OPS. He finally chose, as one of his measuring sticks, runs created, which includes a league/era adjustment that he considered a critical part of the formula. Then, taking the RC results, he introduced a subjective component to rationalize his final rankings. His top six catchers, in order, were Cochrane, Bench, Berra, Campanella, Hartnett, Dickey, and Fisk. Bench moved up from sixth place to second as the result of Neyer's subjective argument that the catchers of the 1920–1965 period were valued for their offense and were not particularly good defensive catchers. He stated, "The mid–1920s through the mid–1960s happen to be when the stolen base was in relative disuse. Which is to say, you didn't have to throw particularly well to be a valuable defensive catcher during that

Carlton Fisk was the most durable catcher in baseball history, catching a total of 2226 games over a memorable 24-year career. *Courtesy Boston Red Sox.*

period. The ability to block pitches was important, because the pitchers were wild and the mitts were flimsy, and of course you always want a backstop who calls a good game." Unfortunately, the statistics do not support Neyer's contention that catchers prior to 1965 couldn't throw very well. From a team standpoint, American League teams posted a 45 percent caught-stealing percentage on 163 attempts per team in 1925 and 41 percent on 128 attempts in 1930. In 1980, American League teams had just a 35 percent success rate on 159 attempts, and in 2000 their success rate had dropped to 31 percent based on 130 attempts. Individually, the two greatest-throwing catchers in baseball history played before 1960. Roy Campanella, the most effective caught-stealing catcher of all time with a 58 percent career success rate, played from 1948 through 1957. And Gabby Hartnett, the number two man, who shot down 53 percent of the 112 runners per year who attempted to steal against him, played from 1922 through 1941. Ken O'Dea (1935–46) was successful 50 percent of the time based on 76 attempts. Gus Mancuso (1928–45) was 48 percent successful on 88 attempts, Bob O'Farrell (1915–35) was 48 percent successful on 125 attempts. And Yogi Berra (1946–65) was 49 percent successful on 73 attempts. Conversely, in the 1960–2004 era, the only catcher to approach the 50 percent CS rate is Ivan Rodriguez (1991–04), who has been successful 49 percent of the time on 97 attempts. Johnny Bench (1967–83) was 43 percent successful on 97 attempts, and Elston Howard (1955–68) was 39 percent successful on 70 attempts. The statistics suggest that a strong-throwing catcher will throw out a high percentage of would-be base stealers regardless of how many attempts are made against him, while a poor-throwing catcher will always have a low caught-stealing rate. The strongest-throwing catchers in the annals of baseball played the game between 1922 and 1965, and even earlier if you go back to the dead-ball days of Schalk, Schang, and Gowdy, whose caught-stealing percentage was in the 48 percent range based on almost 200 attempts per team per year.

There are other catcher rating systems being used at the present time, such as Michael Hoban's batting proficiency (BP) formula, which combines RC and OPS to arrive at a final rating. The system, which Hoban notes is to identify baseball's greatest-hitting catcher, is adjusted for season and for league. And again, Mike Piazza came out on top. There was one internet catcher rating system that measured six different offensive and defensive categories, while producing the usual number of repetitive stats, to arrive at baseball's greatest all-around catcher. The offensive categories were batting average, OBP, SLG, secondary average (SECA), RC, RC per 27 outs minus the league RC27. The defensive categories included games caught (GC) as a percentage of team's games played (GC), assists per game

(ASS), errors per game (E), fielding average minus league fielding average (FA – LFA), double plays per game (DP), and passed balls per game (PB). The winners were, in order, Dickey, Hartnett, Cochrane, Berra, Campanella, Bench, Piazza, Carter, Ivan Rodriguez, and Jason Kendall.

Except for the previous internet rating system, the only other notable Sabermetric rating systems that take into consideration the defensive skills of the players are the popular and sophisticated mathematical models devised by Bill James and Pete Palmer. These two programs, James's runs created and Win Shares system and Palmer's unique Linear Weights system, were reviewed to determine if either of them would be satisfactory for comparing the specific offensive and defensive skills of individual catchers. One of the more widely used statistical systems for measuring the offensive contributions of baseball players is Linear Weights, a brilliantly conceived and designed tool for baseball historians and statisticians. It is favored over Win Shares by many statisticians because it is easy to follow and uses actual game statistics, whereas Win Shares is more theoretical and is difficult for the average fan to follow. The Linear Weights system was invented by Pete Palmer in 1978, when he generated a computer simulation of all major league games played since 1900, to measure all events on a ball field in terms of runs. At the root of this system, as with some other Sabermetric formulas, such as runs created, is the knowledge that wins and losses are what the game of baseball is about. It should be pointed out that Linear Weights is a "value system;" that is, it measures the value of a player to his team, comparing his statistics to the average statistics of his peers. The measurements are predicated on longevity, giving a higher rating to players who play in more games during the season, or in more innings per game. Although it is not designed specifically to measure the skill of individual players, the formula can be adjusted to a skill basis by dividing the results by the number of games a catcher played. The system combines batting runs (BR), base stealing runs (BSR), and fielding runs (FR), to arrive at a value score for each player. The formula for batting runs, as noted previously, is:

$$BR = (.47)1B + (.78)2B + (1.09)3B + (1.4)HR + (.33)(BB + HB) + (.30)SB - (.60)CS - (.25)(AB - H) - .5(OOB).$$

The formula for base stealing runs (BSR) is:

$$BSR = .22SB - .35CS.$$

The fielding runs formula is:

$$FR = .2(PO + 2A - E - PB/2 + DP) \text{ player} - \text{Avg. Pos. Lg.} \times (PO \text{ team}) \times \text{innings, player/innings team.}$$

The formula for catchers also includes one-tenth of the adjusted pitching runs (PR) for the team, times the percentage of games behind the plate by that catcher.

Total player rating (TPR), which is the final value rating of each player, is shown by:

$$TPR = (adj. BR + FR + BSR - Pos. Adj.)$$
divided by runs per win factor for each year.

Pos. Adj. is a position adjustment, which would be the same for all catchers. The adjusted BR includes a normalized park factor that compares the number of runs scored by and against a team in their home park to the average number of runs scored by and against the team in all parks. There is one park factor for each ballpark, and each of the player's statistics are adjusted to that factor, the same factor being used for all members of the home team. Individual performances in specific stadiums are not taken into consideration. So, for Yankee Stadium, there would be one park factor for all members of the team, but as most baseball fans know, *The House That Ruth Built* has a cozy right field porch just over 300 feet from home plate and a 344-foot power alley, while the enormous left center field power alley of 402 feet was historically known as the place where home runs go to die. The park factor for Yankee Stadium is 1.02, but the disparity for right-handed batters and left-handed batters is reflected in the individual park factors of Yogi Berra and Thurman Munson, whose PFs were 1.42 and 0.59 respectively. Yogi's 1.42 means that the Yankee receiver hit 142 home runs in Yankee Stadium for every 100 home runs he hit on the road, while Munson hit just

Thurman Munson's potential Hall of Fame career ended tragically in a plane crash. *Courtesy New York Yankees.*

59 home runs at home for every 100 home runs he hit on the road. Bill Dickey, a notorious left-handed pull hitter, had an even more delightful time swinging the bat in the Stadium than did the spray-hitting Berra, as he compiled a PF of 2.01. Right-handed hitting Elston Howard, with a PF of 0.48, on the other hand, struggled mightily against the cavernous left field wasteland. In 1962 for instance, he could do no better than hit three home runs at home compared to 18 on the road. Yankee Stadium is the most notorious stadium for unequal park factors for right- and left-handed hitters, which is not unusual since it was custom-designed to maximize Babe Ruth's home run output. But it is by no means unique. Many other players have experienced biased individual park factors in certain stadiums over the years, such as Harry Danning (3.07 PF) and Ernie Lombardi (0.79 PF) in the Polo Grounds, Randy Hundley (1.56) in Wrigley Field, Darrell Porter (0.69) in Royals Stadium and Busch Stadium.

The BR formula, as noted, is normalized for each year, providing a common base point by which to measure players against their peers. It is, in effect, an era adjustment in that it permits individual statistical comparisons to be made from one year to another or from one era to another. In this system, the league average is considered to be the zero baseline and each individual player is compared to that baseline. Normalizing a player's statistics tells whether a player is better or worse than his average peer and to what extent he is better or worse. This differential can then be compared directly with the differential from any other year, if desired, to arrive at final comparison.

The fielding component of the Linear Weights system measures all the critical defensive skills of individual players, such as putouts, assists, errors, double plays, and passed balls, but as Pete Palmer noted in the fifth edition of *Total Baseball*, the fielding runs (FR) formula is unsatisfactory for evaluating catchers. In 2002 he said that FR were still inaccurate for catchers. Although he has continued to refine his formula over time to improve the reliability of the ratings, some areas of concern remain.

1. Putouts per se cannot be used to evaluate the relative skills of individual catchers because strikeouts have increased almost exponentially from the 1920s to the new millennium, particularly since the arrival of the guess-hitters in the 1950s and '60s. Strikeouts have been eliminated from the Linear Weights calculations, but that still doesn't solve the problem, as can be seen from the accompanying table.

Catcher Putouts Per Year

Year	Putouts (PO) Per Team	Strikeouts (SO) Per Team	PO – SO
1920	624	454	170
1925	564	418	146
1930	636	496	140
1935	639	501	138
1940	697	566	131
1945	637	503	134
1950	711	598	113
1955	784	677	107
1960	887	801	86
1965	991	916	75
1970	960	886	74
1975	834	764	70
1980	744	686	58
1985	813	762	51
1990	850	810	40
1995	1003	971	32
2000	1025	994	31
2003	1009	976	33

Note: The statistics are based on a 154-game season.

Non-strikeout putouts have been on a continual decline in the major leagues for the past 85 years, from a high of 140 non-strikeout putouts per team per year in 1920 to just 33 non-strikeout putouts per team per year in 2003. Some of the decline is due to the fact that there are fewer attempted bunts that result in pop-ups, and there are fewer attempted steals of home. This is particularly true in the American League, where the designated hitter rule introduced in 1973 has taken much of the strategy out of the American League game. As the above table shows, one of the largest decreases in non-strikeout putouts occurred between 1975 and 1980, which coincides with the introduction of the designated hitter. Most non-strikeout putouts today are the result of foul pop-ups that are caught, and they are dependent, to a large extent, on the size of the foul territory around home plate to the backstop. Since this foul territory has been significantly reduced over the years, it would be unfair to modern-day catchers to measure that statistic. Although many early major league parks had a 60-foot distance from home plate to the backstop, similar to today's more uniform design, some of them ranged from 75 feet to 90 feet. Mickey Cochrane, for instance, had 90 feet to roam in when he was catching in Shibe Park, and Bill Dickey had 84 feet of pasture in Yankee Stadium. The big field in the Bronx still has an 84-foot backstop distance, as does the other New York ballpark, Shea Stadium. Most other modern stadiums, however, conform to the 60-foot distance. The foul territory from first base around to third base has also been reduced over the years to provide additional seating capacity.

2. FR includes a factor for pitching effectiveness, which is primarily out of a catcher's control and punishes a catcher who plays for a team with a poor pitching staff.

3. Total assists are included in FR, but 50 percent to 75 percent of these assists are the result of a catcher's caught-stealing success rate, which is not presently part of the Linear Weights system. Since a catcher's caught-stealing record is one of the biggest weapons in a catcher's arsenal, it should be a separate part of any defensive measurement system for catchers. Caught-stealing statistics have been compiled for every catcher since 1972, and even for a few select catchers prior to 1972, including Roy Campanella. There are also reasonable estimates available for all catchers back into the nineteenth century. At this time, a caught-stealing comparison is not perfect, but it is better than not using the comparison at all. FR also includes double plays, but most double plays are also covered by a catcher's caught-stealing record since most of them are of the strike-'em-out, throw-'em-out variety. Since more than half of a catcher's total assists are covered by a catcher's CS record and double plays are included in the CS record, the remainder of the unaccounted-for assists could be a separate entry.

Pete Palmer, in his continuing pursuit of perfection, revised FR for the 2004 *Baseball Encyclopedia* to include a catcher's caught-stealing record. In making the adjustment, he said, "The main reason I did the CS research was to correct Bench's fielding rating, which was like–10 wins, where Bill Deane concluded it was more like +10. This was because he had few assists because SB weren't attempted. This of course is true." In addition to adding CS to the FR formula, Palmer also created two new factors, Rng and Thr. Range (Rng) compares a catcher's stolen bases allowed per inning to the league's average stolen bases allowed. Throwing (Thr) compares a catcher's caught-stealing per inning to the average caught-stealing rate for the league. These categories, which are based on the assumption that fewer stolen base attempts are made against good-throwing catchers than against poor-throwing catchers, are not part of the FR formula. They are just another way to look at a player's fielding expertise.

Linear Weights is an excellent mathematical model for determining the contribution of individual players to a team's runs scored and to a team's wins. It is well designed for measuring the value of a player to a team, but there are minor adjustments that need to be made to the formulas before the model can be used to accurately measure and compare the skills of individual catchers. These include the use of an individual park factor in the BR formula, modifications to the FR formula to resolve the putout-less-strikeout dilemma and the double play dilemma, and to review the best way to evaluate a catcher's caught-stealing record.

Win Shares is a highly theoretical and complex mathematical model devised by Bill James to measure the performance of major league baseball teams and to compare teams, not only within the same year and era, but also from one era to another. It is, as he said, "A system which summarizes a player's value each season into a simple integer." James also devised a method to utilize the team Win Shares in conjunction with his runs created (RC) formula and such concepts as total marginal runs, marginal runs scored, marginal runs saved, and sub-marginal runs to measure the value of each individual player. Each player's Win Shares is a measure of his contribution to his team. However, the mathematical manipulations required to compile the individual player Win Shares for a season is complicated and time-consuming, and it cannot easily be verified by the average baseball historian or statistician. For example, when Bill James was asked for the calculations that were used to arrive at Joe DiMaggio's 1937 Win Share total, he replied, "It would take me eight to 10 hours, at least, to recreate all of this data and write out an explanation of it. To figure Win Shares for any individual, you have to figure the whole team."

Win Shares measures players for both skill and value by evaluating their contributions to their team, but it does not appear to be suitable as a component for comparing the skills of individual players, for several reasons. First, the player's Win Shares are derived from their team's statistics and not specifically from individual statistics. The ratings are considered to be a combination of skill and value; therefore an average player who played for many years would have a higher rating than a superstar who enjoyed only a short career. The Win Shares rating system is a combination of six different factors. In addition to a player's career Win Shares, it also includes a player's Win Shares for his three best seasons, his Win Shares for his five best seasons, his career Win Shares per 162 games, an era adjustment, and a subjective component.

There are several components of this system that present problems in the comparison of individual catchers, such as the type of era adjustment used, the use of a generalized team park factor, and a subjective component, which allows the statistician to add points to a player's totals for reasons that may have nothing to do with skill. One of the more curious assumptions made by the creator is the assumption that baseball players are becoming more talented every year; therefore today's players deserve bonus points over players from earlier eras. To achieve that objective, the formula includes a timeline element, which is year of birth minus 1800 divided by 10. Using that formula, Mike Piazza would receive an extra 16.8 points for being born in 1968 (1968–1800 divided by 10), Johnny Bench would receive 14.7 points for being born in 1947, Yogi Berra would receive 12.5 points for being born in 1925, and Mickey Cochrane would receive 10.3 points for being born in 1903. However, there is considerable doubt in the baseball establishment that the skills of baseball players have actually improved over the past 80 years. The fact that several records, particularly home run records, have been broken in recent years may be a function of such factors as better equipment, the construction of the baseball, the continually shrinking dimensions of the major league ballparks, artificial turf, and expansion, rather than the size and skill of the players. Or it may be a function of a player's steroid intake. Certainly Babe Ruth was the same player in 1920 when he slammed 54 home runs as he was in 1919 when he set a new home run record with 29. The culprit was not Ruth. It was the baseball, which had a little jackrabbit added to it. And the Babe wasn't the only one to prosper from the new lively ball. Everyone in the major leagues benefited. The 16 major league teams averaged 37 home runs per team per year in 1919, but by 1929 that figure had increased to 97. National League players were no better in 1930 when the entire league hit .303 than they were in 1928 when they hit .281. It was the ball again. The period from 1940 to 1960 experienced a sudden surge in the level of play in the major leagues, but it was integration, not bigger and better players that caused it. Newly admitted Negro league players, who accounted for about 10 percent of the major league rosters by 1960, triggered a renewed interest in the home run. In 1961, American League home runs jumped up 15 percent, not because the players all of a sudden got bigger and stronger, but because the league expanded from eight to 10 teams, diluting the pitching talent. In the 1970s expansion continued, and the player mentality gave birth to the free swinger, a guess-hitter who utilized an all-or-nothing approach to batting designed to hit more home runs, along with more strikeouts and a lower batting average. In the 1990s it was more expansion, an even livelier baseball manufactured in Costa Rica, and smaller ballparks that were beginning to resemble Japanese-league bandboxes. Much of the home run outbursts between 1993 and the present time are, at least partially, attributable to the livelier baseball and to the smaller ballparks. It is a fact that the playing field dimensions of modern baseball stadiums are about 20 percent smaller than the playing field dimensions of sixty or eighty years ago. For example, the left center field power alley in Yankee Stadium was 460 feet in 1923 and 463 feet in

1967. Today it is a comfortable 399 feet. The right center field power alley was 429 feet in 1923. Today it is 385 feet. Center field in Shibe Park, Philadelphia, was 468 feet until 1956. Forbes Field in Pittsburgh had a left field foul line of 365 feet, power alleys of 406 and 416 feet, left and right, and 435 feet to center field. Griffith Stadium in Washington, D.C., measured 405'–421'–320', left to right, in 1950. And the famous Polo Grounds measured 505 feet to straightaway center field in 1949. Today, most parks have 330-foot foul lines and 400-foot center field walls, a veritable chip shot for sluggers like Babe Ruth and Jimmie Foxx.

A statistical analysis of Barry Bonds's 73 home runs in 2001 showed that if Bonds had played in the same parks Babe Ruth played in, his home run total would have been 58, not 73. The American League ballparks in 1927 were 15 feet deeper in the left center field and right center field power alleys and a whopping 40 feet deeper in center field than the 2001 National League parks. And that's without even considering the livelier baseball that Bonds took aim at. Conversely, William J. Jenkinson, in an article in *Baseball Weekly* in 1995, converted Ruth's 1927 homers to a standard present-day ballpark and determined that Ruth would have hit 83 home runs today. And then there's the steroid issue! That problem, if it proves to be a contributing factor in the home run wars, could result in all home run records set between 1993 and 2004 being marked by an asterisk or being removed from the books completely. It is interesting to note that androstenedione, the body-building supplement that Mark McGwire was taking in 1998 when he hit 70 home runs, has now been outlawed by Major League Baseball.

Some people believe baseball players are better today because the population of the country has increased dramatically over the past 85 years. The facts show otherwise. In 1940, prior to integration, the population of the United States was approximately 120 million people, of which about 100 million were eligible to play in organized baseball. When Jackie Robinson integrated baseball, the population was 152 million, and there were another eighteen million people who lived in Puerto Rico, the Dominican Republic, and Venezuela, who became part of the mix. By 1960, the population had grown to about 205 million people, including those outside the U.S., to supply sixteen major league baseball teams, or about 11.7 million possible prospects per team. The period from 1947 through 1960 has been called The Golden Age of Baseball, the time when an integrated sport had the largest population draw in the country's history. During that time, other professional sports were just beginning to flex their muscles and were beginning to attract young athletes, sports like basketball and football, but they had not yet made an impact on baseball prospects. In 1961,

Major League Baseball experienced its first expansion, with the American League being increased from eight teams to 10 teams with a corresponding dilution in talent. By 1970, there were 24 major league baseball teams, by 1980 there were 26 teams, and by 2000 the leagues had grown to 30 teams. The available talent couldn't keep up with the expansion. The population of the U.S., Puerto Rico, the Dominican Republic and Venezuela, reached approximately 328 million people in 2000, or about 10.9 million people per team, a 7 percent decrease from 1960. There were, of course, players entering organized baseball from other countries as well, such as Cuba, Japan, Mexico, and other Central and South American countries, but their effect on population statistics was minimal. Overall, the population of the United States, Puerto Rico, the Dominican Republic, and Venezuela have increased 60 percent since 1960, while the number of major league baseball teams has increased by 88 percent. The dearth of talent in the major leagues is magnified by the situation in the minor leagues. In 1949, there were 58 minor league teams feeding more than 8000 players up to the major leagues. Today, there are about 18 leagues with fewer than 4000 players. If the minor league system had kept pace with the population growth over the past half-century, there should be about 16,000 players in the minor leagues today. Some people claim there is no difference between the minor league system today and that of fifty years ago, that the 4000 players in the system today are the more talented players, and the missing 12,000 players are the less talented players, a fanciful excuse at best. Organized baseball is also receiving stiff competition from the NFL and NBA. Many talented college players over the years, including potential major league baseball players, have opted for the easier routes into professional football and professional basketball rather than challenging baseball's minor league route. Also, as the population has become more educated, many college baseball players have opted for the security of the business world, where their future is more stable, and their family life is more normal. Fifty years ago, not many baseball players had a college degree. Today it is almost the rule rather than the exception. All things considered, it is difficult to believe the game is better today than it was in 1960, and it is even more difficult to believe it is getting better and better every year. In fact, if it hadn't been for the heavy influx of talent from Puerto Rico, the Dominican Republic, and Venezuela over the past 10 to twenty years, with players like Sammy Sosa, Pedro Martinez, Omar Vizquel, Albert Pujols, and Mariano Rivera constituting 18 percent of the major league rosters, (158 players out of 895 players at last count), the major league scene would be a disaster.

Pete Palmer added one other fact. "...from 1901 [to] 1960 the population more than doubled and the number of teams stayed the same. I think if you go overall from 1901 to the present, the population has increased more rapidly than expansion (280/75 compared to 30/16). This would state that the best players must have been in the 1950–60 period, after integration and before expansion."

The Win Shares system includes a generalized park factor for each baseball stadium, comparing the number of runs scored by the team at home against the number of runs scored by the team on the road. The park factor is similar to the one utilized by the Linear Weights system, crediting Bill Dickey and Elston Howard, both of whom played their home games in Yankee Stadium, with the same park factor, in spite of the fact that Dickey hit 135 of his 202 career home runs in friendly Yankee Stadium, while Elston Howard, a straightaway right-handed hitter, hit only 54 of his 167 career home runs out of the Stadium. It is obvious that individual park factors are required if an accurate comparison of one player to another is to be realized. That will be discussed in more detail in the next chapter.

And finally, there is a subjective component added to each player's total in the Win Shares system, based on the researcher's personal opinion of that player's non-measurable contributions, such as clutch hitting, leadership, and "special contributions." As one example of the subjective factor, Bill James in his *Historical Baseball Abstract*, noting that a "quirk" in the rating system gave Mickey Mantle a higher overall rating than Ty Cobb, said, "So I gave Cobb a higher subjective factor than I gave Mantle, and allowed him to edge back ahead. My heart is not in it, but as I see it, the world believes that Cobb was a better player than Mantle, and I would be unable to sustain a logical argument to the contrary under rigorous attack. I have to give Cobb the edge." The subjective factor also includes World Series performance and defensive value beyond that accounted for in the Win Shares system. This scientific "fudge factor" is a non-measurable component that allows the statistician to add points to a player's total if he feels such an adjustment is necessary. Using a subjective component to adjust a player's final rating can never be equitable. It is an impossible exercise when evaluating players whose careers might have begun as long ago as 1920. Certainly, no one living today knows the value of every player's intangible contributions over the entire twentieth century. There is no question it would be advantageous to be able to use a subjective measurement for catchers since a significant part of their skills fall into the intangible area — skills like calling pitches, handling a diverse pitching staff, directing infielders, serving as the manager's field general, blocking the plate, backing up bases, and outrunning the batter to first base on infield hits. It is well known that Campanella, Berra, Bench, Hartnett, Cochrane, and Dickey all received high marks from their peers for their baseball intangibles, but to extend that evaluation to every catcher who played in the major leagues since 1920 is impossible. The same holds true for clutch hitting, leadership, and the other non-measurable factors introduced by James.

The fielding component of the Win Shares system is also based on the team concept and is not an individual measurement. The system includes all of a catcher's putouts less strikeouts, but as was noted previously, the continual reduction in foul territory around home plate, as well as fewer attempted bunts and fewer attempted steals of home, makes the value of that measurement questionable. The system also operates on the assumption that catchers on poor teams face many more attempted steals than catchers on good teams. However, since Win Shares does not include a catcher's caught-stealing record, the formula makes an adjustment for a catcher's total assists, depending on whether the catcher played on a good team or a bad one. That assumption may be true to a certain extent, but as will be shown in the individual catcher's statistics, a catcher's caught-stealing record is not dependent on whether he played for a good team or a bad team. Catchers with strong, accurate arms throw out a high percentage of the runners attempting to steal, while catchers with weak arms or scatter arms have a low success rate, regardless of what team they played for or the number of attempted steals against them, as noted earlier. Mike Piazza is a good example of that reality. He has played for much better teams than Ivan Rodriguez during his career and has faced the incredible number of 176 stolen base attempts for every 154 games played, while throwing out just 25 percent of them. Pudge Rodriguez, on the other hand, has had only 97 attempts against him, gunning down 49 percent of them. The average number of attempts in both leagues at present is 141, so the difference between Piazza's numbers and Rodriguez's number is solely the result of their caught-stealing success rate. The fact that the Win Shares system does not include a catcher's caught-stealing record is another reason why this system cannot be used to compare the skills of individual catchers, since that skill is one of the most important skills in a catcher's repertoire. With regard to Win Shares fielding evaluation in general, James said, "There are some players who are given subjective ratings higher or lower than the mid point (25) because I'm not convinced the Win Shares system makes an adequate evaluation of their defensive contribution." Win Shares is a complex mathematical tool that was devised to compare the performances of teams over the years as well as the value of the team's players. It is a very complicated scientific exercise that has many uses, but in my opinion, comparing the skills of individual players is not one of them. As Bill James once said referring to an opinion of his, I may be entirely correct. I may be partly correct. Or I may be all wrong. It will be up to the reader to make that determination.

Win Shares and Linear Weights are both monumental achievements in the study and analysis of baseball games. For many years statisticians and mathematicians struggled to develop formulas that would allow the game of baseball to be broken down into its simplest form, but all attempts were unsuccessful until James and Palmer appeared on the scene. The Win Shares and Linear Weights models are designed to measure a player's value to his team, but that is a completely different concept from measuring the skills of individual players. Neither system has all the factors that are considered to be critical for measuring the skills of individual catchers and for comparing them side by side, although Linear Weights is much closer than is Win Shares. Win Shares is based on the performance of individual teams, and the players are rated on their contributions to the team. The formulas are predicated on the assumption that the skills of baseball players have continued to improve year by year, even though adjusted statistics do not support that theory. The system also includes a subjective factor that allows the statistician to introduce his or her bias into the equation. Win Shares also lacks an individual park factor that is absolutely crucial for calculating the adjusted slugging average, particularly for players like Dickey, Berra, Howard, and Campanella, whose home runs were significantly affected by the geometrical configurations of their home parks. An equitable era adjustment is also a necessity. Linear Weights is very close to achieving its secondary value of measuring a player's skills. BR does include an era adjustment that considers every season to be the equal of every other season, but it needs an individual park factor before it can be used to compare the individual skills of one player against another with any degree of confidence. And the FR formula should be reviewed, as noted above. This is not meant to minimize the accomplishments of either Pete Palmer or Bill James, because both men are pioneers in their field and both men have done a tremendous job breaking the game of baseball down into its basic components. Their work has been truly revolutionary. Palmer's feat of computerizing all the major league baseball games played since the early 1900s and devising the complex mathematical models he presents is mind-boggling. And James's statistical analysis of complete major league teams places him in the forefront of the game's sweeping new technological advances. James and Palmer have continued to refine their systems over the years, and it is reasonable to assume that, in the near future, one or both of them will modify their formulas to include individualized park factors, a more equitable era adjustment where necessary, a better method of handling a catcher's putouts, and a catcher's caught-stealing percentage that will permit their formulas to be used to evaluate and compare individual catchers.

Until that time arrives, other Sabermetric formulas will have to be used to evaluate and compare the skills of individual catchers. The factors to be used for measuring the offensive and defensive contributions of the individual catchers in this study were determined by the author. They are admittedly less sophisticated than James's and Palmer's formulas, but they are geared to individual players as opposed to teams, and they should be more accurate in measuring the skills of one player against another, particularly where catchers are concerned. They are adjusted for each player's individual park factor as well as for the era in which the individual played. The objective is to put all players on a level playing field so that no player benefits from his home park or from the era in which he played.

The offensive factors that were studied are:

Adjusted on-base-percentage (OBPA) = OBP adjusted for the era in which the individual played.

Adjusted slugging average (XSLG) = SLG adjusted for singles which are accounted for in OBP and adjusted for the player's individualized park factor.

Final adjusted slugging average (XSLGA) = XSLG adjusted for the era in which the individual played.

Stolen bases (SB)

Sacrifice hits (SH)

Double plays grounded into (GIDP)

At first glance, the above factors may seem to be similar to the factors used in other formulas that are designed to evaluate the offensive performance of individual players, but there are several important differences. First, the OBPA derived from OBP included an individualized era adjustment. The XSLGA factor had no less than three adjustments from SLG. First, in calculating XSLG, the singles were eliminated because they were accounted for in OBP. Then the statistics were adjusted to an individualized park factor to eliminate the home field advantage or disadvantage of players like Dickey, Berra, Howard, and Porter. And finally, the XSLGA equation modified XSLG by the inclusion of an era adjustment.

An era adjustment was included because there was no factual basis for assuming that yesterday's players were better than today's players or vice versa. It was concluded therefore that talented players would be just as talented in any era, and the year-to-year or era-to-era fluctuations in batting averages, slugging averages, fielding averages, etc., had to be adjusted to a common base point. In both the adjusted OBPA and the final adjusted XSLGA, the era adjustment was determined in the following manner. A base point year was selected, and the final OBP and XSLG were adjusted to that base point. The base point year selected was 1960, primarily because it fell midway between the high and low limits of both statistics. Coincidentally, it was also about halfway between 1920 and 2004, the range of the study. To arrive at a player's OBPA, the individual's OBP was adjusted up or down depending on the difference between the league average during his career and the base point OBP. For example, Mickey Cochrane's career OBP was .419, the American League average OBP was .349, and the Base Point OBP was .331, a difference of eighteen points, giving Cochrane an OBPA of .419 – (.349 – .331), or .401. The calculation for XSLGA was more complicated. Before making an era adjustment, it was first necessary to calculate XSLG, which involved two adjustments. First, since OBPA included a player's total base hits, it was decided that singles should be eliminated from the XSLG calculation, because the inclusion of singles in calculating the slugging average would be a duplication of effort and would unfairly punish the player who had a low number of singles. Therefore, only the extra-base hits were included in the XSLG calculation. The formula was then 2D + 3T + 4HR1 divided by (550 at-bats—singles). The adjusted home runs (HR1) in the calculation were arrived at by taking a player's park factor and determining his "standard" home runs. For instance, Bill Dickey averaged 18 home runs for every 550 at-bats. But he averaged 24 home runs at home (one team) and only 11 home runs on the road (seven teams), so his HR1 would be $[(11 \times 7) + (24 \times 1)] \div 8$ (the number of teams in the league) = 12.6 home runs. The review of the park factors uncovered the fact that the change in a player's home runs due to the park factor was not the only adjustment that had to be made. Home runs lost or gained by making the PF adjustment are often offset by a similar but opposite change in doubles. So if a player loses five home runs off his home run average because of a high PF, he might gain additional doubles. In making the final adjustment to Bill Dickey's XSLGA, the XSLG was adjusted for the era in which Dickey played. His XSLG was .328, the league SLG during Dickey's career was .391, and the base point SLG was .388, so Dickey's final XSLGA was .328 – (.391 – .388) or .325. Before leaving OBPA and XSLGA, two additional comments should be made regarding runs scored and runs batted in. Neither of these factors was included separately in the formulas for determining a player's offensive contribution, for two very important reasons. Runs scored were not included as a separate entry because they are directly proportional to OBP, and again, to account for them separately would be a duplication of effort. The same holds true for

RBIs. They were not included because they exhibit an extremely strong correlation to SLG. The other offensive statistics used in this study, stolen bases (SB), sacrifice hits (SH), and double plays grounded into (GIDP), are direct measurements as published and do not require an additional explanation at this time.

In arriving at a final offensive rating, the weights of the individual measurements had to be determined. Each factor was rated from 1 to 50, to cover the 50 catchers included in the study. The player with the highest OBPA, in this case Mickey Cochrane, was rated #1, while the player with the lowest OBPA, in this case Tony Pena, was rated #50. The same system was used to measure XSLGA, with the players rated from #1 to #50. The other factors, stolen bases, sacrifice hits, and grounded into double plays, were rated in the same manner, but their rating was then multiplied by .05, since they were not considered to be nearly as significant as OBPA or XSLGA. The resulting offensive point total was arrived at by adding the ratings of the five individual factors together. So if a player was rated #1 in all five categories, his final score would be $1 + 1 + .1 + .1 + .1 = 2.3$, where the .05 factor was rounded off to .1 since carrying the rating out two decimal points was considered to be unrealistic. Conversely if a player finished last in all categories, his final score might read $50 + 50 + 2.5 + 2.5 + 2.5 = 107.5$, where last place of #50 multiplied by .05 is 2.5. And the score could be lower if there were two or more players tied for last place.

The final formula for measuring the offensive skills of the players was:

$$TOP = OBPAR + XSLGAR + .05SBR + .05SHR + .05GIDPR$$

Where:

$$TOP = \text{Total offensive points.}$$
$$OBPAR = \text{OBPA rating, etc.}$$

The final offensive rating (FOR) was determined by the player's final point total, with the player having the lowest point total being rated the best offensive player (1), the player with the second lowest point total being rated (2), and so on down the line to (50).

The defensive factors to be measured in this study included:

Fielding average (FA)
Caught stealing percentage (CS%)
Passed balls (PB)
Wild pitches by the pitching staff (WP)
Range factor (RF)
Adjusted assists (assists minus caught-stealing assists) (ASSA)

Since putouts are a significant part of a catcher's performance, the most tantalizing question was how to utilize them without biasing the results in favor of catchers who benefited from high pitcher strikeouts or from wide expanses of foul territory. It was finally decided that the standard fielding average compilation would be the most acceptable statistic to use because it could be compared to the league average, similar to Pete Palmer's normalization, and the differential could be used to compare the fielding skills of catchers from the same era or from different eras. There would be a slight "double dipping" for assists, which were also measured separately, but that seemed to be the lesser of the evils if an evaluation of a catcher's fielding skills was to be realized. Errors have decreased over the years as a result of better equipment such as gloves, improvements in field grooming, and the use of artificial turf, and fielding average differential appeared to be the most efficient way to evaluate them also. Another calculation that included putouts was the range factor (RF), which is a measurement of the number of assists and putouts a catcher makes per game. This is also an important statistic because it is an indication of a catcher's reflexes, quickness and agility. And it can be compared to the league average, to measure how a catcher compares to his peers.

A catcher's fielding average (FA), like the fielding averages of all positions, has increased continually over the years, as noted above, because of improvements in equipment and facilities. Therefore, a direct comparison of fielding averages could not be made between catchers from different eras. In order to be able to compare the fielding skills of catchers from one era to another, it was first necessary to put the statistics on a level playing field. This was accomplished by comparing a catcher's fielding average to the normal fielding average of all the catchers in the league. This differential (DFA) was then compared to the fielding average differential of catchers from other eras to determine the best-fielding catcher. A similar method was utilized to compare the caught-stealing accomplishments of the various catchers. After a thorough study of all aspects of a catcher's caught-stealing record, it was decided that a catcher's caught-stealing percentage would be the most accurate and equitable way to measure a catcher's skill at throwing out prospective base thieves. It is also the best way to compare one catcher with another, as will be discussed in more detail in chapter nine. The caught-stealing percentage (CS) of a catcher was compared to the normal caught-stealing percentage of all the league's catchers (DCS). This differential was then compared to the caught-stealing differential for catchers from other eras to identify the catcher with the best caught-stealing record. Catchers are responsible for passed balls (PB), so their skill at minimizing passed balls was measured and compared directly. They also must share some responsibility for their pitching staff's wild pitches (WP), since they are not completely blameless in that area. They can contribute to wild pitches through their lack of agility or quickness, or because of faulty catching techniques. Perhaps as many as 25 percent of wild pitches can be prevented by better catching mechanics. The WP total was measured against the average league WP total to obtain a differential, which could then be compared to the WP differential of catchers from other eras.

Range factor (RF) is not an ideal statistic to use because range factors have declined over the years as a result of the increased number of strikeouts, which results in fewer plays being made by position players. After much soul-searching, it was decided that range factor would still be a good yardstick to measure the agility and reflexes of a catcher if the number was compared to the league average for the period covered by the individual's career. The final measurement that was used to arrive at a catcher's overall defensive skill level was a catcher's assists other than those obtained by throwing out prospective base stealers (ASSA). This calculation, like several of the other defensive calculations, included a league differential, which was then used to compare catchers from one era to another.

Pete Palmer, in his Linear Weights system, measures putouts less strikeouts as 0.2 runs, assists at 0.4 runs, caught-stealing at 0.35 runs, and passed balls at 0.125 runs. Those factors compare favorably with the formulas being used for this study, with the exception that passed balls were originally factored at just 0.1 units in this study. Fielding average, which is essentially putouts plus assists divided by errors, gives a final result of 0.4 runs in Palmer's system, which would be equal to 1.0 unit in this study. Caught-stealing is also 1.0 units, while passed balls in this study were increased to 0.3 units to conform to Palmer's system. Wild pitches were set at 0.075 units and catcher assists were factored at 0.5 units.

The formula for measuring the defensive skills of the player is:

$$TDP = DFAR + DCSR + .3PB + .075DWPR + DRFR + 0.5DASSAR$$

where:

TDP = Total defensive points

DFAR = Fielding average rating of the differential from the league average

DCSR = Caught-stealing rating of the differential from the league average

PB = Passed balls

DWPR = Wild pitch rating of the differential from league average

DRFR = Range factor rating of the differential from the league average

DASSAR = Adjusted assist rating of the differential from the league average

As an example, if a player finished first in all categories, he might have a fielding average differential (DFA) of .993 – .983 = + 10, a caught-stealing differential (DCS) of 61% – 41% = +20, five passed balls (PB), a wild pitch differential (DFA) of 23 – 39 = -16, a range factor differential (DRF) of 6.07 – 4.96 = +1.11, and an assist differential (DASS1) of 38 – 30 = + 8. His #1 ratings would give him a point total of:

$$TDP = 1 + 1 + .3 + .1 + 1 + 1 = 4.4$$

The final defensive rating (FDR) was then determined by the player's final total defensive points, with the player having the lowest point total rated number one, the player with the next lowest score being rated number two, and so on down to 50.

8

THE GAME'S
BEST-HITTING CATCHER

Arguments continue to rage within the baseball community. Are today's players better than yesterday's players? Were yesterday's players better than today's players? Or do all eras have equally talented players? There are arguments for all three positions. Advocates in support of today's players point to Nolan Ryan's seven no-hitters, Cal Ripken's 2,632 consecutive-game streak, and Barry Bonds's 73 home runs as proof that now is better. The old-timers point to the all-time All-Star teams that are selected on the basis of skill, not popularity, by various baseball experts. They are almost always dominated by players from a bygone era, such as Walter Johnson, Honus Wagner, Lou Gehrig, and Babe Ruth as proof that the game "ain't what it used to be." They also point to a dilution of talent as discussed in chapter seven. And the middle-of-the-road group (including the author) points to changes in the equipment, smaller ballparks, a livelier ball (including the new Costa Rican ball introduced in 1994), and a different mental approach to the game as reasons for the higher home run totals, higher fielding averages, and higher stolen base totals. They believe that dilution has reduced the overall playing quality of the major leagues, but that the skill level of some of today's individual players, such as Roger Clemens, Mike Piazza, and Barry Bonds, is equal to the skill level of yesterday's players.

This study will, hopefully, help to resolve that debate by comparing catchers from all eras as far back as 1920 in order to identify baseball's greatest all-around catcher. Catchers whose playing careers were primarily in the dead-ball era prior to 1920 were not included in the study because it was not possible to convert their statistics, particularly their defensive statistics, to the lively-ball era. Fifty of the most prominent catchers of the last 85 years were evaluated for both their offensive and defensive skills.

Then the two talents were combined, after first being weighted to account for the relative importance of a catcher's offense to his defense. The strategy of the game has changed numerous times over the past 130 years, at various times emphasizing offense and at other times stressing defense. In the nineteenth century, catchers were expected to excel offensively. The two legendary catchers of the era were Michael "King" Kelly and William "Buck" Ewing, who were large men for their time. In an era when the average major league player stood about 5'7" tall and weighed a wispy 150 pounds, the two catchers stood three inches taller and weighed between 180 and 190 pounds. Both were powerful .300 hitters, and both were also feared for their gloves and their arms. Although Kelly had an advantage in caught-stealing percentage with a 46 percent success rate based on 150 attempts a year to Ewing's 37 percent rate, Ewing was considered to be the better of the two, all around. When the twentieth century got under way, the strategy of the game changed from a slugger's game to a more scientific game, which focused on small, fast, players who could run like the wind, hit-away or bunt, and were skilled fielders. The big, six-foot, 190-pound sluggers like "Big Dan" Brouthers, Roger Connor, and Sam Thompson, who were often accused of "clogging up the base paths," were no longer in demand. Most of the catchers of the day were quick and agile with strong throwing arms. The typical catcher topped the scales at about 160 pounds and hit in the .250–.260 range with little power. But when the lively ball was introduced in 1920, Babe Ruth brought the romance of the long ball back into the game, and the strategy of baseball swung back to offense once again.

Gabby Hartnett was the first of the long ball hitting backstops, but he wasn't a one-dimensional player. His glove was as potent a weapon as his bat. And down through the years, great all-around catchers have been the rule rather than the exception, from Cochrane to Dickey, to Berra and Campanella, to Bench, to Rodriguez. The question is, who was the best? The individual leaders in the most important offensive categories are shown below.

Career Leaders

Carlton Fisk	2499 games played
Carlton Fisk	8756 at-bats
Carlton Fisk	1276 runs scored
Carlton Fisk	2356 base hits
Carlton Fisk	421 doubles
Bill Dickey	72 triples
Mike Piazza	397 home runs (all positions through 2005)
Mike Piazza	377+ home runs (games as catcher — still active)

Yogi Berra	1430 runs batted in
Carlton Fisk	128 stolen bases
Mickey Cochrane	151 sacrifice hits
Mickey Cochrane	.320 batting average

Leaders per 550 at-bats

Mickey Cochrane	110 runs scored
Mickey Cochrane	176 base hits
Mickey Cochrane	35 doubles
Bill Dickey	35 doubles
Bob O'Farrell	8 triples
Mike Piazza	35 home runs (through 2005)
Mike Piazza	108 runs batted in (through 2005)
Carlton Fisk	8 stolen bases
Ivan Rodriguez	8 stolen bases
Mickey Cochrane	16 sacrifice hits

The study undertaken in this chapter, called the final offensive rating (FOR), assumes that the skill level of major league players has remained constant from year to year. That assumption was made because there has been no proof to the contrary. The significant year-to-year variations that have occurred over the past 85 years have been traced to many things, such as changes in the field dimensions, better equipment, improved field grooming, and the construction of the baseball. But no changes have been proven to be the result of differences in the skills of the players. To account for those year-to-year and era-to-era variations, an era adjustment was made by selecting a base point that was midway between the upper and lower statistical limits. The year 1960 was chosen as the base point year because it met those requirements. Coincidentally, it was also about midway between 1920, when the study began, and the present. Pete Palmer used a year-to-year normalization for his era adjustment. The difference between Palmer's normalization and the base point approach outlined above can be seen in the following slugging average example. Suppose Bench, Piazza, Campanella, and Hartnett all had .450 career slugging averages. And suppose the slugging average base point was .388. The following table shows the average league slugging average during the listed player's career, as well as the base point slugging average.

Player	Theoretical Player SLG.	League SLG	Base Pt SLG	Diff.
Johnny Bench	.450	.371	.388	+17
Mike Piazza	.450	.407	.388	-19
Roy Campanella	.450	.396	.388	-8
Gabby Hartnett	.450	.394	.388	-6

In comparing the differences between the Linear Weights method and the base point method, there appears to be little to choose from. For example, in the Linear Weights system, Johnny Bench's SLG of .450 would be compared to the average league SLG of .371, giving him a +79 differential. In the base point method, Bench's final adjusted slugging average (XSLGA) would be .377 (XSLG) − (.371 − .388) = .394, a difference of +17. Both systems seem to be acceptable as era adjustments. Johnny Bench was the big winner in both cases. Mike Piazza was the big loser. And Roy Campanella and Gabby Hartnett were close together in the middle of the pack.

Since the other Sabermetric formulas that were reviewed were missing some of the statistical categories that were deemed critical for measuring and comparing the relative skills of individual catchers, a new formula was devised to accomplish this goal. The formula, identified as final offensive rating (FOR), measured each of the candidates in five different offensive categories: on-base percentage, slugging average, stolen bases, sacrifice hits, and double plays grounded into. When a person thinks of a player's offensive contributions to his team, he often thinks of a player's base hits and runs scored first. Why? Because base hits produce runs, and runs, as Palmer reminded us, are what the game of baseball is all about. If your team scores more runs than the opposing team, your team is the winner. If your team scores fewer runs, your team is the loser. Even more than base hits, however, it's a player's total on-base percentage that contributes to his team's run production. Initially, runs scored and on-base percentage were both included in the FOR formula. But after reviewing all the statistics, and after running a correlation coefficient, the runs scored were eliminated from the formula because there was a fairly strong correlation between runs scored and OBP, and including both of them in the formula might be considered, in some areas, as 'double-dipping'. The OBP calculation was incorporated into the FOR formula, after first correcting it for the era in which the individual catcher played, to put all players on a level playing field. The next factor in the formula was a player's slugging average (SLG). As discussed in the previous chapter, the SLG was modified to eliminate singles from the calculation, again to prevent a duplication of effort since singles were also included in OBP. The next modification, which was extremely important for the accuracy of the formula, was an individualized park factor. Some Sabermetric formulas that used a team park factor gave erroneously high slugging averages for players like Dickey and Berra and correspondingly low slugging averages for other players like Howard and Porter. Finally, the adjusted slugging average (XSLG) was further adjusted to account for the era in which the catcher played. Runs batted in, which were originally considered for the formula, were not included as a separate entity, because of their strong correlation to SLG. The OBPA and XSLGA were the most important factors in rating baseball's great catchers, but stolen bases, sacrifice hits, and double plays grounded into were also incorporated into the FOR formula, although not at the same weight as OBPA and XSLGA.

On-Base-Percentage

Historically, many catchers have been liabilities with the bats. There are exceptions, of course, like Mike Piazza, Mickey Cochrane, Bill Dickey, and Ernie Lombardi. Cochrane was unquestionably the greatest-hitting catcher in baseball between 1925 and 1993. His statistics speak for themselves.

G	AB	R	H	D	T	HR	RBI	BB	OBP	SLG	BA
1482	5169	1041	1652	333	64	119	832	857	.419	.428	.320

Close behind Cochrane as a powerful hitter was Bill Dickey of the New York Yankees.

G	AB	R	H	D	T	HR	RBI	BB	OBP	SLG	BA
1789	6300	930	1969	343	72	202	1209	678	.382	.486	.313

Finally, there was Ernie "Schnozz" Lombardi, the likable backstop of the Cincinnati Reds.

G	AB	R	H	D	T	HR	RBI	BB	OBP	SLG	BA
1853	5855	601	1792	277	27	190	990	430	.358	.460	.306

These three catchers, plus Bubbles Hargrave and Babe Phelps, were the only career .300 hitters in the modern world class catching fraternity until Mike Piazza came along in 1993. Piazza immediately surged to the front of the pack as an offensive powerhouse, hitting both for average and for distance. In his rookie season with the Los Angeles Dodgers, Piazza served notice on the league that he was a force to be reckoned with. He hit a hard .318 with 35 home runs and 112 runs batted in and followed that up with averages of .319, .346 and .336. Then, in 1997, he put it all together. He blistered opposing pitchers to the tune of .362, tying Bill Dickey for the highest single-season batting average by a catcher with more than 350 at-bats, in the modern game. He also sent 40 balls screaming into orbit and drove in 124 runs. Piazza completed his 12th year in the major leagues in 2003, with a .319 career batting average and 358 home runs, 347 as a catcher. He went on to break Carlton Fisk's career home run record of 351 home runs for a catcher on May 4, 2004. Mickey Cochrane still has the highest career batting average of any of the 50 catchers in the study, at .320 with Piazza close behind, but Piazza has seen his batting average drop dramatically since he left Los Angeles, and at age 35, it is unlikely he will finish his career with an average higher than .319. In his seven years with the Dodgers he sported a .331 batting average, but he has hit just .308 over the last six years and has dropped into the .280 range for the last two. Cochrane was also more adept at coaxing bases on balls out of a pitcher than Piazza is, showing 91 walks for every 550 at-bats, while Piazza has averaged 60 walks per 550 at-bats. The hits plus walks gave Cochrane a top-rated .419 on-base-percentage (OBP).

Another .300-hitting catcher who is still active is Ivan "Pudge" Rodriguez. The squat 5'9", 190-pound right-handed hitter owned a .304 career batting average through the 2003 season. At the age of 32, Pudge still has a few good years left, but it is questionable if he can retain his .300 career batting mark until his retirement. Broken down into a 550-at-bats season, the stats for the seven .300-hitting catchers are:

Left: Ernie Lombardi was a rarity in the baseball world, a .300-hitting catcher. *Right:* Mike Piazza is the most explosive hitting catcher ever to play the game. *Author's collection.*

Catcher	R	H	D	T	HR	RBI	BB	BA
Mickey Cochrane	110	176	35	7	13	89	91	.320
Bill Dickey	81	169	30	7	18	106	59	.313
Bubbles Hargrave	68	171	34	12	6	82	47	.310
Babe Phelps	62	171	37	5	14	90	42	.310
Ernie Lombardi	56	168	26	3	18	93	40	.306
Mike Piazza	93	175	27	1	38	119	60	.319
Pudge Rodriguez	82	167	33	3	22	86	29	.304

It would appear, from reviewing the above statistics, that one of the those seven catchers would walk off with the number one ranking as baseball's greatest offensive catcher. But handing one of them the title before all the results were in would have been premature. There were "sleepers" among the catchers, players who don't seem to be contributing much offense, but who put up surprising numbers in statistics like on-base percentage. Three who come to mind in the latter category are Gene Tenace, Mickey Tettleton, and Darrell Porter. Tenace, a career .241 hitter, had an on-base percentage of .388, which increased to .392 when adjusted for the era in which he played. Tettleton, another .241 hitter, had an OBP of .369, adjusted to .366, and Porter, who hit a mediocre .247 during a 17 year career, posted a .354 OBP, adjusted to .362. Their secret was their patience at the plate and their knack for drawing bases on balls. Gene Tenace walked an average of 123 times for every 550 at-bats, while Mickey Tettleton coaxed 111 walks out of opposing pitchers and Darrell Porter drew 90 walks over the same distance. All three scored in the neighborhood of 80 runs per year as a result of their patient plate presence. Their statistics, based on a 550-at-bat season, are:

Catcher	AB	R	H	D	T	HR	RBI	BB	BA
Gene Tenace	550	82	133	22	3	25	84	123	.241
Mickey Tettleton	550	83	133	25	2	29	86	112	.241
Darrell Porter	550	76	136	24	5	19	82	90	.247

Their statistics at first glance are not very impressive, with all three men hitting below .250, but they all possessed above-average power as shown by their home runs totals, and they were all patient hitters who made opposing pitchers work hard.

An era adjustment (EA) made to the OBP played a significant part in the final adjusted on-base-percentage (OBPA). The formula for OBPA is:

$$OBPA = OBP - EA$$

Where:

EA = Era adjustment, as described above.

EA = LOBP – BPOBP

Where:

LOBP = League OBP

BPOBP = Base point OBP, identified as the OBP for the year 1960, which is .322 for the National League and .331 for the American League.

The following table shows the fluctuation in OBP as well as SLG (which will be discussed in the next section).

League OBP and SLG

	NL		AL	
Year	OBP	SLG	OBP	SLG
1920	.322	.357	.347	.387
1925	.348	.414	.360	.408
1930	.360	.448	.351	.421
1935	.331	.391	.351	.402
1940	.326	.376	.342	.407
1945	.333	.364	.325	.346
1950	.336	.401	.356	.402
1955	.328	.407	.336	.381
1960	.322	.388	.331	.388
1965	.311	.374	.311	.369
1970	.329	.392	.322	.379
1975	.327	.369	.328	.379
1980	.320	.374	.331	.399
1985	.319	.374	.327	.406
1990	.321	.383	.327	.388
1995	.331	.408	.344	.427
2000	.342	.432	.349	.443
2003	.332	.417	.333	.428
Range	.311–.348	.357–.448	.311–.360	.346–.443
Median	.330	.403	.336	.395

The EA eliminated any unfair advantage (or disadvantage) that might have been caused by changes in the game from one era to another, such as the construction of the balls, the size of the stadiums, improvements in equipment or stadium facilities, etc. The era adjustment was a boon to Earl Battey, who saw his OBP increase by ten points. Darrell Porter realized an eight-point increase, Bill Freehan a 14-point increase, and Elston Howard a nine-point increase. Conversely, Ivan Rodriguez took an eight-point hit. Some other players who experienced the downside of the era adjustment included Wes Westrum, who saw his OBP go from a healthy .356 to .342, dropping him to 28th place. Bob O'Farrell had a fine .360 OBP before a 21-point era loss put him in 31st place. And Muddy Ruel saw his .365 OBP plummet to .338 after the era adjustment, giving him a 33rd-place finish. Cochrane, who lost 18 points off his OBP because of an unfavorable era adjustment, still finished in first place with an OBPA of .401. Surprisingly, Mike Piazza was not as lucky. He did not finish in second place in OBPA as expected. His .388 OBP, based on his 60 walks plus a negative 11-point era adjustment, dropped him down to third place. Gene Tenace, who had a mediocre .241 batting average as noted above, climbed into second place with an OBPA average of .392. Tettleton and Porter, with their high walk totals, fared better than at first suspected, as will be seen below. Bill Dickey finished high in the rankings thanks to his .313 career batting average and 59 bases on balls. Rick Ferrell, a decent hitter with a .281 batting average, drew 85 walks for every 550 at-bats, giving him a fine .365 OBPA, in spite of losing a 13-point era adjustment. Yogi Berra finished 21st with a .346 OBPA, and Johnny Bench was 25th at .345.

Darrell Porter averaged 19 home runs and 82 runs batted in during his 17-year career. *Courtesy Jay Sanford.*

The importance of the era adjustment (EA) on the final on-base percentage (OBPA) is evident from the following illustration.

	OBP	Ranking	EA	OBPA	Ranking
Bob O'Farrell	.360	#11	-21	.339	#31
Roy Campanella	.360	#11	-9	.351	#15
Earl Battey	.349	#18	+10	.359	#10

Bob O'Farrell lost 20 places in the final OBPA rankings as a result of the era adjustment. Roy Campanella lost four places, but Earl Battey gained eight places, passing Campanella in the OBPA standings on his way to a 10th-place finish.

The top ten places in the OBPA ratings, in order, were:

Catcher	*OBPA*	*Catcher*	*OPBA*
Mickey Cochrane	.401	Rick Ferrell	.365
Gene Tenace	.392	Jason Kendall	.363
Mike Piazza	.377	Joe Torre	.363
Bill Dickey	.368	Darrell Porter	.362
Mickey Tettleton	.366	Earl Battey	.359

The complete list for the OBPA for all 50 catchers can be found in the Appendix.

Slugging Average

In order to arrive at a fair measure of a player's slugging skills, several adjustments had to be made to the standard slugging average formula (SLG). First, singles were eliminated from the calculation since they were counted in the calculation for on-base percentage (OBP), and to count them again would be a duplication of effort. The most significant component of the slugging average was a player's home runs. The following table lists the average home runs per year per major league team, based on a 154 game schedule.

Home runs Per Team Per 154 Games.

Years	HR's	Years	HR's	Years	HR's
1885–1891	39	1960	133	1996	168
1892-1899	24	1970	136	1997	165
1903-1909	19	1980	112	1998	160
1910-1919	31	1990	125	1999	175
1920	39	1991	124	2000	181
1920-1930	73	1992	111	2001	173
1930	98	1993	137	2002	161
1940	98	1994	159	2003	165
1950	130	1995	156		

Home runs have increased dramatically at times over the past 80 years, for various reasons. After the lively ball was introduced in 1920, home runs increased over the next decade to 98 home runs per team per year. The next jump, in the late '40s and early '50s, was attributable to a combination of events. First there was the "Ralph Kiner syndrome." When the Pittsburgh Pirate slugger led the National League in home runs his first seven years in the league and made his now-famous remark, "Home run hitters drive Cadillacs. Singles hitters drive Chevys," a whole generation of young boys began to emulate the big slugger in swinging for distance. Integration, which brought a bevy of long-ball-hitting Negro Leaguers into the major leagues, sluggers like Larry Doby, Monte Irvin, Roy Campanella, Luke Easter, Ernie Banks, and Willie Mays, also drove up the home run production. And another contributing factor to the rise in home runs has been the heavy exodus from South America and the Caribbean basin over the past twenty years. Sluggers like Sammy Sosa from the Dominican Republic, Juan Gonzalez from Puerto Rico, Rafael Palmeiro from Cuba, and Andres Galarraga from Venezuela have popularized the romance of the long ball. These four players have compiled almost 2000 career home runs between them. When questioned about his obsession with home runs and his numerous strikeouts (144 for every 550 at-bats), Sosa said that poor children in the Dominican Republic believe their only hope of becoming successful in life is to become a major league baseball player, and to hit a lot of home runs. And if they have to strike out 144 times a year to realize their goal, it's OK with them. Other factors that have affected home run levels, such as a player's size, expansion, baseball stadium dimensions, night baseball, etc. are discussed in more detail in my books *The King of Swat* and *The Single-Season Home Run Kings*.

The Sabermetric formulas in this study incorporated individual park factors (PF) into the equation, in order to eliminate any unfair advantage (or disadvantage) that might result from the geometrical configuration or atmospheric conditions associated with a particular park. Some statistical programs use a team park factor, so every player who played on a particular team in the same park would have the same park factor. Obviously using one park factor for every player on a particular team could lead to serious errors in individual statistics caused by the unique character of the individual parks, as noted earlier. As with other studies that made adjustments to the data in order to put all the contenders on the same basis, the park factor adjustments (PF) resulted in more than a few surprises. Yogi Berra, for example, had a decided edge in home runs as a result of playing half his games in friendly Yankee Stadium. The left-handed slugger compiled a favorable 1.42 park factor while taking aim at the cozy right field stands in the Bronx, meaning he hit 42 percent more homers there than in other parks around the American League. Elston Howard, a right-handed batter who had to face the immense left field expanse at the Stadium, had a PF of just 0.48. And Thurman Munson, another Yankee mainstay, could manage only 42 homers at home against 71 homers on the road, for a PF of 0.58. The wide swings in PFs shown above reinforced the belief that individual park factors (PF) were needed in order to level the field. There were some big winners in the slugging sweepstakes when individual park factors were used to eliminate the effects of the team PF, and there were also a few big losers. Elston Howard was a huge winner in the park factor adjustment as his 0.48 PF sent his adjusted home runs per 550 at-bats up, from 17 to 21. Thurman Munson saw his homer total increase from 12 to 14, Darrell Porter enjoyed an increase from 19 to 22, and Jim Sundberg's total went from nine to 11. The big losers included Bill Dickey, whose 2.02 PF caused his homers to plummet from 18 per 550 at-bats to 13. Yogi Berra took a big hit in the power department, with his home runs going from 26 to 22, and Roy Campanella's home runs dropped from 32 to 29.

Using individual park factors gave some unexpected results in the slugging sweepstakes. Many of the most productive power hitters had unfavorable HRFs that affected their statistics. When the playing field anomalies were taken into consideration and individual park factors were used, their output soared. Mike Piazza, not surprisingly, had the highest unadjusted slugging average at .579. Roy Campanella was next at an even .500, followed by Gabby Hartnett at .489, Bill Dickey at .486, and Ivan Rodriguez at .485. Walker Cooper had a respectable .464 slugging average (SLG), while Darrell Porter came in at .409. When singles were erased from the equation and individual park factors were used to adjust a player's statistics, including his doubles, triples, home runs, and batting average, all SLGs took a big hit. Piazza still led the parade, but his slugging average plummeted to .485. Then it fell to .466 when adjusted to the era in which he played. Bill Dickey, who had a 2.01 PF, saw his XSLGA bottom out at .325, Berra's fell from .482 to .350, Campanella's dropped to .374, and Thurman Munson's went from .410 to .267. But again there were a few surprises. Some players who had unfavorable PFs benefited from the adjustment. Ernie Lombardi, who had a 0.79 PF, came in with an adjusted slugging average (XSLGA) of .346, and Elston Howard finished at .324. Walker Cooper, who had to hit into the wide-open spaces in left center field at the Polo Grounds, giving him a PF of 0.70, compiled a slugging average of .364 when all adjustments were made. Gene Tenace, who combined a lowly .241 batting average and 25 home runs for every 550 at-bats with a 0.88 park factor, finished eighth in slugging with an average of .347. And Darrell Porter, who had a 0.69 PF based on 77 homers at home and 111 homers on the road, put up a fine .322 adjusted slugging average, to finish a strong 16th out of 47 contenders.

The final adjustment to the slugging average formula was the inclusion of an era adjustment (EA). The table in the preceding section shows the average league slugging averages for both the National League and the American League from 1920 to the present. Once again, there were many swings in the final results. Bill Freehan was one of the big winners in the (EA) stakes, increasing his slugging average by 21 points. Johnny Bench gained 17 points, Ernie Lombardi gained 14 points, while Gary Carter, Ted Simmons, and Joe Torre each picked up 13. On the other side of the coin, many catchers, most of them in the 1990s, suffered disastrous decreases. The '90s, with livelier balls and bats, smaller ballparks, and other questionable advantages, had the highest slugging averages since the balls were constructed without raised seams, in 1930. Jorge Posada lost 45 points. Ivan Rodriguez lost 36 points, and Charles Johnson lost 31.

The final formula for the adjusted slugging average (XSLGA) is:

$$XSLGA = XSLG - (LSA - BPSA)$$

Where:

$$XSLG = (2D1 + 3T1 + 4HR1) / 550 - S$$

Where:

D1, T1, and HR1 = Doubles, triples, and home runs adjusted for the individual PF

LSA – BPSA represents the era adjustment

LSA = League slugging average during player's career

BPSA = Base point slugging average, identified as the SLG for the year 1960, which is .388 for both the National League and the American Leagues.

S = Singles

The importance of using an individual park factor as opposed to a team park factor can be seen in the following example.

Bill Dickey's Statistics

	AB	H	D	T	HR	BA
Actual stats per 550 ABs	550	169	30	6	18	.313
Stats at home (Yankee Stadium)	550	170	24	6	24	.309
Stats away from home	550	174	35	7	11	.316
Stats adjusted for individual PF	550	174	34	7	13	.316

Dickey's adjusted slugging average using his actual published statistics would be:

XSLGA (Actual stats) = (60 + 18 + 72) divided by 431 = .348 – 3 (Era Adj.) = .345

However, his adjusted slugging average, after incorporating the individual park factor, was:

XSLGA (Adj. Stats) = (68 + 21 + 52) divided by 430 = .328 – 3 (ERA Adj) = .325

If a team park factor were used, Bill Dickey would have been ranked tenth out of 50 catchers. But by using an individualized PF, Dickey was rated 13. Obviously that difference in his XSLGA could have had a significant effect on his total offensive ranking and his final all-around ranking.

Stolen Bases

Catchers are not noted for their base stealing skills, but stolen bases are an important part of the game of baseball, and it is a tremendous advantage to a team if a player can steal a base at an opportune time. No catcher has ever won a stolen base title, and in all probability, no catcher ever will, because of the constant abuse his body takes behind the plate, but some catchers, even today, are threats to steal. In the modern era, only three catchers have stolen more than 100 bases during their careers: Kendall, Rodriguez and Fisk. Fisk swiped 128 bases over a 25-year career, but Kendall already has 148 and is still adding to his total. The Pittsburgh Flier stole 26 bases in 1988, followed by 22 in each of the following two years. At 31 years of age, he has slowed down somewhat, but he may still reach the 200 stolen base mark before he retires. Fisk's high was 17, reached in both 1982 and 1985. Ivan Rodriguez, with 107 stolen bases through 2005, may yet crack the 150 career mark. Charles Johnson, with only four stolen bases in eleven years, most likely won't. In the "old days," catchers stole bases as a matter of routine. The nineteenth-century legends, King Kelly and Buck Ewing, stole 315 and 354 bases respectively during their careers. The early twentieth-century catchers, Roger Bresnahan, Ray Schalk, and Wally Schang, swiped 212, 176, and 122, in that order. Broken down into a 154-game season, the stolen base leaders among modern-day catchers are Kendall with 18, Fisk and Rodriguez with eight, followed by Mickey Cochrane, Muddy Ruel, and Tony Pena with seven, and Bob O'Farrell, Johnny Bench, Gene Tenace, and Thurman Munson with five each.

Sacrifice Hits

Another important skill of catchers is the ability to bunt for a base hit at a critical time in the game, or to move a runner along with a well placed sacrifice. As with other skills, the ability to lay down a sacrifice has taken a big hit over the decades, not only from catchers, but from all players. In today's game, teams tend to wait for the three-run homer, particularly in the American League where the designated hitter bats for the pitcher. From a career standpoint, the leader in sacrifice hits is Mickey Cochrane with 151, followed by Muddy Ruel with 143 and Gabby Hartnett with 137. However, as Pete Palmer pointed out, some of the sacrifice hits attributed to Cochrane, Ruel, and Hartnett were actually sacrifice flies. At the other end of the spectrum, Mike Piazza is the only catcher in the study who does not have a single sacrifice bunt to his credit in his entire career, and that chink in his offensive armor may have cost his team a division title. The Dodgers were tied with the San Diego Padres for first place in the National League Western Division on the last day of the season in 1996, and they entertained the Padres in a game for all the marbles. In the bottom of the ninth inning of a scoreless game, the Dodgers put the first two men on base for Piazza, but the big catcher, disdaining the bunt, fanned, and the next batter, Eric Karros, hit into an inning-ending double play. San Diego won the game and the division title two innings later. On a 154-game basis, the leaders in sacrifice hits are Ruel with 17, Cochrane with 16, Ray Mueller with 12, Bob O'Farrell with 11, and Jim Sundberg, Gabby Hartnett, and Ken O'Dea with 10 each.

Grounded Into Double Plays (GIDP)

Another key strength of a great catcher is his ability to stay out of the double play. The apparent career leader in hitting into the fewest double plays is Bill Dickey, whose incomplete records credit him with 49 GIDPs in 1844 recorded at-bats. The "turtles" of the profession are Ted Simmons with 287 in 8680 at-bats, Joe Torre with 284 in 7874 at-bats, and Ernie Lombardi with 261 in 5664 at-bats. On a 154-game basis, the best catchers at avoiding hitting into double plays are John Roseboro with seven GIDPs, followed by Tom Haller with eight, and Mickey Tettleton, Darrell Porter, Mickey Cochrane, and Gene Tenace with 10 each. The slow man in the study, as might be expected, is Ernie Lombardi with 25 GIDPs per 154 games. He is followed by Ray Mueller with 21 and Tony Pena and Joe Torre with 20.

Final Offensive Rating (FOR)

The total offensive points for catchers were explained in the previous chapter, with the best performance for OBPA and XSLGA being rated (1), the second best (2), down to the lowest rated performance (50). Stolen bases were rated from best to worst, from one to 50, using a .05 multiplication factor, since stolen bases were considered to be only five percent as important as either OBPA or XSLGA. Sacrifice hits and grounded into double plays were handled in the same manner, using a similar .05 multiplication factor. The equation for the final offensive rating (FOR) is:

FOR = OBPAR + XSLGAR + .05SBR + .05SHR + .05GIDPR

Where:

OBPAR = OBPA rating
XSLGAR = XSLGR rating, and so on

The catcher with the fewest total points is the top offensive catcher, the catcher with the next lowest point total is number two, and so on down to 50.

The top eleven places for offensive catcher follow. The complete list can be found in the Appendix.

Catcher	OBPAR	XSLGAR	SBR	SHR	GIDPR	Total Points	FOR
M. Piazza	3	1	2.2	2.5	2.1	10.8	1
G. Tenace	2	8	0.6	1.4	0.2	12.2	2
M. Cochrane	1	17	0.3	0.1	0.2	18.6	3
G. Hartnett	12	5	1.6	0.3	1.1	20.0	4
B. Dickey	4	13	1.1	1.1	1.1	20.3	5
R. Campanella	15	3	1.1	1.1	2.1	22.3	6
J. Torre	7	12	1.6	2.2	2.4	25.2	7
D. Porter	9	16	0.7	1.7	0.2	27.6	8
E. Lombardi	15	9	2.2	1.7	2.5	30.4	9
J. Bench	25	2	0.6	2.2	1.0	30.8	10T
Y. Berra	21	6	1.1	2.2	0.5	30.8	10T

The final ratings revealed several interesting facts. Only Mike Piazza, Gene Tenace, Joe Torre, and Gabby Hartnett finished in the top twelve in both OBPAR and XSLGAR. Piazza had below average performances in the three categories that rely on good bat control and good speed — stolen bases, sacrifice hits, and grounding into double plays, but he was so dominant in the more important categories of OBPAR and XSLGAR that he easily captured the coveted title of baseball's greatest-hitting catcher. Gene Tenace missed his chance at the title, out-slugged by Piazza, who left all the other challengers in his dust. The number two man in XSLGAR was Bench, and he finished a full 72 points behind the champ. And his 25th-place finish in OBPAR cost him dearly in the final offensive ratings. Mickey Cochrane was hurt by his 18th-place finish in XSLGAR, the result of his modest 13 homers for every 550 at-bats, and his 16-point negative era adjustment. Bill Dickey lost valuable points because of his poor individual park factor adjustment. In the OBPAR rating, Hartnett was hurt by a huge 16-point negative era adjustment, while Campanella and Bench were penalized by their modest batting averages and, in Bench's case, by his low walk totals. Cochrane was greatly aided by his outstanding speed, finishing near the top in stolen bases and in first place for both sacrifice hits and fewest double plays grounded into. His speed allowed him to beat out both Hartnett and Campanella in the race for third place. Hartnett edged past Campanella thanks to his fine record in sacrifice hits and in grounding into fewer double plays. Campanella's outstanding slugging record gained him a sixth-place finish behind Dickey, while his stronger showing in OBPAR gave him a big advantage over Bench. Yogi Berra, a notorious bad-ball hitter who considered taking a base on balls an insult, suffered in the OBPAR category as a result. His 51 walks per 550 at-bats, one of the lowest totals for world-class catchers, relegated him to an 11th-place finish.

A summary of the other finishers in the offensive competition follows, in order of their ranking, from number 12 to 50.

12. Mickey Tettleton was another surprise in the offensive sweepstakes, parlaying his 112 bases on balls into a high overall finish. He came in a strong fifth in OBPAR, finished in the top half in XSLGAR, captured second place in the GIDPR category, and was outstanding in the SBR and SHR categories also.

13T. Ted Simmons was a solid offensive performer who finished in the top 18 for both OBPAR and XSLGAR, thanks to his 16 home runs for every 550 at-bats and his .285 batting average. He lost valuable points because of poor showings in the SBR, SHR, and GIDPR categories.

13T. Chris Hoiles was one of the most underrated catchers of the twentieth century. He was an outstanding all-around receiver, with longball power and one of the steadiest gloves in major league history.

15. Carlton Fisk was a powerful offensive threat whose 24 homers for every 550 at-bats and 1.0 HRF carried him to a 10th-place finish in the XSLGAR category. He finished in the top half of the OBPAR stat although his low bases on balls total and his .269 batting average cost him several positions. He also finished near the top in both the SBR and GIDPR category.

16. Bill Freehan was a talented all-around catcher who starred both offensively and defensively. He finished 12th in OBPAR and 22nd in SLGAR, and his above-average speed gave him good scores in SBRs and SHRs, and seventh-place finish in GIDPRs.

17. Earl Battey finished in the top third of the offensive ratings on the basis of his fine 10th-place finish for OBPAR. His 16 home runs for every 550 at-bats and his .270 batting average gave him a 30th-place finish for XSLGAR. He grounded into 19 double plays, a figure exceeded by only four other players.

18. Joe Ferguson's 14th-place finish in OBPA was the major factor in his high offensive rating.

19. Bubbles Hargrave was a hard-hitting catcher of the 1920s. He hit for average and he hit with power, as reflected in his 21st-place finish in OBPAR and his 22nd-place finish in XSLGAR.

20. Jason Kendall played his ninth year in the National League in 2004, so his rating may decline as his career winds down.

21. Walker Cooper, the long-ball-hitting backstop for the powerful New York Giants of the late '40s, posted a fourth-place finish for XSLGAR to offset his mediocre results in the other categories. He finished number 42 in OBPAR and grounded into 19 double plays.

22. Babe Phelps was one of the original good-hit, no-field catchers. His 17th-place finish in XSLGAR and his 30th-place finish in OBPAR were the keys to his high offensive rating.

23. Thurman Munson was 15th in OBPAR but finished 33rd in XSL-GAR, primarily because of his low home run total. He showed well in SB, but his other results were middle of the road.

24. Rick Ferrell, with his .281 batting average and 85 bases on balls, came in a surprising sixth in OBPAR and was strong in SBR, SHR, and GIDPR, but that wasn't enough to offset a 45th-place finish in XSLGAR.

25. Elston Howard cemented 25th place on the strength of a strong 14th-place showing in XSLGAR. He finished number 36 in OBPAR and was generally below average in SBR, SHR, and GIDPR.

26. Smoky Burgess had an excellent 18th-place finish for OBPAR. The hard-hitting southpaw swinger could do no better than a 34th-place finish in XSLGAR in spite of a tough .295 batting average, with 15 homers and 83 RBIs a year.

27. Gary Carter was also strong in XSLGAR, finishing in 20th place. He also excelled in GIDPR, grounding into only 12 double plays for every 154 games. He finished near the middle of the pack in OBPAR because of his .262 batting average and 59 walks.

28. Darren Daulton continued to show superior offensive numbers throughout his 14-year career, compiling a .378 OBP and a .463 SLG in his final season.

29. Javy Lopez, another active player, powered his way to a number seven finish in the XSLGAR category, offsetting his below-average results in the other categories. He holds a solid .287 batting average, but his scant 37 bases on balls for every 550 at-bats dropped him to 46th place in OBPAR.

30. Ivan Rodriguez, who is still active, was in the middle of most categories, with a high of 21st place in XSLGAR. He was near the top of the list for SBR with eight successful attempts a year.

31. Tom Haller was consistent in all categories, finishing 31st in OBPAR and 27th in XSLGAR.

32. Ed Bailey was a solid all-around offensive player during his 14-year career and maintained that consistency in the ratings, finishing 27th in OBPAR and 31st in XSLGAR.

33. Sherm Lollar, the mainstay of the Chicago White Sox during the

'50s, cemented his position with an 21st-place finish in OBPAR. His .264 batting average relegated him to 37th place in XSLGAR, and his slow foot speed hurt him in both the GIDPR and SBR categories.

34. Lance Parrish had a strong 14th-place finish for XSLGAR, but could do no better than 47th place for OBPAR. His defense, as will be seen, was exceptional.

35. Mike Scioscia's position was based on his strong 28th-place rating in OBPAR, which was helped by his 71 bases on balls a year.

36. Gus Triandos, the long-ball-hitting backstop of the Baltimore Orioles, rode into 36th place on the basis of a 24th-place finish in XSLGAR.

37. Birdie Tebbetts posted a strong 20th-place finish in OBPAR thanks to a fine .270 batting average and 58 bases on balls. But unfortunately, because of his low base on ball rate and his lack of power, six home runs for every 550 at-bats, he came in 49th in XSLGAR. He was above average in the SBR and SHR categories.

38. Bob O'Farrell was near average for OBPAR and XSLGAR, while excelling in the other categories.

39T. Charles Johnson was above average for XSLGAR, finishing in 25th place, but was no better than 43rd in OBPAR. He was average to slightly below average in the other categories.

39T. John Roseboro, the favorite receiver of Sandy Koufax and Don Drysdale, was not only an outstanding defensive catcher. He was also dangerous with a bat in his hand.

41. Wes Westrum finished 26th OBPAR, but could do no better than 47th for XSLGAR.

42. Del Crandall finished 29th for XSLGAR thanks to his 20 home runs a year, but his .254 batting average condemned him to 49th place for OBPAR. He was strong, however, in both SBR and SHR.

43T. Muddy Ruel, a veteran of the old dead-ball days, finished a respectable 33rd in OBPAR, but could do no better than 50th in slugging. He was near the top of the list for SBR, SHR, and GIDPR.

43T. Manny Sanguillen was one of the top all-around catchers of the 1970s, always giving Johnny Bench a battle for the number one spot.

45. Ken O'Dea, a noted defensive specialist, was at or near the top in both the SHR and GIDPR categories. But his .255 batting average and 10 home runs consigned him to 39th place in OBPAR and 43rd place in XSLGAR.

46. Jim Sundberg, another defensive genius who batted a modest .248 with nine home runs per year during his career, was slightly below average in most categories. He finished 38th in OBPAR and 46th in XSLGAR. He excelled in SHR and GIDPR.

47. Buddy Rosar, an outstanding defensive catcher, was a decent hitter with a .261 average, but he had little power and drew only 54 walks a year. He finished 37th in OBPAR and 48th in XSLGAR, but was above average for SBR and SHR.

48. Ray Mueller, a noted defensive specialist, batted only .252 with 11 home runs and 47 bases on balls, banishing him to 48th place for OBPAR and 39th place for XSLGAR. He was above average for SBR and SHR, but near the bottom for GIDPR.

49. Harry "The Horse" Danning, another defensive stalwart, was 43rd in OBPAR, 44th in XSLGAR, and average in the other categories.

50. Tony Pena, the man who made the one-legged catching stance popular, was outstanding on defense, but not a force to be reckoned with on offense. He batted .260 with nine homers and 39 walks, putting him in 50th place for OBPAR and 42nd place for XSLGAR. He was strong in SBR and SHR, but third from the bottom in GIDPR.

The final offensive ratings, broken down into eras and leagues, gave the following results.

Offensive Leaders by Era and by League

National League	American League
1920–1940	**1920–1940**
1. Gabby Hartnett	1. Mickey Cochrane
2. Ernie Lombardi	2. Bill Dickey
3. Bubbles Hargrave	3. Rick Ferrell
4. Babe Phelps	4. Muddy Ruel
5. Bob O'Farrell	
1940–1960	**1940–1960**
1. Roy Campanella	1. Yogi Berra
2. Walker Cooper	2. Sherman Lollar
3. Smoky Burgess	3. Gus Triandos
4. Ed Bailey	4. Birdie Tebbetts
5. Wes Westrum	5. Buddy Rosar
1960–1980	**1960–1980**
1. Joe Torre	1. Gene Tenace
2. Johnny Bench	2. Darrell Porter
3. Ted Simmons	3. Bill Freehan
4. Joe Ferguson	4. Earl Battey
5. Tom Haller	5. Elston Howard
1980–2000	
1. Mike Piazza	1. Mickey Tettleton
2. Chris Hoiles	2. Carlton Fisk
3. Jason Kendall	3. Ivan Rodriguez
4. Gary Carter	4. Lance Parrish
5. Darren Daulton	5. Jim Sundberg

The previous chapter reviewed several other statistical studies that were conducted to identify baseball's greatest-hitting catcher. Some of these studies are compared with the FOR to determine if there are any differences and, if so, the reasons for those differences. Charles Rosciam compared the offensive systems of Bill James (RC), Pete Palmer and John Thorn (BR), and Jim McMartin (RG), finally averaging all three systems to arrive at a consensus batting leader. The ratings are shown below.

Ratings

Catcher	RC	BR	RG	AVG	FOR
Mike Piazza	2	1	1	1	1
Mickey Cochrane	1	2	2	2	3
Roy Campanella	6	4	3	3	6
Mickey Tettleton	7	8	4	6	12
Bill Dickey	3	9	5	5	5
Gabby Hartnett	4	5	6	4	4
Johnny Bench	11	7	7	7	10T
Yogi Berra	9	11	8	8	10T
Javy Lopez	14	21	9	10	29
Ernie Lombardi	11	8	10	9	9

The above ratings, which measure only a player's offensive skills, have been adjusted to include only the catchers that are among the 50 catchers being evaluated in this study. Actually the first nine positions are untouched. Only the tenth position has been adjusted. One interesting absentee from the list of 38 catchers reviewed by Rosciam was Gene Tenace, usually considered one of the top offensive catchers of his time. In reviewing the individual systems, it appears that Tenace would have finished in second place on the average list, the same place he finished on the FOR list. The biggest discrepancies between the FOR formula and the other formulas occurred with Mickey Tettleton and Javy Lopez. Tettleton, who finished between fourth and eighth in the other formulas, and 12th in FOR, may have suffered in the FOR rating because of the loss of 22 points in an era adjustment. And Javy Lopez took a huge hit, losing 44 points in an era adjustment. The batting runs (BR) formula gave the best agreement to the FOR formula, particularly with regard to Javy Lopez's rating. It rated Lopez number 21 compared to number 29 for the FOR formula, while the other two formulas rated him ninth and 14th. The BR formula, which is one of the Linear Weights formulas developed by Pete Palmer, has an era adjustment that normalizes a player's statistics to the league average, but it also includes a generalized park factor. The RC formula of Bill James, which claims the baseball talent is getting better every year, gave Lopez extra points because he is a modern-day player.

Don Zminda produced a Relativity Index that compared runs created (RC) per 27 outs to a league RC (LRC) per 27 outs, to compare individual catchers. His ratings are shown below, again adjusted to show only the catchers that are in this study.

Catcher	Index	FOR
Mike Piazza	173.2	1
Mickey Cochrane	149.9	3
Gene Tenace	148.8	2
Bill Dickey	140.0	5
Joe Torre	138.7	7
Roy Campanella	137.7	6
Yogi Berra	137.7	10T
Gabby Hartnett	137.2	4
Johnny Bench	134.6	10T
Smoky Burgess	129.0	26

Michael Hoban's system, which combines runs created (RC) with Pete Palmer's OPS to produce a rating he calls batting proficiency (BP), gave the results listed below.

Catcher	Batting Proficiency	FOR
Mike Piazza	289	1
Johnny Bench	265	10T
Ted Simmons	262	13
Yogi Berra	252	10T
Mickey Cochrane	254	3
Gary Carter	251	27
Bill Dickey	247	5
Carlton Fisk	243	15
Gabby Hartnett	243	4
Ivan Rodriguez	233	30
Roy Campanella	232	6

There was no surprise in the number one man. It was Mike Piazza again, but there were many wild swings that left the BP in considerable disagreement with other systems. It was probably due to James's era adjustment that favors modern players. For instance, Ted Simmons, Gary Carter, Carlton Fisk, and Ivan Rodriguez do not appear on Zminda's Relativity Index or on the RG, RC, or BR formulas, and none of the four are in the top 11 of the FOR formula. Two of them, Rodriguez and Carter, finished 30th and 27th respectively.

Kevin Fullam listed the top-hitting catchers by seven different offensive categories, but he didn't combine the categories. One category he listed was OPS (on-base percentage plus slugging average). It is interesting to view the raw OPS data alongside the adjusted OPS (AOPS) from

Pete Palmer's latest tome, *The Baseball Encyclopedia*. AOPS is normalized for the league and is adjusted for the team park factor.

Catcher	OPS	AOPS
Mike Piazza	0.971	156
Mickey Cochrane	0.889	127
Gabby Hartnett	0.878	126
Roy Campanella	0.877	123
Yogi Berra	0.851	126
Carlton Fisk	0.848	116
Bill Dickey	0.842	128
Ernie Lombardi	0.834	126
Smoky Burgess	0.819	116
Joe Torre	0.817	129
Gene Tenace	0.816	137
Johnny Bench	0.815	127

AOPS is more accurate than OPS because it is adjusted for the era in which a catcher played, but it is still plagued by the use of a general park factor.

The best system for rating the offensive skills of individual catchers at the present time, other than the one presented in this book, is the adjusted batting runs (ABR) formula devised by Pete Palmer in his 2004 publication, *The Baseball Encyclopedia*. The formulas for determining ABR are:

$$BR = .33(BB + HBP) + .47H + .38D + .55T + .93HR - ABF(AB-H)$$

Where ABF = .33(BB + HBP) + .47H + .38D + .55T + .93HR, all divided by (AB − LGF × H). Note: All the statistics in the ABF formula are league statistics, as opposed to the statistics in the BR formula, which are individual statistics.

Then

$$ABR = BR - (Batters\ PF - 1) \times RPA \times PA/BPF$$

Where:

ABF = League batting factor. Value of an average batter = 0.
RPA = Number of runs per plate appearance, league
BPF = Batters park factor
LGF = League factor

ABR Ratings

Catcher	Games	ABR	ABR/154 G.	Rating	FOR
Mickey Cochrane	1482	250	26.0	3	3
Bill Dickey	1789	257	22.1	4	5
Gabby Hartnett	1990	242	18.7	6	4
Roy Campanella	1215	141	17.9	7	6
Yogi Berra	2120	244	17.7	8	10T
Johnny Bench	2158	270	19.3	5	10T
Mike Piazza	1461	429	45.2	1	1
Gene Tenace	1555	277	27.4	2	2
Ted Simmons	2456	218	13.7	11	13
Darrell Porter	1782	123	10.6	13	8
Ernie Lombardi	1853	198	16.5	9	9

The ABR formula gave reasonably good agreement to the FOR formula, particularly in the top three positions, but there were a couple of significant differences. The lack of an individualized park factor gave Berra and Dickey a big advantage in the ABR formula, while Darrell Porter was penalized for his unfavorable park factor. Hartnett and Campanella had higher ratings in the FOR formula than the ABR formula, while Bench, Lombardi, and Simmons had higher ratings in the ABR formula.

Jorge Posada, the New York Yankees' exceptional catcher, has had only six full seasons in the major leagues, so he was not included in this study. However, his statistics are so outstanding they will be presented in both the offensive and defensive sections, even though his point totals were not counted. His approximate offensive rating is shown below along with his approximate rating in individual categories.

OBPAR	XSLGAR	SBR	SHR	GIDPR	Total Points	Final Rating
.369 (4)	.304 (19)	1.6	2.5	1.4	28.5	9 Estimated

As is evident in the above presentation, Jorge Posada has some of the finest offensive statistics of any catcher in the study. In 2003, he batted .281 with 135 base hits in 481 at-bats. His hits included 24 doubles and 30 home runs, with 101 runs batted in. He has also coaxed 89 bases on balls per year out of opposing pitchers over his major league career. The 33-year old switch-hitter appears to be just reaching his peak at this relatively advanced age for a catcher, so he may have another six or seven years ahead of him in the Big Show, if his knees hold up. It will be interesting to see how Posada's numbers shape up when his career has been completed.

Two other catchers who were ineligible for this study will also be reviewed here because their careers are of interest to many people. Jimmie Foxx and Josh Gibson were two of the greatest hitters ever to strap on a chest protector. Foxx originally came up to the Philadelphia Athletics in 1925 as a catcher, but Mickey Cochrane was there ahead of him, so it was obvious one of them would have to move to another position. Unfortunately for the man known as "The Beast," he was versatile and had experience at both third base and first base, while Cochrane couldn't play anywhere else except catcher. Foxx therefore moved to first base, where he became one of the top two first basemen in baseball history, along with Lou Gehrig. In his major league career, Jimmie Foxx caught 108 games, including 63 games for the A's between 1925 and 1935 and 45 for the Boston Red Sox, 42 of them in 1940. Had he been a

Jimmie Foxx, a converted catcher, became one of the two best first baseman in the annals of baseball.

catcher during his entire career, he might well have beaten out Mike Piazza for the title of baseball's greatest-hitting catcher, as evidenced by the following statistics. However, in fairness to Piazza, Foxx might not have been able to duplicate his offensive statistics if he had been forced to crouch behind the plate 130 or 140 times a year. The wear and tear on his body and the typical injuries suffered by catchers, like Campanella, whose batting average fluctuated wildly from .207 to .325 depending on his physical condition, might have seriously affected his batting average as well as his home run totals.

OBPAR	XSLGAR	SBR	SHR	GIDPR	Total Points	Final Rating
.411 (1)	.488 (1)	0.5	1.1	1.1	4.7	(1)

Josh Gibson was arguably the greatest-hitting catcher in Negro League history. His .362 Negro League average, along with a .353 average in the Cuban Winter League, a .355 average in the Puerto Rican Winter League, and a .373 average in the Mexican League, would convert to .318 batting average in the major leagues, as discussed in my book, *Baseball's Other All-Stars*. His 48 home runs for every 550 at-bats in the Negro Leagues would give him an incredible 61 homers a year in the major leagues. According to the following statistics, he would be battling Jimmie Foxx and Mike Piazza for the position of baseball's greatest-hitting catcher.

OBPAR	XSLGAR	SBR	SHR	GIDPR	Total Points	Final Rating
.411 (1)	.463 (3)	1.0	1.7	1.2	7.9	(2)

9

THE NUMBER ONE DEFENSIVE
CATCHER OF ALL TIME

As noted in the previous chapter, some baseball historians claim that today's players are the best who have ever played the game. Bill James thought that was the case when he formulated his Win Shares system, because he included an era adjustment that was based on giving the highest point total to the most recent players, based on their birth date. Player point totals decline as the player's birth date recedes. The traditionalists believe the greatest players in baseball history were active from the turn of the twentieth century to the 1940s based on the fact that the most popular All-Time all-star teams usually include Walter Johnson as the pitcher, Lou Gehrig at first base, Rogers Hornsby at second, Honus Wagner at short, Ted Williams in left field, and Babe Ruth in right field. Center field usually belongs to either Joe DiMaggio or Willie Mays. The only so-called modern players to be selected to an all-time All-Star team are Mays, who played from 1951 to 1973, catcher Johnny Bench, who played from 1967 to 1983, and third baseman Mike Schmidt, who played from 1972 to 1989. A third group of historians find no evidence that either the modern-day players or the early players were superior. They believe the skills have remained essentially constant from one decade to the next. The only things that have changed are the quality of the equipment, the size of the ballparks, the liveliness of the balls, the size of the players, and the number of major league teams now operating. Bigger players, in general, hit more home runs than smaller players, which should be obvious to the most casual fan. But size alone doesn't create home run champions. The most successful sluggers combine decent size with excellent hand-eye coordination and quick wrists. The present home run king, Hank Aaron, weighed only 180 pounds. Willie Mays also checked in at 180, and Mickey Mantle topped the scales at 197. Mike Piazza has already given modern-day catchers a big boost by being crowned baseball's greatest offensive catcher, but is he also the game's greatest defensive catcher, or the game's greatest all-around catcher? Or is some other modern-day catcher the best with the mitt? And is some modern-day catcher the best all-around catcher in the annals of major league baseball? The next two chapters will attempt to answer those questions.

There are numerous statistical formulas in use today to measure the individual offensive skills of major league baseball players, but there are essentially no statistical systems in use today that are designed to measure the defensive skills of major league catchers, with the exception of Bill James's and Pete Palmer's systems, which were addressed earlier. The 2004 updated FR formula in Palmer's Linear Weights system, which is probably the most widely accepted statistical formula in use today for measuring the defensive skills of major league players, is outlined below.

$$FR = PFR/(PO - SO \text{ for team}) - LFR/(PO - SO \text{ for league}) \times \text{player innings}$$

Where:

PFR is the player fielding rate, which for catchers is described below.
$$PFR = .2 \times (PO - SO + 2(ASS - CS) - E + DP + PB/2)$$
Then, a SB/CS factor is added, which is $+CSF \times CS - .22 \times SB$, where CSF is a league factor to make the average catcher 0.
CSF = .22(SB-league – SB-team)/(CS-league – CS-team), which is the league average not counting player on the catcher's team, whom he does not have to face.
LFR is the league fielding rate, which has a similar formula.

The formula also includes an adjustment for pitching runs (PR) for the team. The problems with using this formula for evaluating the defensive skills of catchers, as viewed from this perspective, are the use of putouts minus strikeouts, the exclusion of a catcher's caught-stealing percentage, the inclusion of pitching runs, and the inclusion of terms like innings player, which is a value measurement, not a skill measurement.

The following table lists a team's putouts minus strikeouts for the last 85 years. As can be seen, POs – SOs have declined continually during this period, making it unsuitable for measuring a catcher's skills.

Catcher Putouts Per Team Per 154 Games

Year	Total POs per Team	SOs per team	POs – SOs
1920	624	454	170
1925	564	418	146
1930	636	496	140
1935	639	501	138
1940	697	566	131
1945	637	503	134
1950	711	598	113
1955	784	677	107
1960	887	801	86
1965	991	916	75
1970	960	886	74
1975	834	764	70
1980	744	686	58
1985	813	762	51
1990	850	810	40
1995	1003	971	32
2000	1025	994	31
2003	1009	976	33

Pete Palmer noted that FR does include longevity, but that dividing by the games played would eliminate that problem. He also said, "Catcher FR are quite inaccurate however." According to Pete, catcher FR is still a work-in-progress. Some of the more popular statistical programs, including FR, appear to use Johnny Bench as a benchmark for determining the accuracy of the formulas. If Bench is rated lower than the statistician thinks he should be rated, the equations are reviewed and, in some cases, modified in such a way that Bench's position is improved. Bill James once said that Bench "was a brilliant defensive catcher, winning ten straight Gold Gloves," and that feeling has carried over into the thinking processes of other baseball statisticians. *Total Baseball,* for instance, listed Bench as number 130 in its total player rating (TPR) in the eighth edition, but showed him in 46th place several years later.

Many people use a player's Gold Glove awards to describe his defensive skills, but that may not be a valid argument. The Gold Glove award was initiated by the Rawlings Sporting Goods Company in 1957 to recognize the best defensive players at their positions each year. It was the defensive counterpart of the Hillerich and Bradsby Silver Bat award, given to the league's best hitters each year. Two Gold Glove awards are presented for each position every year, one for the National League and one for the American League. The awards are voted on by major league coaches and managers. The judges may not vote for a player on their own team or for a player in the other league. It is interesting to note that Pete Palmer identified 60 players as the best defensive players in their league between 1957 and 1986, and only 28 of them won their respective Gold Glove awards. The awards appear to be, in some cases, popularity contests, or votes based on a player's reputation rather than on what he had accomplished in a particular season. Of 366 fielding average leaders between 1957 and 1987, only 118 of them, or 32 percent, won Gold Gloves. One criticism of the award is that a player's batting performance often plays a role in the selections. *USA Today* baseball editor Hal Bodley said, "A player who is outstanding on defense and respectable on offense has a much better chance of getting a Gold Glove than a counterpart whose forte is fielding alone." Wes Parker, a six-time Gold Glove winner, expressed his dissatisfaction with the voting procedure in *Total Baseball.* "Many, if not most, coaches and managers fail to take their voting responsibility seriously ... they are usually much more concerned with their team and the pennant race, and as a result, tend to zip through the ballots.... So they wind up voting for the most recognizable names.... Reputation has a lot to do with (the award) .... In 1966, Bill White won the award (for the seventh consecutive time) although even White admitted that I probably deserved it. It takes a couple of years for your reputation to catch up with you, but that can work to your advantage at the end of your career." Some critics claim that since a manager and his coaches cannot vote for a player on their own team, they often won't vote for a player on another team who is contending with their team's player. From a catching standpoint, Johnny Bench and Ivan Rodriguez have both won ten Gold Gloves, although it is generally agreed that several of those awards were on reputation only and not on skill. Gold Gloves, it seems, are of questionable value in measuring a player's defensive skills.

It is difficult to make a case for the modern catcher as the best ever based on the statistics that show them to trail their pre–1970 counterparts in almost all phases of the defensive game, from caught-stealing percentage to passed balls to wild pitches by their pitching staffs to assists. Conversely, the catchers from the dead-ball era cannot match the modern-day catchers in offensive firepower. But the men behind the mask in the '20s, '30s, '40s, '50s and '60s combined both offensive skills and defensive skills to create some of the best all-around catchers the game has ever seen. Fans can easily monitor the defensive skills of today's catchers by focusing on their pitch-to-pitch actions. In addition to their more obvious moves such as runners caught stealing, pop-ups caught, and errors committed, there are several important areas that define a great catcher. Notice if the catcher races to first base to back up the first baseman on ground balls to the infield. All the legendary catchers did, from Hartnett to Campanella to Berra. And Campanella frequently beat the runner to the base. Hartnett, more than once, made a putout at first base after backing up the first baseman. And when a pitch is thrown outside to a right-handed batter, notice if the catcher shifts his body in front of the ball, or if he nonchalantly backhands it. The great catchers shifted their body. In fact, it was one of the first lessons Gabby Hartnett's father drilled into the ten-year old boy when he was starting out. Catchers who backhand the ball are either lazy or they have poor catching technique. They also generally have a high number of passed balls and wild pitches allowed.

The biggest problem in rating catchers is the inability to measure their intangibles, such as field leadership, handling a pitching staff, calling a game, backing up bases, and positioning infielders. Bill James attempted to solve that problem by use of a "subjective element," where the statistician can add points to a player's totals for such "intangibles." But, as noted in chapter seven, that manipulation cannot be used equitably because there is no one living today who can realistically evaluate the intangibles of catchers who played as far back as 1925. That unfortunate situation means that some of the contenders in this study will fall victim to the study's shortcomings. In the search for baseball's greatest catcher, Bob Boone is one of those victims. Boone was an outstanding defensive catcher, but he suffered in the ratings because a significant part of his value was in the area of intangibles. As Bob McCullough noted, "Bob Boone was one of the game's consummate defensive catchers, a thinking man's player who improved every pitching staff he worked with." Boone handled his pitching staffs to perfection, he called a great game, and he was one of the most durable catchers ever to crouch behind the plate. His major league record of appearing in over 100 games in each of fifteen years is almost incomprehensible. Unfortunately, many of his greatest skills cannot be measured. It should also be noted that this study is a comparison of the top 50 catchers in baseball history. The player who is rated number 50 is not a failure. Over the course of the past 85 years of major league history, somewhere between 1000 and 2000 catchers have exhibited their skills in the Big Show with, according to Palmer, 794 who caught at least 25 games. The man who finishes number 50 in this study is considered to be the 50th best catcher ever to play the game — 50 out of 794. That's quite an honor.

Six different defensive factors were selected to measure the defensive skills of the individual catchers and to compare one catcher with another, in order to identify the greatest defensive catcher ever to play the game. These factors are:

Fielding average (FA)
Caught stealing percentage (CS%)
Passed balls (PB)
Wild pitches by the pitching staff (WP)
Range factor (RF)
Adjusted assists (total assists minus caught-stealing assists) (ASS1)

A catcher's fielding average (FA) was measured against his peers, and the differential (DFA) was compared to the DFA of players from other eras to produce an equitable rating. The same procedure was used for measuring a catcher's caught-stealing rating, his adjusted assists, and the wild pitches allowed by the pitching staff. Passed balls were measured and compared directly. The relative weights of the individual factors in this formula compare favorably with the relative weights used by Pete Palmer in his fielding runs formula. The formula for measuring the defensive skills of the player is:

$$TDP = DFAR + DCSR + .3PBR + .075DWPR + DRFR + 0.5DASSR$$

where:

TDP = Total defensive points
DFAR = Fielding average rating of the differential from the league average
DCSR = Caught-stealing rating of the differential from league average
PBR = Passed balls rating
DWPR = Wild pitch rating of the differential from league average
DRFR = Range factor rating of the differential from the league average
DASSAR = Adjusted assist rating of the differential from the league average. Adjusted assists are the total assists minus caught-stealing assists.

The final defensive rating (FDR) was then determined by the player's final total defensive points, with the player having the lowest point total rated number one, the player with the next lowest score being rated number two, and so on down to 50.

There have been many superb defensive catchers in the major leagues over the past century. The leaders in some of the more important defensive categories are listed below.

Defensive Leaders — Career

Charles Johnson	.994 fielding percentage (still active)
Buddy Rosar	DFA of +10 to league average (.992 vs .982)
Roy Campanella	58% caught stealing percentage
Roy Campanella	DCS of +18 to league average (58% vs 40%)

Charles Johnson	Fewest passed balls— 5
Al Lopez	Fewest passed balls – 5
Buddy Rosar	Fewest passed balls— 5
Ray Mueller	Fewest passed balls— 5
Sherman Lollar	Fewest passed balls – 5
Mike Piazza	7.29 range factor
Roy Campanella	DRF of +1.32 to league average (5.98 vs 4.66)
Muddy Ruel	61 (assists minus CS assists)
Javy Lopez	DASSA of +9 to league average (39 assists vs 30)

As can be seen from the above listing, all eras are represented from Muddy Ruel in 1917–34 to Johnson, Piazza, and Javy Lopez in the 1990s. Still, it is obvious to baseball historians that a catcher's life was much harder in the old days. Bob Carroll, in *Oldtyme Baseball News* Vol. 7, No. 3, in 1995, pointed out many of the difficulties encountered by those early-day catchers. There were frequent doubleheaders before the advent of night ball, and catchers almost never caught both games because of the heat, making it difficult to catch a high number of games during a season or in a career. "In Rick Ferrell's time, most games were played in the daytime. What must it have been like catching nine innings in St. Louis? With the sun out? On an August day? Wearing one of those old flannel uniforms? And all that heavy catcher's padding? With everything twice as heavy because of soaked-in sweat?" The bulky, rigid catcher's mitt presented another, more dangerous, problem to the catcher. It required that the catcher have his bare hand ready to cover the ball as soon as the ball hit the mitt so it wouldn't bounce out. A slight miscalculation in the timing of that technique could result in a painful injury, such as a broken finger. As Carroll said, "You could identify veteran catchers in the dark by shaking hands with them. Their right hands were misshapen. Their fingers were gnarled, their knuckles like walnuts from being broken and broken again."

The development of the hinged mitt and the advent of night ball made life much easier for the catcher. The hinged mitt was devised by Randy Hundley and improved upon by Johnny Bench. It permitted the catcher to put his bare hand behind his back "out of harm's way," as Carroll said. "Because it snaps shut like a Venus flytrap at the critical instant, the hinged glove allows the hand it protects to bear the whole burden of catching the ball…. A modern catcher does catch the ball like a first baseman. The ball slams into the part of the glove that shields the space between his thumb and his index finger. Catching that way — where the palm of the left hand doesn't take the impact of the pitch — helps catchers hit better. They used to talk about how a catcher's left hand was puffed up after a game. If he caught regularly, the puffing became permanent. That had to affect how he gripped a bat." Bench was quoted as saying that the hinged mitt allowed him to "snap up wide, bouncing pitches that regular-mitted catchers could only flap at. Moreover, the hinged mitt made catching pop fouls much more certain."

There is still an ongoing debate about the technical skills of the modern-day catcher. Harry Danning of the New York Giants once said that today's catchers are not as good as catchers were years ago because they don't work at it. They prefer to spend their time practicing hitting. Today, most catchers don't shift their bodies in front of pitches like they did years ago, and as Branch Rickey said, "You cannot stop a pitch in the dirt with just your glove." Campy shifted his body with the pitch if it was outside. Bench didn't. His one-handed style, which was flashy but not necessarily effective, may have infected thousands of young boys over the past 30 years and may have resulted in an increase in the number of wild pitches and passed balls in today's game.

Fielding Average (FA)

Bill James noted that catcher's fielding averages are of questionable value because most of the putouts are the result of strikeouts, which "virtually never result in catcher's errors." He suggested removing strikeout putouts from the formula, which would put the statistic on a level playing field. But James overlooked one key factor. Non-strikeout putouts have been on a continuous decline throughout the twentieth century, as shown above, the result of many factors, including the reduction in foul territory around home plate, fewer attempted steals, and fewer attempted bunts. James also said, "Catcher's assists have to be modified by consideration of a team's won-lost record. Many more stolen bases occur when the team is ahead than when they are behind." That may be true, but it might need to be accounted for differently. A catcher's assists fall into two categories: caught-stealing assists and other assists. Both those factors were measured separately in this study and were compared against their peers to once again provide a level playing field. However, since there are no perfect measurements for comparing a catcher's putouts, and since it is important to be able to evaluate a catcher's ability to field his position adequately, it was decided that fielding average would have to suffice. Admittedly, it contains some double-dipping with assists, and it includes the pitcher's strikeouts, but the result were compared against the league averages, which help to offset those deficiencies.

Caught Stealing (CS)

The ability of a catcher to throw out a runner attempting to steal is one of the most important weapons in his repertoire. As will be seen, a catcher with a strong throwing arm will keep runners glued to their bases, not running around the base paths. Base runners who are intimidated by a catcher attempt fewer stolen bases and take more conservative leads off their base in fear of being picked off. This, in turn, reduces their ability to advance to another base or to score a run on a base hit, a fly ball, or an infield grounder. Caught-stealing (CS) percentages for catchers make for an interesting study. Before reviewing the individual career caught-stealing statistics of the 50 catchers in this study, a general review of the history of stolen bases in the major leagues was conducted in order to confirm or refute the theories of some statisticians, noted earlier, that a catcher's caught-stealing percentage was due to the number of attempts against him. The argument asserts, for instance, that Johnny Bench's 43 percent CS rate is equivalent to, or better than, Roy Campanella's 58 percent CS rate because Bench had 97 attempts against him while Campanella faced only 54 challenges a year. The following chart shows the average major league caught-stealing statistics from 1920 to the present time.

| | National League | | | American League | | | Major League Avg. Att/Team/ | |
Year	Att.	CS	%CS	Att.	CS	%CS	154 games	%CS
1920	1831	862	47	1461	710	49	206	48
1925	1189	517	43	1302	586	45	156	44
1930	1021	423	41	128		41		
1935	809	329	41	101		41		
1940	811	333	41	102		41		
1945	826	373	45	103		45		
1951	746	293	39	724	311	43	92	41
1955	666	289	43	564	247	44	76	43
1960	814	313	38	656	234	36	92	37
1965	1174	429	37	1059	355	34	140	36
1970	1561	516	33	1445	562	39	125	36
1975	1734	558	32	2159	811	38	162	35
1980	2674	835	31	2230	775	35	189	33
1985	2352	716	30	2176	715	33	174	31
1990	2514	727	29	2286	783	34	185	31
1995	2273	671	30	1917	586	31	150	30
2000	2363	736	31	1884	587	31	142	31

If the decade of the '20s is considered to be a transitional period, then there is definitely a strong relationship between the number of stolen base attempts and a catcher's caught-stealing rate. Over the years, the number of attempted steals varied considerably from decade to decade as the strategy of the game changed. From a Ty Cobb running game in the teens and '20s, baseball evolved into a Babe Ruth slugging match during the '20s,

'30s, and '40s. The first indication that the situation might revert back to a running game came in 1947, when Jackie Robinson joined the Brooklyn Dodgers. The fiery second baseman terrorized opposing pitchers when he was on base, and he led the league in stolen bases with 29 and 37 in 1947 and 1949 respectively. At that time, however, there was no justification for him to steal bases in bunches since the Dodgers had one of the most awesome slugging teams in major league history. The 1953 team slammed 206 home runs and averaged 6.2 runs a game, with six different players crossing the plate more than 100 times. The running game became more popular in the 1950s when Luis Aparacio and the Go-Go Chicago White Sox drove opposing teams crazy. Little Luis led the league in stolen bases his first nine years in the American League and the Sox were always around the 100-steal mark as a team, with a high of 122 in 1960. In 1962, Maury Wills of the Los Angeles Dodgers swiped 104 sacks to break Ty Cobb's single-season stolen-base record of 96 steals set in 1915. The situation finally came to a head in 1979 when Rickey Henderson, the Oakland Hot Dog, arrived on the scene. The 5'10" speedster swiped 100 sacks in his sophomore season and two years later he set a modern major league record by stealing 130 bases in 172 attempts, a 76 percent success rate. He went on to lead the league in stolen bases twelve times, eclipsing Max Carey's major league record of ten stolen base titles and Ty Cobb's American League mark of seven titles. Henderson's 1406 career steals, 509 more than Cobb's previous record, may never be equaled. Other jackrabbits who popularized the stolen base during the '60s, '70s, and '80s included Lou Brock, an eight-time stolen base leader with 938 career steals, Tim Raines, who stole 70 or more bases six times, and Vince Coleman, who stole over 100 bases each of his first three years in the National League.

A graph of the stolen base attempts versus the catcher's caught-stealing success rate appears to be a linear relationship, and it hasn't changed in the past 85 years. The graph shows that an average major league catcher can throw out about 30 percent of runners attempting to steal against him if he faces 190 attempts a year, and 45 percent of runners attempting to steal if he faces only 70 attempts a year. That would tend to confirm the theories noted above. However, there is more to the story than that. There is considerable scatter in the data indicating that the skill of the catcher also plays a role in the relationship. A study of the individual catchers reveals that most of the 50 world-class catchers in this study have caught-stealing percentages that are better than the average caught-stealing percentages shown on the graph. There are usually fewer stolen base attempts against a strong-throwing catcher than against a weak-throwing catcher, although there are still considerable differences between catchers having the same number of attempts against them. For instance, Johnny Bench faced 97 challenges a year and compiled a 43 percent success rate. The average catcher during Bench's career, according to the above statistics, had a 41 percent success rate, giving Bench a two percent advantage. But Ivan Rodriguez, who also had 97 stolen base attempts against him, had a 49 percent success rate, a full six percent higher than Bench, and 13 percent higher than the average catcher during his career. Mike Piazza and Gary Carter both faced 170 stolen base challenges a year, but while Piazza stopped only 25 percent of them, Carter was successful 35 percent of the time. Bill Dickey and Gabby Hartnett were each challenged 93 times a year, with Hartnett out-gunning Dickey by a healthy 12 percent, 53 percent to 41 percent. Jim Sundberg and Carlton Fisk each had 136 attempts against them, with Sundberg winning the battle 41 percent to 34 percent. A catcher's reputation also has an effect on the number of attempts against him, as shown in the statistics for the first half of the 2004 season. Although the American League attempts totaled 64 per team for 73 games (136 annualized to a 154-game season), only 21 runners (55 annualized) challenged

Jim Sundberg compiled a .993 career fielding average. *Courtesy Texas Rangers.*

the arm of Pudge Rodriguez, with six of them being gunned down, a 29 percent success rate against a league average 32 percent. In the National League, stolen base attempts averaged 52 (109 annualized). There were 22 attempts to steal against Mike Piazza in 27 games (125 attempts annualized), with seven of them being caught, a 32 percent success rate, the same as the league average. It appears that a catcher's caught-stealing percentage is a combination of the number of attempts against him plus his skill at throwing out prospective thieves, at least at the present time. In the period between 1920 and 1940, base runners did not seem to be intimidated by a catcher's reputation. They attempted just as many stolen bases against the likes of Gabby Hartnett, Muddy

Ruel, and Ernie Lombardi as they did against weaker-throwing catchers. Roy Campanella was one of the first catchers to intimidate base runners. He faced 34 percent fewer runners attempting to steal than the league average. Johnny Bench faced 37 percent fewer runners, and Ivan Rodriguez faced 32 percent fewer runners. Yogi Berra faced only nine percent fewer runners, indicating that opposing base runners never quite appreciated his enormous talent. At the other end of the spectrum, Mike Piazza faced 24 percent *MORE* base runners attempting to steal than the average catcher of the period.

That there are more stolen base attempts today than there were 50 years ago is a fact. And that the caught-stealing percentage is down from 45 percent fifty years ago to 30 percent today is also a fact. The question is, in view of the evidence presented above, are there more attempts and lower caught-stealing percentages today because catching skills have deteriorated over the years, or because runners today are bigger and faster? Some baseball historians claim the reason for the decline is because teams are looking for big, strong, power hitters and are willing to sacrifice some defense to improve their offense. That new management philosophy may be part of the answer, but the argument that bigger, faster runners are stealing more bases doesn't seem valid based on available statistics. The leading base stealers today don't have any higher stolen base percentages than players from earlier decades. Ty Cobb was successful 83 percent of the time, Max Carey was successful 79 percent of the time, Willie Mays was successful 77 percent of the time, and Mickey Mantle was successful 80 percent of the time. Modern base stealers include Henderson at 81 percent successful, Wills at 74 percent, Aparacio at 79 percent, Ichiro Suzuki at 77 percent, Barry Bonds at 78 percent, and Juan Pierre at 75 percent. Some catchers, even today, throw out a high percentage of runners attempting to steal. As noted above, Pudge Rodriguez throws out in the neighborhood of 50 percent of all runners attempting to steal on him, putting him in the upper echelon of caught-stealing catchers all-time. The fact that there are more runners attempting to steal today is more than likely due to their 70 percent stolen base success rate. Baseball statisticians have determined that if a runner is successful stealing a base more than 67 percent of the time, it is worth the risk. And big league managers apparently believe what they read and are utilizing that strategy. That being the case, stolen base attempts will probably remain at a high level until catchers can reduce the stolen base success rate to less than 67 percent. Pudge Rodriguez is a good example of what is needed in the catching fraternity today. In a time when an average of 145–150 steals are attempted each year, he is facing only 96 attempts a year thanks to his 50 percent success rate.

As Roy Campanella once said, "A catcher has to assume that a base runner is going to steal on every pitch, and he must come up in a throwing position on every pitch in case the runner goes. That way he's never surprised." Maybe that philosophy is the reason Campanella tossed out 58 percent of all the runners who attempted to steal on him. Another argument defending the poor caught-stealing rate of today's catchers is that they are victims of their pitcher's inability to hold runners on base. That may be a minor consideration, but pitching staffs are always in a state of flux, with men coming and going. Over the course of 162 games a year for 10 to 20 years, it is not reasonable to assume that one catcher is going to be the victim of poor pitching habits year after year while other catchers always enjoy the benefits of 10 or 12 talented pitchers. Ivan Rodriguez's caught-stealing percentage has ranged from a low of 33 percent in 2002 to a high of 60 percent in 2001, due to any number of reasons such as injuries, a young pitching staff, or a wild pitching staff. Over the years, these things tend to equal out.

Roy Campanella was, by far, the most dominant caught-stealing catcher in the annals of professional baseball. He gunned down an average of 58 percent of all the runners who had the audacity to challenge his arm. No one else has come close to matching his success rate. Campanella had the perfect blend of arm strength, quick release, and accuracy. Gabby Hartnett, the number two man, who has been credited with owning baseball's strongest throwing arm, but did not have Campy's quick release or accuracy, boasted a 53 percent average. Other major league catchers who equaled or exceeded a 50 percent caught-stealing rate include Wes Westrum (51 percent), Hank Gowdy (51 percent), Ken O'Dea (50 percent), and Ray Mueller (50 percent). Yogi Berra enjoyed a 47 percent success rate, while Johnny Bench checked in at 43 percent. In his best year, Bench tossed out 57 percent of all men attempting to steal on him. That's an imposing number, but it pales in comparison to Roy Campanella's high mark of 68 percent.

Catchers' caught-stealing percentages cannot be compared directly from era to era due to the periodic changes in baseball strategy that affect the number of bases that runners attempt to steal each year, as well as changes in the design of catcher's mitts. There are differing opinions as to whether the hinged mitt is better or worse than the old rigid, overstuffed mitt for throwing out base runners. Harry Danning was quoted as saying, "We used what we called the 'snap throw.' You'd come up and throw from behind your ear. This was how all the old catchers used to throw. With the gloves that we had, you could bounce the ball into your hand. Today they can't. It gets in there and many times they can't get hold of it, it gets in there so deep." Johnny Bench had a different opinion. According to Carroll, Bench said the hinged mitt allowed him to be in a better position to throw after receiving a pitch, thus cutting the time it took to get the ball to second. It also reduced his transfer time from glove to hand.

As noted above, the number of attempts has an effect on a catcher's CS%, with more attempts resulting in a lower average CS%. However, it was also noted that world-class catchers almost always exceeded the average CS%. In order to give all catchers a level playing field, this study compared a catcher's caught-stealing percentage to the league's average percentage, and that differential was then compared to the differentials of catchers from other eras to determine the top caught-stealing catcher. To no-one's surprise, Roy Campanella emerged as the number one man in caught-stealing differential also. His 58 percent CS rate exceeded the league average by a whopping 18 percent. To many people's surprise however, he was closely shadowed by Ivan "Pudge" Rodriguez, whose 49 percent CS rate was 17 percent ahead of the league average. Gabby Hartnett was third at +12, followed by Charles Johnson and Wes Westrum at +10, Johnny Bench at +8, Thurman Munson at +7, and Jim Sundberg, Ken O'Dea, Ray Mueller, and Del Crandall at +6. One of the hazards of the catching position is reflected in the career of Munson. He had a rifle arm when he first joined the Yankees, throwing out 52 percent of all runners who tried to steal on him during his first five years in the league, including a sensational 61 percent success rate in 1971. However, shoulder problems reduced his effectiveness later in his career, limiting his caught-stealing percentage to just 33 percent between 1974 and 1979. Roy Campanella and Johnny Bench also suffered major injuries during their careers that sapped their throwing effectiveness. Campanella, who enjoyed a 63 percent caught-stealing success rate during his first six years in the National League, suffered nerve damage in his throwing hand that reduced his percentage to just 48 percent during his last four years. Bench, who was hampered by a variety of injuries saw his caught-stealing percentage fall to just 37 percent during his last five years of full-time catching. And the wear and tear of catching over 100 games a year for ten years may be catching up with 32-year-old Pudge Rodriguez. He has seen his caught-stealing percentage drop from the 50 percent range during his first eleven years in the major leagues to under 35 percent in the past three years.

Passed Balls (PB)

Harry Danning's statement that "A passed ball catcher is not a catcher" was partially correct. But there are exceptions to every rule. It is true that most passed ball catchers are poor defensive catchers, but occasionally a strong defensive catcher will have one or more weak spots. One catcher might be outstanding at throwing out prospective base stealers, but be weak on catching balls in the dirt. Another catcher might be strong at preventing passed balls but weak on catching foul pop-ups. No two catchers, like no two pitchers, are alike. They each have their own unique strengths and weaknesses. There has never been a perfect catcher.

In general, the catchers with the highest number of passed balls have lower defensive ratings than their competitors. For instance, Gus Triandos, recognized as a strong offensive backstop, averaged 21 passed balls for every 154 games, compared to a league average of 14. However as Palmer pointed out, he had to catch knuckleball artist Hoyt Wilhelm, which contributed to his high total. Joe Ferguson, another catcher preferred for his bat, allowed 17 passed balls, while Ted Simmons and Tom Haller permitted 16 passed balls each. But Lance Parrish was an exception to the rule. The big 6'3" backstop of the Detroit Tigers, a recognized defensive specialist, also allowed 16 passed balls against a league average of 13. At the other end of the spectrum, the leaders in preventing passed balls were almost all recognized as strong defensive catchers. The top five in preventing passed balls were Buddy Rosar, Ray Mueller, Sherm Lollar, Charles Johnson, and Chris Hoiles.

Lance Parrish hit 324 home runs and fielded .991 during his 19-year major league career. *Courtesy Jay Sanford.*

Wild Pitches (WP)

There are more wild pitches thrown today than there were 60 to 80 years ago. That's a fact. The Philadelphia A's pitching staff of Mickey Cochrane's time uncorked an average of 24 wild pitches per year. Bill Dickey's Yankees had 25, Gabby Hartnett's Cubs had 23, Yogi Berra's Yankees had 23, and Roy Campanella's Dodgers had 29. Johnny Bench's Reds of the 1970s were guilty of 43 wild pitches, while Gary Carter's

Expos and Mets had 37 and Carlton Fisk's Red Sox and White Sox had just 23. Mike Piazza's Dodgers and Mets have uncorked 40 wild pitches, while Ivan Rodriguez's Rangers have been guilty of 55 and Charles Johnson's teams have compiled a total of 46 wild pitches per year. Some of the possible reasons for the increases are listed below.

1. Talented catchers can reduce the number of wild pitches thrown by their pitching staffs by their quick reflexes, agility, and speed. A study of a catcher's passed balls, plus his pitching staff's wild pitches, over the past 85 years indicates that low passed ball catchers also direct pitching staffs that have low wild pitch percentages, while high passed ball catchers guide pitching staffs that have a higher incidence of wild pitches. The correlation between the two is not extremely strong. It is an indication only, but it does deserve further study.

2. Expansion has diluted the pitching staffs, so there are more wild-throwing pitchers in the major leagues today that, years ago, would still be in AAA ball learning the fundamentals of their craft.

3. There are more pitches thrown in a game now — about 140 or more pitches a game compared to about 120 pitches 80 years ago. Actually Larry Jansen, when he was the pitching coach for the San Francisco Giants in the 1960s, logged the pitches for each game. His count was 123 pitches a game.

Based on the information that has been uncovered during this study regarding the overall skills of today's catchers, it can be assumed that the average catcher today is just as talented as the average catcher of 50 to 80 years ago. That being the case, it can also be assumed that one of the major reasons for the higher wild pitch rate today is because of the higher number of pitches thrown in a game. That would be a reflection of the skills of today's pitchers rather than their catchers. In order to put all the catchers on the same base point, the same procedure that was followed in comparing CS% was followed in comparing wild pitches allowed. A catcher is obviously not the primary cause of wild pitches. That fault lies with the pitcher. But like passed balls, a talented catcher can minimize the number of wild pitches thrown by his pitching staff by his quick reflexes, agility, and speed. The number of wild pitches thrown by a catcher's pitching staff was compared to the average number of wild pitches thrown by a league team. That difference was then compared to catchers from other eras. The best catcher at preventing wild pitches by his pitching staff was Carlton Fisk of the Boston Red Sox and Chicago White Sox, whose speed and agility held his teams' wild pitch count to an average of 23 a year, 16 WPs below the league average. Elston Howard was at –14, followed by Javy

Lopez at –11, Mike Piazza at –9, Ray Mueller, Yogi Berra, and Del Crandall at –7, and Sherm Lollar at –6.

Range Factor (RF)

Great catchers usually have exceptional reflexes and agility. Roy Campanella was nicknamed "The Cat" by the sports journalists in New York because of his quickness around home plate, pouncing on bunts, running down foul pop-ups, and racing a batter to first base on a ground ball. Other receivers who were noted for their outstanding speed and reflexes include Mickey Cochrane, Yogi Berra, and Gary Carter. Gabby Hartnett, who slowed down in his later years, was a tall, slim speedster when he was younger. And Tim McCarver is still the only catcher to lead his league in triples, a feat he accomplished in 1966. A catcher's reflexes and agility play an important part in his overall contributions to his team. After much soul-searching as to the best way to measure a catcher's reflexes, it was decided to rely on the range factor (RF), a measure of the number of putouts and assists a catcher makes during a game. It was not the perfect solution to the problem because of the concerns expressed about total putouts and the double-dipping situation with assists, but it seemed to be the best measurement available. The range factor, like fielding average and caught-stealing, could not be compared directly with range factors from other eras, because catcher's range factors have been declining over the years due to the changes in the game noted previously, an increase in strikeouts, fewer bunts attempted, and so on. But when compared to the league average, it provided a reasonable evaluation of a catcher's skills against those of his peers. That differential was then compared to the differentials of catchers from other eras in order to arrive at a ranking.

Roy Campanella emerged from the pack to claim first place in the range factor comparison. His 5.98 RF was a significant 1.32 points higher than the National League average during his career. John Roseboro captured second place with a strong +1.08 differential. The remainder of the top ten, in order, were Bill Freehan,

Tony Pena was one of the greatest defensive catchers in the game. *Courtesy Jay Sanford.*

the quiet leader of the Detroit Tigers at +1.03, Mike Scioscia at +0.93, Yogi Berra at +0.88, Mickey Cochrane at +0.87, Bill Dickey at +0.86, Gary Carter at +0.84, Gabby Hartnett at +0.74, and Tony Pena and Lance Parrish at +0.70. The remainder of the rankings can be found in the appendix.

Adjusted Assists (ASSA)

Adjusted assists (ASSA) are the difference between a catcher's total assists and his caught-stealing assists. They, like the caught-stealing assists, are one of a catcher's primary weapons in keeping the opposing team under control. Most non-caught-stealing assists, or adjusted assists, are the result of dropped third strikes, attempted bunts, topped balls, and pickoffs. A catcher's adjusted assists were compared to the league average, as was done with caught-stealing, fielding average, and wild pitches. This seemed to be the best method of comparing catchers because adjusted assists have declined over the years as a result of many factors, including bigger and better gloves that have reduced the number of dropped third strikes, fewer pickoffs attempted, and an increase in the number of pitcher strikeouts, which affect the number of balls actually put in play by the batter. In fact, adjusted assists have been in a free-fall since the mid 1920s, as shown in the following table.

Catcher Assists by Team Per 154 Games

Year	Total Assists	Caught-Stealing Assists	Adjusted Assists
1920	179	98	81
1925	131	69	62
1930	93	49	44
1935	92	41	51
1940	97	46	51
1945	92	42	50
1950	76	33	43
1955	75	34	41
1960	77	34	43
1965	81	37	44
1970	75	43	32
1975	86	54	32
1980	79	55	24
1985	71	49	22
1990	76	51	25
1995	79	48	31
2000	73	42	31
2003	71	36	35

Fifty years ago, there were approximately 3.5 strikeouts a game. Today there are almost seven strikeouts a game, meaning there are three to four fewer balls put into play by the batter, resulting in fewer opportunities by the catcher to record an assist. There are also fewer sacrifice bunts attempted and fewer bunts attempted for base hits, in this age of the long ball. A study of all World Series games played since 1920 produced some interesting results. Overall, 53 percent of all assists resulted from runners caught stealing, although the number of actual outs recorded due to runners being caught stealing, and the caught-stealing percentage, has declined over the years. An additional 11 percent of all assists were attributed to dropped third strikes, 11 percent from double plays (usually the strike-em-out, throw-em-out variety), 11 percent from sacrifices, and 10 percent from topped balls.

Adjusted assists (ASSA) totaled approximately 81 assists per team per year in 1920. Then they quickly dropped to 62 assists in 1925, perhaps because the long-ball syndrome reduced the number of sacrifice hits and caused base runners to be more cautious, reducing the number of pickoffs. They leveled out in the low 50s from 1935 to 1950, when they fell once again, to the low 40s. Adjusted assists then remained relatively stable until 1970 when they began another decline, probably caused, to some extent, by the American League's adoption of the designated hitter, which reduced sacrifice bunts in the league drastically from 68 sacrifices per team in 1970 to 36 sacrifices per team in 2001, as shown in the following table.

Sacrifice Hits and Sacrifice Flies

	National League			American League		
Year	Total Sacs	Sac Hits	Sac Flies	Total Sacs	Sac Hits	Sac Flies
1925	135	85	50	185	117	68
1935	95	60	35	100	63	37
1945	108	68	40	105	66	39
1955	114	71	43	125	79	46
1965	103	68	35	112	74	38
1975	131	87	44	108	63	45
1980	124	78	46	128	72	56
1985	112	72	40	90	44	46
1996	111	67	44	90	39	51
2001	105	60	45	83	36	47

Sacrifice bunts in the National League have been relatively stable since 1930, ranging from 60 per team to 72 per team, with a "blip" of 87 in 1975. Adjusted assists seemed to reach a low point of about 22 assists in the mid '80s, but are now on the rise again, reaching 35 adjusted assists per team per year in 2003.

Curiously, only 10 of the 50 catchers in this study had positive adjusted assist differentials (DASSA). Five were zero, and 35 were negative. Also, surprisingly, the periods from 1920 to 1940 and from 1980 to 2004 were more evenly distributed between positive and negative results, while the two periods from 1940 to 1960 and 1960 to 1980 were strongly negative. The distribution of players and their results is shown below.

ASSA Results

Period	Positive	Zero	Negative	Number of Catchers
1920–40	3	1	7	11
1940–60	2	0	10	12
1960–80	1	2	10	13
1980–04	4	2	8	14

It is difficult to explain the above results. The first thing that is obvious is that the catchers in the 1920–40 period and the players in the 1980–04 period had adjusted assists close to the league average, while the catchers in the other two periods fell below the league average. One explanation for the negative results between 1940 and 1980 is that the great catchers of those periods intimidated batters and base runners to the extent that batters attempted fewer sacrifice bunts and base runners stayed close to their bases, reducing the number of runners who were picked off. That is pure conjecture, of course. The real answer may be entirely different. The catchers who produced positive adjusted assists numbers were:

Javy Lopez	+4	Lance Parrish	+6
Birdie Tebbetts	+7	Bob O'Farrell	+2
Gabby Hartnett	+2	Tony Pena	+1
Thurman Munson	+9	Jim Sundberg	+1
Rick Ferrell	+3	Ray Mueller	+1

Total Defensive Points (TDP)

The total defensive points (TDP) for measuring a catchers defensive skills, as discussed in chapter seven, awarded the best performance for DFAR, DCSR, DFAR, and DASSAR, one point for each category. The second best received two points, etc. Passed balls were rated from best to worst, from one to 50, using a .3 multiplication factor, and wild pitches (DWPR) from one to 50 using a .075 multiplication factor. The equation is:

$$TDP = DFAR + DCSR + .3PB + .075DWPR + DRFR + DASSAR$$

Where:

TDP = Total defensive points
DFAR = Fielding average rating of the differential from the league average
DCSR = Caught-stealing rating from the differential from the league average
PB = Passed balls
DWPR = Wild pitch rating from the differential from the league average
DRFR = Range Factor rating from the differential from the league average
DASSAR = Adjusted assists rating from the differential from the league average

As an example, if a player was rated number one in all the categories, his final point total might be 1 + 1 + .3 + .1 + 1 + 1 = 4.4. And if a player finished last in all the categories, his point total might be 50 + 50 + 15 + 4 + 50 + 50 = 219.

Final Defensive Rating (FDR)

The final defensive rating was determined by the player's total defensive points, with the player having the lowest point total recognized as the best defensive catcher (number one), the player with the next lowest total number two, down to 50. The top ten places for defensive catcher follow.

Catcher	DFAR	DCSR	.3PBR	.075DWPR	DRFR	DASSAR	Total Points	FDR
G. Hartnett	5	3	9.6	2.0	9	3.0	31.6	1
R. Campanella	15	1	3.3	2.0	1	15.0	37.3	2
Jim Sundberg	2	8	9.6	3.1	15	4.0	41.7	3
Gary Carter	9	15	1.8	1.0	8	8.0	42.8	4
Lance Parrish	9	12	14.1	3.1	10	2.0	50.2	5
Tony Pena	15	18	4.8	2.5	11	4.0	55.3	6
Yogi Berra	23	12	3.3	2.0	1	15.0	56.3	7
H. Danning	9	23	1.8	3.4	18	6.0	61.2	8
Bill Dickey	5	29	3.3	2.5	7	14	60.8	9
Ray Mueller	2	8	0.3	0.6	48	1.0	62.9	10

Gabby Hartnett deservedly won the title of baseball's greatest defensive catcher. He had essentially no weaknesses. He finished fourth in fielding average, third in caught-stealing percentage, ninth in range factor, and third in adjusted assists. Roy Campanella finished number one in both caught-stealing percentage and range factor, but came in 15th in fielding average even though his .988 FA was four points better than the league average. Jim Sundberg was outstanding in fielding average, caught-stealing percentage, and adjusted assists, but his 15th place finish in range factor cost him the top spot. Gary Carter, the loquacious backstop for Montreal and New York, was outstanding in all categories except caught-stealing, where his 15th-place finish scuttled his hopes for the title. His 35 percent CS rate was four points above the league average, but still left him in the middle of the pack. Lance Parrish came in fifth in the defensive catcher race, thanks to a third-place finish in adjusted assists, a ninth-place finish in FA, and a 10th-place finish in RF. Tony Pena was particularly strong in RF, where he came in 11th, and ASSA, where he came in 11th, to nail down sixth place. Harry "The Horse" Danning, a New York Giants fixture in the late '30s, had a .985 fielding average, which was five points above the league average, good enough for an ninth-place finish. He came in 15th in ASSA and 18th in RF. Bill Dickey finished fifth in FA but was hurt by a 29th-place finish in CS. Del Crandall finished eighth in caught-stealing and had strong showings in PB and WP. Ray Mueller was the most unfortunate contender. He excelled in most categories, finishing second in FA, eighth in CS, and 11th in ASSA, while showing well in both passed balls and wild pitches, but he finished a disastrous 48th in range factor, dropping him all the way from first place to 10th.

A summary of the other finishers in the defensive competition follows, in order of their ranking, from #11 to #50.

11. Del Crandall was outstanding in CS where he finished 8th. He also excelled in PB and ASSA.

12. Muddy Ruel was a small 5'9", 150-pound receiver, but he was an exceptional fielder, and was above average in range factor and

Gabby Hartnett discusses a pitch call with the umpire. *Courtesy Roy Hartnett.*

adjusted assists. His 113 total assists for every 154 games played, is the best of all the catchers in the study.

13. John Roseboro, another of the great Los Angeles catchers, had catlike agility that gave him a second place finish in range factor.

14. Mike Scioscia was a hard-nosed catcher for the Dodgers who was renowned as the toughest plate-blocking backstop in the major leagues.

15. Elston Howard, the first black player to play for the New York Yankees, was one of their finest receivers. He had a well-rounded game that helped the Yankees capture nine American League pennants and four world championships in fourteen years.

16T. Buddy Rosar had the best fielding average differential of all the catchers in the study, a sensational +10. His .992 career fielding average is tied for fifth best, all-time. He also finished high in the caught-stealing category, but lost valuable points on range factor.

John Roseboro, a defensive stalwart, was also a dangerous clutch hitter who paced the Dodgers to three world championships. *Courtesy Jay Sanford.*

16T. Charles Johnson is one of the top defensive catchers still active, along with Pudge Rodriguez.

18. Ivan "Pudge" Rodriguez, who is still active, is the possessor of the most powerful throwing arm in the past fifty years, averaging almost 50 percent success shooting down prospective base stealers. His only weak area is in his number of errors, and that is probably the result of his aggressiveness in trying to pick runners off base.

19. Johnny Bench was outstanding at cutting down would-be base stealers, finishing sixth, but was average in fielding average and came in 35th in range factor.

20. Ken O'Dea was another receiver who had a cannon for a throwing arm. He finished eighth in caught-stealing percentage.

21. Bill Freehan finished fifth in fielding percentage and third in range factor. His weak throwing arm, however, gave him low ratings in caught-stealing percentage and adjusted assists.

22. Earl Battey, who guided the Minnesota Twins to an American League pennant in 1965, was highly rated in all categories except fielding

average, where his .990 percentage, one point higher than the league average, left him mired in 32nd place.

23. Mickey Cochrane was one of the American League's exceptional catchers, but, like Freehan, his weak throwing arm cost him dearly in the caught-stealing and adjusted assists categories.

24. Chris Hoiles was sensational in all phases of defensive play, except for his caught-stealing record. His 28 percent CS rate left him in 45th place in that category.

25. Rick Ferrell was one of the American League's most respected catchers during the 1930s and was one of a handful of catchers who racked up more than 1000 assists during their careers.

26. Sherman Lollar was outstanding in many facets of the game, including fielding average, where his .992 career average is the fifth best, all-time. He was below average in caught-stealing percentage and range factor.

27. Therman Munson had a deadly throwing arm early in his career, before shoulder injuries reduced his effectiveness. The surly catcher was also the top-rated catcher for adjusted assists.

28. Javy Lopez, one of the best active catchers, is outstanding both offensively and defensively.

29. Wes Westrum was one of the few catchers who had a 50 percent or better career caught-stealing percentage. His 51 percent mark was a full 10 points higher than the league average.

30. Carlton Fisk was outstanding at directing a pitching staff. His pitchers had the lowest wild pitch count in the study. Fisk also had exceptionally quick reflexes around the plate.

31. Bob O'Farrell, Gabby Hartnett's predecessor, was another receiver who excelled in all phases of the defensive game. His 113 total assists for every 154 games played is the second best in the study.

32. Birdie Tebbetts had a solid all-around game and had the second best adjusted assist record in the study.

33. Manny Sanguillen's arm served him well in the ratings. He finished 23rd in CS and sixth in other assists.

34. Joe Torre suffered from poor ratings in passed balls, wild pitches, and range factor.

35. Mike Piazza, baseball's greatest-hitting catcher, was penalized in the defensive competition by his poor throwing on attempted steals. His 25 percent success rate is five percent below the league average and is the lowest CS% of any catcher in the study. He excelled in range factor, minimizing wild pitches, and preventing passed balls.

36. Darren Daulton's poor CS record combined with a 32nd-place finish in FA doomed him to 36th place.

37. Tom Haller's poor caught-stealing record, four percentage points below the 38 percent league average, was the major reason for his 37th-place finish.

38. Gus Triandos had a fine 41 percent CS record, but his FA was two points below the league average.

39. Bubbles Hargrave finished a strong second in FA to offset his low rating in CS.

40. Walker Cooper, an eight-time All-Star, was hampered by a mediocre fielding average of .977.

41. Joe Ferguson was noted more for his bat than his glove.

42. Ed Bailey was more of an offensive threat than a defensive stalwart, with 20 home runs for every 550 at-bats.

43. Gene Tenace, one of the game's greatest offensive catchers, was effective on defense as well. He was particularly strong in fielding average and adjusted assists.

44. Ted Simmons had an outstanding all-around defensive game. He was just beaten by exceptional competition.

45. Ernie Lombardi, another backstop noted for his powerful bat, possessed a solid, but not outstanding, all-around defensive game.

46. Jason Kendall was another of the fine offensive catchers, who carried a .304 batting average into the 2004 season.

47. Mickey Tettleton was among the leaders in career fielding average at .991, two points above the league average.

48. Darrell Porter was rated the eighth best offensive catcher in baseball history. His defense, although outmatched by the other catchers in this study, still left 90 percent of all major league catchers looking up to him.

49. Babe Phelps carried a big bat but an erratic glove. He edged out Smoky Burgess for 49th place with a 13th-place finish in RF.

50. Smoky Burgess was primarily an offensive catcher, but he could hold his own behind the plate, compiling a fine .988 career fielding average.

The top defensive catchers of all-time, by era and by league, are listed below.

Defensive Leaders By Era and By League

National League	American League
1920–1940	**1920–1940**
1. Gabby Hartnett*	1. Bill Dickey
2. Harry Danning	2. Muddy Ruel
3. Ken O'Dea	3. Mickey Cochrane
4. Bob O'Farrell	4. Rick Ferrell
5. Ernie Lombardi	

1940–1960

1. Roy Campanella	1. Yogi Berra
2. Ray Mueller	2. Buddy Rosar
3. Del Crandall	3. Sherman Lollar
4. Wes Westrum	4. Birdie Tebbetts
5. Ed Bailey	5. Gus Triandos

1960–1980

1. John Roseboro	1. Elston Howard
2. Johnny Bench	2. Bill Freehan
3. Manny Sanguillen	3. Earl Battey
4. Joe Torre	4. Gene Tenace
5. Tom Haller	5. Darrell Porter

1980–2000

1. Gary Carter	1. Jim Sundberg
2. Tony Pena	2. Lance Parrish
3. Mike Scioscia	3. Ivan Rodriguez
4. Charles Johnson	4. Chris Hoiles
5. Javy Lopez	5. Carlton Fisk

*Gabby Hartnett was the greatest defensive catcher in baseball history.

Before leaving the "Best Defensive Catcher" category, the final defensive ratings (FDR) were compared to the fielding runs formula, which was described above. Note that the corresponding FDR1 is a relative number corresponding only to the players listed. It does not represent the player's final defensive rating (FDR). The dates 1989 and 1997 correspond to editions of *Total Baseball* and the 2004 date represents the latest edition of *The Baseball Encyclopedia*.

Fielding Runs (FR) Per 154 Games

Catcher	Games Caught	FR 1989	Rtg.	FR 1997	Rtg.	FR 2004	Rtg.	FDR1
Ivan Rodriguez	1564	—	—	6.72	3	16.10	1	13
Tony Pena	1950	12.72	2	9.00	1	14.06	2	6
Johnny Bench	1742	-0.97	12	-7.07	16	7.07	7	14
Gary Carter	2056	13.27	1	4.04	8	10.49	3	4
Lance Parrish	1818	7.08	6	1.27	14	9.98	4	5
Jim Sundberg	1927	10.55	4	7.67	2	9.59	5	3
Gabby Hartnett	1793	5.93	8	6.36	4	9.10	6	1
Yogi Berra	1699	4.89	11	5.04	6	6.54	9	7
Ray Mueller	917	5.21	9	3.53	9	6.72	8	10
Del Crandall	1479	9.79	5	6.35	5	6.46	10	11
Roy Campanella	1183	6.77	7	4.30	7	5.99	11	2
Bill Dickey	1708	-2.07	13	2.16	10	5.14	12	9
Mickey Cochrane	1482	-3.82	14	1.49	13	3.93	14	15
Mike Piazza	1380	—	—	-6.47	15	-8.48	16	16
Harry Danning	801	12.11	3	1.54	12	4.81	13	8
Rick Ferrell	1806	4.95	10	1.71	11	2.05	15	12

The fielding runs formula and the final defensive rating formula were in fair agreement with the exception of Rodriguez, Bench, Hartnett, Campanella, and Danning. Ivan Rodriguez and Johnny Bench finished much higher in the FR formula than they did in the FDR1 formula. Rodriguez actually finished in 13th place out of the 16 catchers listed above in FDR1. Johnny Bench was rated 14th out of 16 catchers in FDR1, which was in good agreement with the 1989 and 1997 FRs. But his rating jumped up from 16th place in 1997 to seventh place in 2004, after the FRs formula was modified. Conversely, Roy Campanella, Gabby Hartnett, and Harry Danning suffered in the new fielding runs computation.

Jorge Posada, who is not included in the official study, had the following estimated defensive ratings.

DFA	DCS	.3PB	.075WP	DRF	DASSA	Total Points	Final Rating
33	38	12.9	1.7	19	2.5	107.1	33 est.

Jimmie Foxx's defensive statistics are not yet available, except for his fielding average and his passed balls. His .990 FA was a full nine points above the league average, which would have given him a second-place finish in that category in the study. His 13 passed balls for every 154 games would have placed him in 39th place.

Josh Gibson's defensive statistics are not available, and probably never will be, due to the poor record keeping in the Negro leagues.

10

BASEBALL'S GREATEST
ALL-AROUND CATCHER

Chapter 8 identified Mike Piazza as the best offensive catcher of all time. Chapter 9 saw Gabby Hartnett emerge from the pack to claim the title of baseball's best defensive catcher. The big question now is, which catcher will be crowned as the greatest all-around catcher in baseball history. Will it be Piazza? Or Hartnett? Or will someone else capture the coveted title? To answer that question, it is important to be able to correctly measure a catcher's offensive and defensive contributions to arrive at the one man who displayed the perfect blend of offense and defense. Perhaps the most important factor in arriving at the final rating is the relative weight to be assigned to a catcher's offense as opposed to his defense. The statistical formulas of both Bill James and Pete Palmer were reviewed to determine the relative weights they allocated to each player's offense and to his defense. It was a surprise to discover that James's Win Shares formula is not a constant for all catchers. James said there are differences in offensive contributions and defensive contributions from catcher to catcher. For instance, according to him, 37 percent of Gary Carter's Win Shares is attributable to his defense, while only 28 percent of Yogi Berra's Win Shares is attributable to his defense. Johnny Bench's Win Shares was also 28 percent defense. Bill Bergen, a notoriously weak-hitting catcher from the early part of the century, had a Win Shares rating that was 100 percent attributable to his defense. On the average, the relative weight of a player's offense is about 2.33 times his defense in the Win Shares scheme of things. Pete Palmer's total player rating (TPR) appears to give a player's offensive contribution about four times the weight of his defensive contribution.

Most baseball people agree that, in general, offense is more important than defense, but it varies considerably from position to position. A pitcher, for instance, is primarily rated on his pitching. Neither his offense nor his fielding carry much weight. A shortstop, on the other hand, is the anchor on a team's defensive structure, and his defense may be just as important as his offense. In analyzing the importance that defense plays in a game, a player's position needs to be taken into account. Certainly a shortstop's defensive contribution is much more critical to the outcome of a game than is a left fielder's defensive contribution, for instance. Many people believe that a shortstop's defensive contribution to the outcome of a game is just as important as his offensive contribution, so in evaluating the best all-around shortstop, his offense and his defense should be rated equally. A third baseman's offense might be twice as important as his defense, although his defensive skills are still very critical to his team's success. A second baseman and a center fielder might have a 3–1 ratio of offense to defense. At the other end of the spectrum, a left fielder or a right fielder, or even a first baseman, are in the lineup for their offense, not their defense. In those cases, offense may be as much as four or five times as important as defense. As far as the catcher is concerned, his defensive skills are extremely important, perhaps as important as a shortstop's defensive skills, but, if not, they are certainly as important as a third baseman's defensive skills. More often than not, over the years, outstanding defensive catchers have been preferred over good offensive catchers because their value in calling a game and handling a pitching staff have been deemed more important than the number of home runs they might hit. Still, overall, a catcher's offense has to be given weight over his defense. For this study, a catcher's offense was weighted at two to one over his defense, the same ratio as for a third baseman. However, for comparison purposes, the ratings of the top ten catchers will be presented not only for the two-to-one final rating, but also for the one-to-one rating and the four-and-a-half-to-one rating. Interestingly, the comparisons will show that there is no change in the top three positions in any of those ratings and, for the most part, the same people are included in the top ten regardless of the offensive weight, although there are minor positional shifts. In only two cases were other players able to crack the top ten rating.

Most of the catchers in this study seem to have been eliminated from consideration as baseball's greatest all-around catcher. The only catchers that appeared to be still in the running were those who finished in the top ten offensively or defensively. The top ten offensive catchers, in order of their finish, were:

Mike Piazza	Joe Torre
Gene Tenace	Darrell Porter
Mickey Cochrane	Ernie Lombardi
Gabby Hartnett	Johnny Bench (T)
Bill Dickey	Yogi Berra (T)
Roy Campanella	

Their defensive counterparts were:

Gabby Hartnett	Tony Pena
Roy Campanella	Yogi Berra
Jim Sundberg	Harry Danning
Gary Carter	Bill Dickey
Lance Parrish	Ray Mueller

That's a total of 17 catchers who were considered to be the favorites for the title of baseball's greatest all-around catcher, counting duplicates. The final ratings, based on a two-to-one offense to defense weighting system, are:

Catcher	Offensive Rating × 2	Defensive Rating × 1	Total Points	Final Catcher Rating
Gabby Hartnett	8	1	9	1
Roy Campanella	12	2	14	2
Bill Dickey	10	9	19	3
Yogi Berra	20	7	27	4
Mickey Cochrane	6	23	29	5
Mike Piazza	2	35	37	6
Johnny Bench	20	19	39	7
Gene Tenace	4	43	47	8
Joe Torre	14	34	48	9
Chris Hoiles	26	24	50	10
Bill Freehan	32	21	53	11
Earl Battey	34	22	56	12
Gary Carter	54	4	58	13
Carlton Fisk	30	30	60	14
Ernie Lombardi	18	45	63	15

The complete list of the FCRs can be found in the Appendix. The estimated FCRs for Jorge Posada can be found in the appendix also.

The first ten places on the list of the world's greatest all-around catchers were players who finished in the top ten either offensively or defensively. But there were several surprises after the tenth position. Bill Freehan, who didn't finish in the top ten either offensively or defensively, captured the number eleven spot all-around on the basis of his well-balanced skills. He finished 16th on offense and 21st on defense. Earl Battey, a number 17 offensive backstop, captured the number 12 spot thanks to a 22nd-place finish on defense. Munson, Howard, and Fisk were successful because they were strong all-around catchers. Some of the other finalists were more one-dimensional. For instance, the game's most productive hitter, Mike Piazza, came in a distant 35th on defense. Gene Tenace, number four on offense, finished 43rd on defense. Darrell Porter, the number eight offensive catcher, was 48th on defense, dropping him to 16th place overall. Conversely, Jim Sundberg, the number three man behind Hartnett and Campanella, on defense, could do no better than 46th on offense, leaving him in 35th place overall. Tony Pena, number six on defense, finished 50th on offense. Lance Parrish, the fifth best defensive catcher, fell to 20th place overall after a 34th-place finish on offense. And Charles Johnson, number 16 on defense, finished 39th on offense, for a final rating of 34.

For the better part of 70 years, the debate over the identity of baseball's greatest all-around catcher has raged. In the 1930s and '40s, the votes for baseball's greatest catcher usually went to either Bill Dickey or Mickey Cochrane, with Gabby Hartnett garnering an isolated vote here or there. In the 1950s and '60s, it was a close call between Roy Campanella and Yogi Berra. And from the 1970s through the 1990s, Johnny Bench was generally acclaimed to be number one, with Mike Piazza peeking over his shoulder. But now the issue has been resolved, once and for all. Facts speak louder than words. Statistics are worth 1000 opinions. In this study, the offensive and defensive statistics of the world's greatest catchers were compared side by side. And in the end, one man emerged as the greatest all-around catcher in baseball history. He was Charles Leo "Gabby" Hartnett, the Hall of Fame catcher of the Chicago Cubs.

Johnny Bench, arguably the greatest catcher of the last 35 years, led the Cincinnati Reds to six National League pennants. *Courtesy Cincinnati Reds Historical Library.*

The final catcher ratings (FCR) confirm Hartnett's superiority in all phases of the game. He finished fourth as baseball's best-hitting catcher, behind Piazza, Tenace, and Cochrane, and he walked off with the title of the game's best defensive catcher. The number two man as best all-around catcher was Roy Campanella of the Brooklyn Dodgers. He and Hartnett were pretty evenly matched, with Hartnett finishing fourth on offense to Campy's sixth-place finish and Campy coming in second behind Hartnett on defense. Campanella lost his opportunity to capture the top spot on defense when he finished 15th in fielding average and 31st in adjusted assists. The competition in the fielding average category was so close that Campy's four-point advantage over the league average lost twelve places in the ratings to Gabby's six-point advantage. Hartnett, the man who was called "A Master of the Pickoff," easily outdistanced Campanella in the adjusted assist category. On offense, it was nip and tuck between the two competitors, with Gabby edging Campy in the on-base category and Campy returning the favor in the slugging average category. The complete statistical tables can be found in the appendix.

Many modern baseball historians favor Johnny Bench as baseball's all-time catcher, with a few votes going to Yogi Berra, Bill Dickey, or Mickey Cochrane. Gabby Hartnett and Roy Campanella, it seems, were the forgotten men, which is strange considering their statistical superiority. In head-to-head competition with his American League counterparts, Dickey and Cochrane, Hartnett easily defeated them in caught-stealing percentage, year after year, for more than a decade. He outgunned each of them nine times in 10 years. The master of the pickoff also had a comfortable advantage in adjusted assists over Cochrane, beating him seven times in 10 years while holding Dickey to a five-five draw. He out-fielded Dickey six times in 10 years, but came in second to Cochrane, six to three with one even. There was only one other major defensive category that Hartnett did not win. He finished behind his two adversaries in range factor. The following table shows his superiority over Cochrane and Dickey in fielding average and total assists.

| | Hartnett | | | | Cochrane | | | | Dickey | | | |
| | | | | LGE | | | | LGE | | | | LGE |
Year	FA	A	SBA	SBA	FA	A	SBA	SBA	FA	A	SBA	SBA
1924	.963	97										
1925	.958	114*	60	84	.984*	79	93	90				
1926	.978	86	42	76	.975	90	78	83				
1927	.973	99*	52	81	.986	85	84	99				
1928	.989*	103*	39	87	.966	71	83	87				
1929	—	—	—	—	.983*	77	89	80	.979	95*	78	80
1930	.989*	68*	47	60	.993*	69*	79	75	.977	51	82	75
1931	.981	68	49	58	.986	63	66	78	.996*	78	71	78
1932	.982	75	29	56	.993*	94*	68	68	.987	53	65	68
1933	.989	77	35	51	.989	67	67	56	.993	82	35	56
1934	.996*	86*	37	45	.988	69	43	68	.986	49	68	68
1935	.984*	77*	45	50	.989	50	44	41	.995*	62	44	41
1936	.991*	75	39	50					.976	61	47	36
1937	.996*	65	47	57					.991*	80	52	70
1938	.995	40	40	44					.987	74	52	68
1939	.992	47	34	46					.989*	57	49	74
1940									.994	55		
1941									.994*	45		
Career	.984	1269	595	845	.985	840	794	825	.988	954	728	853
Per yr.		109	43	60	89	72	75	86		56	66	

Note: * denotes league leader

Where:

FA = Fielding average
A = Total assists
SBA = Stolen bases allowed
LGE SBA = League stolen bases allowed

On offense, he held his own against the American Leaguers. He trailed both Dickey and Cochrane in on-base percentage, but easily outdistanced them in slugging percentage, finishing fifth out of 50 catchers, compared to 13th for Dickey and 17th for Cochrane. Compared to Berra, Gabby dominated the offensive statistics, finishing higher than Yogi in both OBP and SLG, as well as in SH. On defense, it was no contest, with Hartnett piling up such a huge lead in FA, CS, and ASSA that Berra's small advantages in PB, WP, and RF left him far in arrears. Hartnett

Bill Dickey has the second highest career batting average for a catcher in the annals of the game. *Courtesy New York Yankees.*

also excelled in a head-to-head matchup against Johnny Bench, winning the offensive battle in a fairly close competition by taking the OBPA category handily, while losing a close decision in SLG. Gabby ran away with the defensive competition, defeating Bench easily in FA, RF, and ASSA, while taking a closer decision in CS. Bench won only the PB and WP categories against the Cubs' superstar. It is unlikely that Bench could have gained any ground on Hartnett even if the intangibles could have been evaluated, because it was well known that Bench was not one of the best at calling a game or handling a pitching staff. His pitchers shook him off frequently.

Gabby Hartnett led the National League in 22 defensive categories during his career. He won one Most Valuable Player award and played in four World Series. Mickey Cochrane led his league in 14 defensive categories, won two MVP awards, and appeared in five World Series. Bill Dickey led in 14 defensive categories and appeared in eight World Series. Yogi Berra led in 19 defensive categories, won three MVP awards, and appeared in a fantastic 14 World Series. Roy Campanella led in 12 defensive categories and one offensive category, won three MVP awards, and appeared in five World Series. Johnny Bench led in five defensive categories and five offensive categories, and played in four World Series.

Gabby Hartnett's Early Training

Gabby Hartnett was one of Millville's best marbles players as a young-ster. The game involved throwing marbles at a large agate located about fifty feet away. Gabby was tough to beat. He hit the agate often with his overhand throws. He told his buddies, "Throwing marbles overhand is the best way to throw because that way the arm is better directed by the eye." He learned the throwing motion from his father, Fred, who had been a strong-armed semi-pro catcher in the Blackstone Valley of Massachusetts. The oldest of seven Hartnett boys became interested in catching when he was just eight years old, and by the time he was 10, his father had him and his brother Sweetie in the back yard for baseball practice every evening after work. Sweetie would pitch and Gabby would catch, while Fred stood off to the side, instructing them and observing their technique. One time, when Gabby backhanded a wide pitch instead of shifting his body in front of the ball, Fred rushed over and gave him a swift kick in the pants. "Is that the way I taught you to catch the ball? Now do it again, and do it right this time." Fred was a taskmaster who drove his son mercilessly in the art of catching a baseball. By the time he was a teenager, Gabby Hartnett was a polished defensive catcher, blessed with a powerful throwing arm he inherited from his father. Several members of his family also possessed what was known up and down the valley as "The Hart-nett Arm." His best friend and favorite pitcher was Tim McNamara, who later went on to pitch for the Boston Braves. Tim spoke admiringly of the "Hartnett Arm." "I never worried about the runner on first base, because I knew if he tried to steal, [Gabby] would throw him out."

Hartnett on Hartnett

Many of Gabby Hartnett's comments written here, regarding hitting and catching, were taken from an article by Alfred M. McCoy in "The Open Road for Boys," May, 1937.

On Hitting

"Hitting is the heart of the game. You've got to hit to score, and if you don't score, you can't beat anyone, and if you can't win your share of games, there's no sense in playing.

When I was a youngster, I wanted to take a wagon tongue for a bat, dig a good toe-hold, and swing with all my might. But I smartened up fast when I found out I wasn't hitting well. After I settled on a bat of proper weight and length, my batting average improved quickly. If there's any one thing I like better than anything else, it's my base hits.

There's another important point and that's confidence. Just thinking you're going to hit the ball is half the battle. You build confidence when you know you are doing things correctly."

"When you're at bat, think of nothing but hitting, and be ready to hit the first good pitch you see. Major league pitchers have nearly perfect control and pitch only to the corners most of the time. We don't get many cripples to hit.

"Another thing. When you hit the ball — run! Don't look to see where it's going. Even if it looks like a sure putout, keep on running. Don't quit until you're actually out. Nothing looks worse, and you never can tell. Even the best of them make errors."

On Catching

"Part of my job is to try to get a batter's mind off his work. One day, for instance, we were playing Boston, and Elbie Fletcher, their first baseman, was at bat. The score was tied, three men on, two out in the ninth inning, and the count three and two. Tex Carleton was on the mound when I went to work on Elbie. I told him to watch the next one for he was sure going to see something different from anything that had ever been served up to him before. The pitch cut the heart of the plate, and Fletcher just stood there looking at it, being struck out without ever taking his bat off his shoulder. We won the game in the last half of the inning."

"I study the base runners. It's my business to find out when a runner is going to steal. By studying their actions, I pick up certain give-away signs. They get tense or turn a bit. Then I call for a pitchout with a signal everyone on our team knows, so they can back up the play."

"I can throw to second base from a crouch, but I believe in stepping in the direction you are going to throw. It's easier on the arm, and I'm careful of that old soup-bone since I almost lost the use of it in 1929."

"A catcher has to have good footwork. He has to be able to step to the side he wishes to go, starting with the foot on that side, so as to keep the pitch directly in front of him, yet he must always be in a position to throw."

"A catcher has to direct the team in general from his position behind the plate. I don't position outfielders normally, but if I see a man clearly out of position for a certain batter, I signal him to shift. When a couple of infielders are going after a pop-up, I call out the name of the one to make the catch, and keep calling his name until the ball is caught. Between innings, the pitcher and I go over the batters coming up the next inning so we are in agreement how we're going to pitch to them."

"And a catcher always has to protect his hands. He will hurt his hands if he doesn't catch the ball in his glove. If he points his fingers toward the ball, there's a danger of a split finger. By keeping his bare hand closed into a fist, most of this chance is eliminated. Get in front of the ball and don't get careless, and the likelihood of injury is very slim. When I catch a pop-up, I get directly under the ball if I can, then lift my hands high to catch it so that, in case of a fumble, there's another chance to catch it."

"Blocking the plate is also an important responsibility of the catcher. We are well protected with shin guards and I usually try to catch the ball, tag the runner, and get out of the way."

Comments about Gabby by His Peers and by Baseball Historians

Sheriff Blake, who pitched to Hartnett for eight years, once said, "Gabby was the greatest catcher I ever saw. If you got a man on first base who was a good base runner, you didn't have to keep your mind too much on him; you could concentrate on the hitter. Because if the runner got too far off first, Hartnett would pick him off."

Charlie Grimm said "When Gabby was catching, there were two umpires behind the plate."

Joe McCarthy, who managed Bill Dickey for 14 years and who saw Mickey Cochrane in action for more than a dozen years, called Gabby Hartnett "the perfect catcher. He was the greatest catcher I ever saw. He was super smart. Nobody ever had more hustle, and nobody could throw with him. There have been few great clutch hitters, and he was the best."

Carl Hubbell said Hartnett was the toughest hitter he ever faced.

Paul Richards, who managed in the major leagues for 12 years between 1951 and 1976, said "The best throwing arm I ever saw on a catcher probably belonged to Gabby Hartnett. Better than Bench? Yes. The fans used to come out early to watch infield practice just to watch Hartnett throw the ball around. He made a theatrical performance out of it."

Casey Stengel, who saw every catcher from Ray Schalk to Johnny Bench, called Gabby Hartnett the greatest catcher ever to play the game.

Bill Klem, the dean of umpires, who umpired for 36 years, including 18 World Series, saw every catcher from 1905 to 1951, and he selected Gabby Hartnett as the catcher on his all-time All-Star team.

Comments about Campanella by His Peers and by Baseball Historians

Some of baseball's greatest players, managers, and executives left numerous testimonials to Campanella's greatness. Paul Richards, a major league player for eight years and a major league manager from 1951 to '61 and again in 1976, was quoted in *The Ballplayers* as saying Campanella was "the best catcher in the business—major or minor leagues." Ty Cobb seconded that opinion when he said, "When they look for players to put in the Hall of Fame, they'll have to start with Roy Campanella." And Tris Speaker, arguably baseball's greatest center fielder, agreed. "Of all the men playing baseball today, the one they will talk

Roy Campanella challenged Gabby Hartnett for the title of baseball's greatest catcher.

about the most 20 or 30 years from now will be Campanella." Brooklyn Dodgers general manager Branch Rickey, who knew Campanella better than most people, said he was a master at handling the low pitch. He always shifted his body when the pitch was outside, something many of the modern catchers don't do. "He was the perfect receiver. He took charge of his pitchers. He assumed authority." Author Al Hirshberg, who saw Campanella catch hundreds of times in his capacity as a sportswriter for the *Boston Post*, noted, "Campy had one of the greatest throwing arms of any catcher. He had a snap throw, which meant that he could get the ball away faster because he didn't have to draw his arm back ... [his] arm was deadly, and he could throw to any base with equal facility.... He ran the ballgame from behind the plate. A take-charge guy who never stopped talking or moving around, he was the boss on the field. When a pitcher seemed to be sagging, Campy woke him up with a yell and a bullet throw, yet he was never tense or upset. Fresco Thompson, the Dodgers' vice president, called him 'the most relaxed ballplayer I've ever seen.'"

Best All-Around Catchers by Era and by League

National League	*American League*
1920–1940	
1. Gabby Hartnett*	1. Bill Dickey
2. Ernie Lombardi	2. Mickey Cochrane
3. Bubbles Hargrave	3. Rick Ferrell
4. Babe Phelps	4. Muddy Ruel
5. Harry Danning	
1940–1960	
1. Roy Campanella	1. Yogi Berra
2. Walker Cooper	2. Sherm Lollar
3. Del Crandall	3. Birdie Tebetts
4. Smoky Burgess	4T. Buddy Rosar
5T. Ray Mueller	4T. Gus Triandos
5T. Ed Bailey	
1960–1980	
1.Johnny Bench	1. Gene Tenace
2. Joe Torre	2. Bill Freehan
3.Ted Simmons	3. Earl Battey
4.Joe Ferguson	4. Elston Howard
5. John Roseboro	5. Thurman Munson
1980–2004	
1. Mike Piazza	1. Chris Hoiles
2. Gary Carter	2. Carlton Fisk
3. Mike Scioscia	3. Mickey Tettleton
4. Jason Kendall	4. Lance Parrish
5. Darren Daulton	5. Ivan Rodriguez

* Gabby Hartnett was baseball's greatest all-around catcher.

This work is the first in-depth study to evaluate catchers for both their offensive and defensive skills, and it is the first study to compare the caught-stealing percentages of the individual catchers. Only direct statistical measurements of the individual catchers were utilized, and these were adjusted for era and compared to the league average. There were no generalizations for such things as park factor, there were no pitching statistics factored in, there were no positional adjustments, and the statistics were all based on a 154-game and 550-at-bat season, so everyone was measured on the same basis. The study measured the skill of the individual catchers and not their value to a team. It is unfortunate that many of a catcher's skills fall into the category of intangibles, those skills that cannot be measured, such as leadership, pitch calling, handling the pitching staff, backing up bases, and blocking the plate. But it is unlikely that any of the catchers in the study could have surpassed either Hartnett or Cam-

Gabby Hartnett surpassed all other catchers in the ratings as the game's greatest all-around catcher.

panella, had the intangibles been measured, because both men were drilled by their mentors in all aspects of the position, including those mentioned above. And both men excelled in all those categories.

The following table compares the final catcher rating (FCR) with Pete Palmer's new rating system for all position players, the batter-fielder wins (BFW) rating outlined in *The Baseball Encyclopedia*, as well as *Total Baseball's* total player rating. The formula for BFW is:

$$BFW = (BR + FR + BSR - Pos. Adj.) / Runs Per Win$$

Where:

BFW is batter-fielder wins
FR is fielding runs
BSR is base stealing runs
BR is batting runs

Although BFW is a value system like TPR, it can be easily converted to a skill rating, based on a 154 game season, by dividing the total BFW number by the ratio of 154 to total games caught.

It should be noted that the BFWs in the table below included the ratings for only those catchers whose careers peaked after 1920. The nineteenth-century catchers and the catchers who played between 1900 and 1920 were excluded. It appears from the above comparisons that the BFW and TPR rating systems are much more heavily weighted toward offense than is the FCR system. There seems to be no other way to explain Mike Piazza's number one overall rating, in view of his obvious defensive deficiencies. He finished in 36th place in the final defensive rating (FDR) of the present study. Of course, his 25 percent caught-stealing percentage, which is not included in the BFW and TPR systems, may also be a contributing factor. And that omission may also account for the lower ratings for Roy Campanella and Gabby Hartnett. Other significant differences that exist between the FCR system and the BFW and TPR systems, in addition to the caught-stealing statistics, are the generalized park factors used by BFW and TPR, as well as their use of a pitching factor.

Catcher	FCR	BFW Per 154 G.	TPR Per 154 G.
Gabby Hartnett	1	4	2
Roy Campanella	2	6	5
Bill Dickey	3	5	4
Yogi Berra	4	8	6
Mickey Cochrane	5	2	3
Mike Piazza	6	1	1
Johnny Bench	7	7	8
Gene Tenace	8	11	10
Joe Torre	9	20	15
Chris Hoiles	10	13	11
Bill Freehan	11	21	16
Earl Battey	12	19	13
Gary Carter	13	10	7
Carlton Fisk	14	12	12
Ernie Lombardi	15	14	14
Darrell Porter	16	18	15
Elston Howard	17	23	23
Ted Simmons	18	22	18
Mickey Tettleton	19	16	22
Thurmon Munson	20	9	9

FCR is admittedly a rough measurement and comparison of the overall skills of major league catchers, but the ultimate solution could be close at hand. A slight modification to the BFW system, or the TPR system, could provide incontrovertible scientific ratings. The batting runs (BR) formula could be modified to include an individual park factor. Actually, it would not be a park factor per se. All the critical individual batting statistics, R, H, D, T, HR, BB, BA, etc., would have to be adjusted to an "average park," not just the home runs. Additionally, the pitching runs and the positional adjustment could be eliminated from the formula since the measurement would be strictly for a catcher's skills. The normalization of the results would be retained so the player's offensive skills could be compared directly with the offensive skills of catchers from any era. The fielding runs (FR) formula could measure and compare a catcher's normalized fielding average, which would include total putouts, total assists, and errors. A catcher's stolen base record could be presented in the most effective configuration, perhaps as a caught-stealing percentage, which seems to be the most equitable method of comparing catcher's skills in that critical category. That result could also be normalized for era comparison purposes, as could adjusted assists (A – CS). And double plays could possibly be eliminated since they would be covered under PO, A, and CS%. Passed balls would still be included, and a catcher's responsibility for a percentage of his team's wild pitches could be reviewed for possible inclusion in the formula.

When new, more sophisticated, studies are conducted in the future, the most important results of this study should still be valid.

- Gabby Hartnett and Roy Campanella should still be a step above the other catchers and will probably run one-two in any new statistical study to identify baseball's greatest all-around catcher, although Campanella could be pressed by Bill Dickey.
- Mickey Cochrane, Johnny Bench, Mike Piazza, and Yogi Berra should finish in the top ten and probably in the top six or seven.

APPENDIX 1:
OFFENSIVE STATISTICS

Catcher	Years	G	AB	R	H	D	T	HR	RBI	BA
Bailey, Ed	1953–66	1212	3581	432	915	128	15	155	540	.256
Battey, Earl	1955–67	1141	3586	393	969	150	17	104	449	.270
Bench, Johnny	1967–83	2158	7658	1091	2048	381	49	389	1376	.267
Berra, Yogi	1946–65	2120	7555	1175	2150	321	49	358	1430	.285
Burgess, Smoky	1949–67	1691	4471	485	1318	230	33	126	673	.295
Campanella, Roy	1948–57	1215	4202	627	1161	178	18	242	856	.276
Carter, Gary	1974–92	2295	7971	1025	2092	371	31	324	1225	.262
Cochrane, Mickey	1925–37	1482	5169	1041	1652	333	64	119	832	.320
Cooper, Walker	1940–57	1473	4702	573	1341	240	40	173	812	.285
Crandall, Del	1949–66	1573	5026	585	1276	179	18	179	657	.254
Danning, Harry	1933–42	890	2971	363	847	162	26	57	397	.285
Daulton, Darren	1983–97	1161	3630	511	891	197	25	137	588	.245
Dickey, Bill	1928–46	1789	6300	930	1969	343	72	202	1209	.313
Ferguson, Joe	1970–83	1013	3001	407	719	121	11	122	445	.240
Ferrell, Rick	1929–47	1884	6028	687	1692	324	45	28	734	.281
Fisk, Carlton	1969–93	2499	8756	1276	2356	421	47	376	1330	.269
Freehan, Bill	1961–76	1774	6073	706	1591	241	35	200	758	.262
Haller, Tom	1961–72	1294	3935	461	1011	153	31	134	504	.257
Hargrave, Bubbles	1913–30	852	2533	314	786	155	58	29	376	.310
Hartnett, Gabby	1922–41	1990	6432	867	1912	396	64	236	1179	.297
Hoiles, Chris	1989–98	894	2820	415	739	122	2	151	449	.262
Howard, Elston	1955–68	1605	5363	619	1471	218	50	167	762	.274
Johnson, Charles	1993–03	1060	3485	418	859	187	4	154	518	.246
Kendall, Jason	1996–03	1105	4032	620	1226	224	29	64	420	.304
Lollar, Sherman	1946–63	1752	5351	623	1415	244	14	155	808	.264
Lombardi, Ernie	1931–47	1853	5855	601	1792	277	27	190	990	.306
Lopez, Javy	1993–03	1156	4003	508	1148	190	14	214	694	.287
Mueller, Ray	1935–51	985	2911	281	733	123	23	56	373	.252
Munson, Thurman	1969–79	1423	5344	696	1558	229	32	113	701	.271
O'Dea, Ken	1935–46	832	2195	262	560	101	20	40	323	.255
O'Farrell, Bob	1915–35	1492	4101	517	1120	201	58	51	549	.273
Parrish, Lance	1977–95	1988	7067	856	1782	305	27	324	1070	.252

Catcher	Years	G	AB	R	H	D	T	HR	RBI	BA
Pena, Tony	1980–97	1988	6489	667	1687	298	27	107	708	.260
Phelps, Babe	1931–42	726	2117	239	657	143	19	54	345	.310
Piazza, Mike	1992–03	1461	5350	888	1708	264	6	358	1107	.319
Porter, Darrell	1971–87	1782	5539	765	1369	237	48	188	826	.247
Posada, Jorge	1995–03	866	2920	449	788	181	5	135	526	.270
Rodriguez, Ivan	1991–03	1623	6167	942	1875	381	31	231	914	.304
Rosar, Buddy	1939–51	988	3198	335	836	147	15	18	367	.261
Roseboro, John	1957–70	1585	4847	512	1206	190	44	104	548	.249
Ruel, Muddy	1917–37	1468	4514	494	1242	187	29	4	534	.275
Sanguillen, Manny	1967–80	1448	5062	566	1500	205	57	65	585	.296
Scioscia, Mike	1980–92	1441	4373	398	1131	198	12	68	446	.259
Simmons, Ted	1968–88	2456	8680	1074	2472	483	47	248	1389	.285
Sundberg, Jim	1974–89	1962	6021	621	1493	243	36	95	624	.248
Tebbetts, Birdie	1936–52	1162	3704	357	1000	169	22	38	469	.270
Tenace, Gene	1969–83	1555	4390	653	1060	179	20	201	674	.241
Tettleton, Mickey	1984–97	1485	4698	711	1132	210	16	245	732	.241
Torre, Joe	1960–77	2209	7874	996	2342	344	59	252	1185	.297
Triandos, Gus	1953–65	1206	3907	389	954	147	6	167	608	.244
Westrum, Wes	1947–57	919	2322	302	503	59	8	96	315	.217

Catcher	SB	SH	OBP	OBPA	SLG	XSLGA
Bailey, Ed	17	20	.355	.343	.429	.269
Battey, Earl	13	39	.349	.359	.409	.276
Bench, Johnny	68	11	.342	.345	.476	.394
Berra, Yogi	30	9	.350	.346	.482	.350
Burgess, Smoky	13	13	.364	.348	.446	.266
Campanella, Roy	25	30	.360	.351	.500	.374
Carter, Gary	39	33	.335	.337	.439	.307
Cochrane, Mickey	64	151	.419	.401	.478	.313
Cooper, Walker	18	44	.332	.321	.464	.364
Crandall, Del	26	68	.315	.307	.404	.287
Danning, Harry	13	22	.330	.320	.415	.208
Daulton, Darren	50	12	.357	.346	.427	.265
Dickey, Bill	36	51	.382	.368	.486	.325
Ferguson, Joe	4	3	.358	.353	.409	.290
Ferrell, Rick	29	103	.378	.365	.363	.207
Fisk, Carlton	128	26	.341	.345	.457	.343
Freehan, Bill	24	38	.340	.354	.412	.299
Haller, Tom	14	35	.340	.339	.414	.292
Hargrave, Bubbles	29	70	.372	.346	.452	.299
Hartnett, Gabby	28	137	.370	.354	.489	.359
Hoiles, Chris	5	11	.366	.356	.467	.311
Howard, Elston	9	29	.322	.331	.427	.324
Johnson, Charles	4	16	.331	.320	.438	.295
Kendall, Jason	129	8	.385	.363	.422	.212
Lollar, Sherman	20	47	.357	.346	.402	.241
Lombardi, Ernie	8	18	.358	.351	.460	.346
Lopez, Javy	8	6	.337	.316	.502	.348
Mueller, Ray	14	64	.314	.308	.368	.228

Catcher	SB	SH	OBP	OBPA	SLG	XSLGA
Munson, Thurman	47	21	.346	.351	.410	.267
O'Dea, Ken	3	39	.338	.325	.374	.209
O'Farrell, Bob	35	83	.360	.339	.388	.212
Parrish, Lance	28	23	.313	.309	.440	.324
Pena, Tony	80	68	.309	.298	.364	.211
Phelps, Babe	9	16	.362	.341	.472	.316
Piazza, Mike	17	0	.391	.377	.579	.466
Porter, Darrell	39	18	.354	.362	.409	.322
Posada, Jorge	9	1	.375	.369	.474	.304
Rodriguez, Ivan	90	17	.341	.333	.485	.302
Rosar, Buddy	29	44	.330	.329	.334	.163
Roseboro, John	67	44	.326	.323	.371	.268
Ruel, Muddy	61	143	.365	.338	.332	.117
Sanguillen, Manny	36	28	.326	.319	.398	.247
Scioscia, Mike	29	57	.344	.342	.356	.236
Simmons, Ted	21	11	.348	.348	.437	.327
Sundberg, Jim	20	118	.327	.326	.348	.201
Tebbetts, Birdie	29	44	.341	.347	.358	.132
Tenace, Gene	36	21	.388	.392	.429	.347
Tettleton, Mickey	23	21	.369	.366	.449	.294
Torre, Joe	23	13	.365	.363	.452	.326
Triandos, Gus	1	26	.322	.323	.413	.298
Westrum, Wes	10	11	.356	.342	.373	.186

NOTE: The offensive and defensive statistics used in this study for the six active catchers— Piazza, Rodriguez, Javy Lopez, Charles Johnson, Kendall, and Posada — are inclusive of the 2003 baseball season. It has been determined that the inclusion of the 2004 and 2005 season statistics would have very little effect on the final ratings and would have no effect on the top twenty positions.

APPENDIX 2:
OFFENSIVE RATINGS

Catcher	OBPA	Rating	XSLGA	Rating	SB	Rating ×.05	SH	Rating ×.05	GIDP	Rating ×.05
Bailey, Ed	.343	27	.269	31	2	1.6	3	1.4	10	.2
Battey, Earl	.359	10	.276	30	2	1.6	6	.7	19	2.1
Bench, Johnny	.345	25	.394	2	5	.6	1	2.2	14	1.0
Berra, Yogi	.346	21	.350	6	3	1.1	1	2.2	11	.5
Burgess, Smoky	.348	18	.266	34	2	1.6	2	1.7	15	1.1
Campanella, Roy	.351	15	.374	3	3	1.1	4	1.1	19	2.1
Carter, Gary	.337	34	.307	20	3	1.0	2	1.7	12	.7
Cochrane, Mickey	.401	1	.313	18	7	.3	16	.1	10	.2
Cooper, Walker	.321	42	.364	4	2	1.6	5	.8	19	2.1
Crandall, Del	.307	49	.287	29	3	1.1	7	.5	18	1.8
Danning, Harry	.320	43	.208	44	2	1.6	4	1.1	17	1.7
Daulton, Darren	.346	21	.265	35	8	.1	2	1.7	11	.5
Dickey, Bill	.368	4	.325	13	3	1.1	4	1.1	15	1.1
Ferrell, Rick	.365	6	.207	45	3	1.1	9	.4	14	1.0
Ferguson, Joe	.353	14	.290	28	4	.7	3	1.4	16	1.4
Fisk, Carlton	.345	25	.343	10	8	.1	2	1.7	13	.8
Freehan, Bill	.354	12	.299	22	2	1.6	3	1.4	12	.7
Haller, Tom	.339	31	.292	27	2	1.6	5	.8	8	.1
Hargrave, Bubbles	.346	21	.299	22	2	.5	15	.1	19	2.1
Hartnett, Gabby	.354	12	.359	5	2	1.6	10	.3	15	1.1
Hoiles, Chris	.356	11	.311	19	1	2.2	2	1.7	13	.8
Howard, Elston	.331	36	.324	14	1	2.2	3	1.4	16	1.4
Johnson, Charles	.320	43	.295	25	1	2.2	3	1.4	16	1.4
Kendall, Jason	.363	7	.212	39	18	.1	1	2.2	11	.5
Lollar, Sherman	.346	21	.241	37	2	1.6	5	.8	19	2.1
Lombardi, Ernie	.351	15	.346	9	1	2.2	2	1.7	25	2.5
Lopez, Javy	.316	46	.348	7	1	2.2	1	2.2	19	2.1
Mueller, Ray	.308	48	.228	39	3	1.1	6	.7	21	2.5
Munson, Thurman	.351	15	.267	33	5	.6	2	1.7	16	1.4
O'Dea, Ken	.325	39	.209	43	1	2.2	10	.3	13	.8
O'Farrell, Bob	.339	31	.212	40	5	.6	11	.2	11	.5

Catcher	OBPA	Rating	XSLGA	Rating	SB	Rating ×.05		SH	Rating ×.05		GIDP	Rating ×.05
Parrish, Lance	.309	47	.324	14	2	1.6		2	1.7		15	1.1
Pena, Tony	.298	50	.211	42	7	.3		6	.7		20	2.4
Phelps, Babe	.341	30	.316	17	2	1.6		4	1.1		17	1.7
Piazza, Mike	.377	3	.466	1	1	2.2		0	2.5		19	2.1
Porter, Darrell	.362	9	.322	16	4	.7		2	1.7		10	.2
Posada, Jorge	.369	4	.304	19	2	1.6		0	2.5		16	1.4
Rodriguez, Ivan	.333	35	.302	21	8	.1		2	1.7		18	1.8
Rosar, Buddy	.329	37	.163	48	3	1.1		8	.5		17	1.7
Roseboro, John	.323	40	.268	32	8	.1		5	.8		7	.1
Ruel, Muddy	.338	33	.117	50	7	.3		17	.1		15	1.1
Sanguillen, Manny	.319	45	.247	36	4	.7		3	1.4		16	1.4
Scioscia, Mike	.342	28	.236	38	4	.7		7	.5		11	.5
Simmons, Ted	.348	18	.327	11	2	1.6		1	2.2		18	1.8
Sundberg, Jim	.326	38	.201	45	2	1.6		10	.3		15	1.1
Tebbetts, Birdie	.347	20	.132	49	4	.7		7	.5		18	1.8
Tenace, Gene	.392	2	.347	8	5	.6		3	1.4		10	.2
Tettleton, Mickey	.366	5	.294	26	3	1.1		2	1.7		10	.2
Torre, Joe	.363	7	.326	12	2	1.6		1	2.2		20	2.4
Triandos, Gus	.323	40	.298	24	0	3.0		4	1.1		18	1.8
Westrum, Wes	.342	28	.186	47	2	1.6		3	1.4		13	.8

Catcher	Total Points	Final Rating
Piazza, Mike	10.8	1
Tenace, Gene	12.2	2
Cochrane, Mickey	19.6	3
Hartnett, Gabby	20.0	4
Dickey, Bill	20.3	5
Campanella, Roy	22.3	6
Torre, Joe	25.2	7
Porter, Darrell	27.6	8
Lombardi, Ernie	30.4	9
Posada, Jorge	28.5	9 est.*
Berra, Yogi	30.8	10
Bench, Johnny	30.8	10
Tettleton, Mickey	34.0	12
Hoiles, Chris	34.7	13
Simmons, Ted	34.6	13
Fisk, Carlton	37.6	15
Freehan, Bill	37.7	16
Battey, Earl	44.4	17
Ferguson, Joe	45.5	18

*Jorge Posada's major league service time did not qualify him for inclusion in this study. However, since he is still active and since he is one of the foremost catchers in the game today, his statistics are included in the tables, and his estimated rating is presented for comparison purposes.

Catcher	Total Points	Final Rating
Hargrave, Bubbles	45.7	19
Kendall, Jason	49.8	20
Cooper, Walker	50.5	21
Phelps, Babe	51.4	22
Munson, Thurman	51.7	23
Ferrell, Rick	53.5	24
Howard, Elston	55.0	25
Burgess, Smoky	56.4	26
Carter, Gary	57.4	27
Daulton, Darren	58.3	28
Lopez, Javy	59.5	29
Rodriguez, Ivan	59.6	30
Haller, Tom	60.5	31
Bailey, Ed	61.2	32
Lollar, Sherman	62.5	33
Parrish, Lance	65.4	34
Scioscia, Mike	67.7	35
Triandos, Gus	69.9	36
Tebbetts, Birdie	72.0	37
O'Farrell, Bob	72.3	38
Johnson, Charles	73.0	39
Roseboro, John	73.0	39
Westrum, Wes	78.8	41
Crandall, Del	81.4	42
Ruel, Muddy	84.5	43
Sanguillen, Manny	84.5	43
O'Dea, Ken	85.3	45
Sundberg, Jim	87.0	46
Rosar, Buddy	88.3	47
Mueller, Ray	91.3	48
Danning, Harry	91.4	49
Pena, Tony	95.4	50

APPENDIX 3:
DEFENSIVE STATISTICS

Catcher	Games Caught	Field'g Avg.	Putouts	Assists	Errors	Caught Stealing %	Passed Balls	Range Factor
Bailey, Ed	1064	.986	5267	450	80	39	48	5.37
Battey, Earl	1087	.990	6176	501	69	40	96	6.14
Bench, Johnny	1742	.990	9249	850	97	43	94	5.80
Berra, Yogi	1699	.989	873	978	110	49	76	5.61
Burgess, Smoky	1139	.988	5214	441	71	34	73	4.96
Campanella, Roy	1183	.988	6520	550	85	58	56	5.98
Carter, Gary	2056	.991	11785	1203	121	35	84	6.32
Cochrane, Mickey	1451	.985	6414	840	111	40	88	5.00
Cooper, Walker	1223	.977	5166	589	138	44	79	4.71
Crandall, Del	1479	.989	7352	759	89	46	60	5.48
Danning, Harry	801	.985	3257	455	57	47	32	4.63
Daulton, Darren	965	.989	5417	455	66	29	64	6.07
Dickey, Bill	1708	.988	7965	954	108	41	76	5.22
Ferguson, Joe	766	.987	3905	376	56	34	84	5.59
Ferrell, Rick	1806	.984	7248	1127	135	43	142	4.64
Fisk, Carlton	2226	.988	11369	1048	155	33	129	5.58
Freehan, Bill	1576	.993	9941	721	72	34	106	6.74
Haller, Tom	1199	.992	7012	511	65	34	121	6.27
Hargrave, Bubbles	747	.983	2420	493	49	39	47	3.90
Hartnett, Gabby	1793	.984	7292	1254	143	53	126	4.77
Hoiles, Chris	819	.994	4830	320	29	28	27	6.29
Howard, Elston	1138	.993	6447	479	51	41	23	6.09
Johnson, Charles	861	.995	5556	438	36	41	32	6.79
Kendall, Jason	1059	.988	6636	526	86	30	56	6.76
Lollar, Sherman	1571	.992	7059	688	62	43	53	4.97
Lombardi, Ernie	1544	.979	5694	845	143	41	152	4.22
Lopez, Javy	1106	.992	7421	542	64	29	80	7.20
Mueller, Ray	917	.988	3095	503	43	50	32	3.92
Munson, Thurman	1279	.982	6253	742	127	44	93	5.47
O'Dea, Ken	627	.983	2450	336	48	50	40	4.44
O'Farrell, Bob	1338	.976	4295	980	130	48	54	3.94

Catcher	Games Caught	Field'g Avg.	Putouts	Assists	Errors	Caught Stealing %	Passed Balls	Range Factor
Parrish, Lance	1820	.991	9647	980	94	39	192	5.85
Pena, Tony	1950	.991	11212	1045	117	35	105	6.26
Phelps, Babe	592	.974	2251	291	69	42	46	4.29
Piazza, Mike	1198	.990	8258	566	102	25	81	7.29
Porter, Darrell	1506	.982	6756	754	134	38	132	4.99
Posada, Jorge	821	.992	5463	366	48	30	74	7.10
Rodriguez, Ivan	1327	.990	7911	731	92	49	71	6.57
Rosar, Buddy	934	.992	3845	511	36	48	28	4.66
Roseboro, John	1475	.989	9291	675	107	41	111	6.72
Ruel, Muddy	1422	.982	5347	1136	116	45	59	4.60
Sanguillen, Manny	1115	.986	5996	540	94	38	89	5.87
Scioscia, Mike	1395	.988	8335	737	114	34	82	6.50
Simmons, Ted	1769	.987	8906	915	130	33	182	5.72
Sundberg, Jim	1927	.993	9767	1007	81	41	130	5.59
Tebbetts, Birdie	1108	.978	4667	666	119	44	64	4.81
Tenace, Gene	893	.986	3945	441	63	36	73	4.92
Tettleton, Mickey	872	.991	3978	346	39	29	64	4.96
Torre, Joe	903	.990	4850	428	56	56	40	6.05
Triandos, Gus	992	.987	5123	448	72	41	138	5.62
Westrum, Wes	902	.985	3639	418	62	51	61	4.49

Catcher	FA	Lge FA	DFA.	CS%	Lge CS%	DCS	RF	Lge RF	DRF	ASSA1	Lge ASSA1	DASSA
Bailey, Ed	.986	.987	-1	39	39	0	5.37	5.32	+0.05	35	43	-8
Battey, Earl	.990	.989	+1	40	36	+4	6.14	5.61	+0.53	42	42	0
Bench, Johnny	.990	.987	+3	43	36	+7	5.80	5.59	+0.21	33	29	+4
Berra, Yogi	.989	.987	+2	49	44	+5	5.61	4.73	+0.88	36	43	-7
Burgess, Smoky	.988	.986	+2	34	40	-6	4.96	5.09	-0.13	34	45	-11
Campanella, Roy	.988	.984	+4	58	40	+18	5.98	4.66	+1.32	39	42	-3
Carter, Gary	.991	.986	+5	35	31	+4	6.32	5.48	+0.84	29	26	+3
Cochrane, Mickey	.985	980	+5	40	42	-2	5.00	4.13	+0.87	46	52	-6
Cooper, Walker	.977	.982	-5	44	43	+1	4.71	4.38	+0.33	41	46	-5
Crandall, Del	.989	.986	+3	46	40	+6	5.48	5.13	+0.35	44	45	-1
Danning, Harry	.985	.980	+5	47	45	+2	4.63	4.18	+0.45	51	51	0
Daulton, Darren	.989	.988	+1	29	32	-3	6.07	5.74	+0.33	27	30	-3
Dickey, Bill	.988	.982	+6	41	40	+1	5.22	4.36	+0.86	45	49	-4
Ferguson, Joe	.987	.986	+1	34	34	0	5.59	5.33	+0.26	29	49	-20
Ferrell, Rick	.984	.982	+2	43	40	+3	4.64	4.32	+0.32	52	49	+3
Fisk, Carlton	.988	.986	+2	33	36	-3	5.58	5.10	+0.48	27	29	-2
Freehan, Bill	.993	.987	+6	34	37	-3	6.74	5.68	+1.06	27	36	-9
Haller, Tom	.992	.988	+4	34	38	-4	6.27	5.88	+0.39	26	46	-20
Hargrave, Bubbles	.983	.975	+8	39	44	-5	3.90	4.01	-0.11	50	76	-26
Hartnett, Gabby	.984	.978	+6	53	41	+12	4.77	4.03	+0.74	58	52	+6
Hoiles, Chris	.994	.990	+4	28	32	-4	6.29	5.67	+0.62	17	20	-3
Howard, Elston	.993	.989	+4	41	38	+3	6.09	5.66	+0.43	38	43	-5
Johnson, Charles	.995	.990	+5	41	31	+10	6.79	6.78	+0.01	31	32	-1
Kendall, Jason	.988	.990	-2	30	32	-2	6.76	7.00	-0.24	36	36	0
Lollar, Sherman	.992	.987	+5	43	42	+1	4.97	4.94	+0.03	37	42	-5
Lombardi, Ernie	.979	.980	-1	41	41	0	4.22	4.10	+0.12	47	51	-4
Lopez, Javy	.992	.990	+2	29	30	-1	7.20	6.86	+0.34	39	35	+4
Mueller, Ray	.988	.980	+8	50	44	+6	3.92	4.22	-0.30	50	49	+1

Catcher	FA	Lge FA	DFA.	CS%	Lge CS%	DCS	RF	Lge RF	DRF	ASSA1	Lge ASSA1	DASSA
Munson, Thurman	.982	.984	-2	44	37	+7	5.47	5.22	+0.25	38	32	+6
O'Dea, Ken	.983	.979	+4	50	44	+6	4.44	4.15	+0.29	45	51	-6
O'Farrell, Bob	.976	.975	+1	48	45	+3	3.94	4.03	-0.09	54	52	+2
Parrish, Lance	.991	.986	+5	39	34	+5	5.85	5.15	+0.70	28	26	+2
Pena, Tony	.991	.987	+4	35	32	+3	6.26	5.56	+0.70	31	30	+1
Phelps, Babe	.974	.980	-6	42	46	-4	4.29	4.22	+0.07	42	53	-11
Piazza, Mike	.990	.990	0	25	30	-5	7.29	6.66	+0.63	29	32	-3
Porter, Darrell	.982	.984	-2	38	36	+2	4.99	5.15	-0.16	20	26	-6
Posada, Jorge	.992	.991	+1	30	31	-1	7.10	6.68	+0.42	31	28	+3
Rodriguez, Ivan	.990	.990	0	49	32	+17	6.57	6.14	+0.43	32	32	0
Rosar, Buddy	.992	.982	+10	48	43	+5	4.66	4.43	+0.23	40	48	-8
Roseboro, John	.989	.987	+2	41	38	+3	6.72	5.64	+1.08	39	42	-3
Ruel, Muddy	.982	.976	+6	45	44	+1	4.60	4.18	+0.42	61	62	-1
Sanguillen, Manny	.986	.987	-1	38	36	+2	5.87	5.58	+0.29	31	31	0
Scioscia, Mike	.988	.987	+1	34	30	+4	6.50	5.57	+0.93	26	28	-2
Simmons, Ted	.987	.986	+1	33	35	-2	5.72	5.53	+0.19	27	28	-1
Sundberg, Jim	.993	.985	+8	41	35	+6	5.59	4.98	+0.61	23	22	+1
Tebbetts, Birdie	.978	.983	-5	44	42	+2	4.81	4.39	+0.42	55	48	+7
Tenace, Gene	.986	.984	+2	36	35	+1	4.92	5.27	-0.35	26	32	-6
Tettleton, Mickey	.991	.989	+2	29	32	-3	4.96	5.32	-0.36	19	24	-5
Torre, Joe	.990	.988	+2	40	38	+2	6.05	6.01	+0.04	34	38	-4
Triandos, Gus	.987	.989	-2	41	39	+2	5.62	5.35	+0.27	41	43	-2
Westrum, Wes	.985	.984	+1	51	41	+10	4.49	4.64	-0.15	41	42	-1

Appendix 4: Defensive Ratings

	DFA	RTG	DCS	RTG	PBR ×.3	DWPR ×.075	DRF RTG	DASSAR ×.5	Total Points
Bailey, Ed	-1	41	0	34	3.3	0.8	38	20	137.1
Battey, Earl	+1	32	+4	15	12.0	1.8	16	6	82.8
Bench, Johnny	+3	21	+7	6	4.8	1.0	35	8	75.8
Berra, Yogi	+2	23	+5	12	3.3	06	5	16	59.9
Burgess, Smoky	+2	23	-6	50	7.5	1.0	44	24	149.5
Campanella, Roy	+4	15	+18	1	3.3	2.0	1	15	37.3
Carter, Gary	+5	9	+4	15	1.8	1.0	8	8	42.8
Cochrane, Mickey	+5	9	-2	39	6.0	2.0	6	21	83.0
Cooper, Walker	-5	48	+1	29	7.5	2.5	26	15	128.0
Crandall, Del	+3	21	+6	8	1.8	0.6	24	8	63.4
Danning, Harry	+5	9	+2	23	1.8	3.4	18	6	61.2
Daulton, Darren	+1	32	-3	41	7.5	3.8	26	11	121.3
Dickey, Bill	+6	5	+1	29	3.3	2.5	7	14	60.8
Ferguson, Joe	+1	32	0	34	14.7	1.7	32	22	136.4
Ferrell, Rick	+2	23	+3	18	11.1	1.7	28	3	84.8
Fisk, Carlton	+2	23	-3	41	6.0	0.1	17	11	98.1
Freehan, Bill	+6	5	-3	41	7.5	1.8	3	22	80.3
Haller, Tom	+4	15	-4	45	14.1	0.5	23	25	122.6
Hargrave, Bubbles	+8	2	-5	48	7.5	1.0	43	25	126.5
Hartnett, Gabby	+6	5	+12	3	9.6	2.0	9	3	31.6
Hoiles, Chris	+4	15	-4	45	0.3	0.2	13	11	84.5
Howard, Elston	+4	15	+3	18	3.3	0.2	19	14	69.5
Johnson, Charles	+5	9	+10	4	0.3	1.0	41	15	70.3
Kendall, Jason	-2	44	-1	37	4.8	3.4	47	6	142.2
Lollar, Sherman	+5	9	+1	29	0.3	0.8	40	15	94.1
Lombardi, Ernie	-1	41	0	34	12.9	2.5	37	17	141.4
Lopez, Javy	+2	23	-1	37	9.6	0.3	25	2	96.9
Mueller, Ray	+8	2	+6	8	0.3	0.6	48	4	62.9
Munson, Thurman	-2	44	+7	6	9.6	2.0	33	1.0	95.6
O'Dea, Ken	+4	15	+6	8	7.5	2.5	29	16	78.0
O'Farrell, Bob	+1	32	+3	18	1.8	1.4	42	4	99.2

	DFA	RTG	DCS	RTG	PBR RTG ×.3	DWPR ×.075	DRF RTG	DASSAR ×.5	Total Points
Parrish, Lance	+5	9	+5	12	14.1	3.1	10	2	50.2
Pena, Tony	+4	15	+3	18	4.8	2.5	11	4	55.3
Phelps, Babe	-6	50	-4	45	11.1	3.1	13	24	146.2
Piazza, Mike	0	39	-5	48	6.0	0.5	12	11	116.5
Porter, Darrell	-2	44	+2	23	12.0	2.9	46	16	143.9
Posada, Jorge	+1	33	-1	38	12.9	1.7	19	2.5	107.1 est.
Rodriguez, Ivan	0	39	+17	2	4.8	1.4	19	6	72.2
Rosar, Buddy	+10	1	+5	12	0.3	2.0	34	21	70.3
Roseboro, John	+2	23	+3	18	11.1	3.6	2	11	68.7
Ruel, Muddy	+6	5	+1	30	1.8	1.8	21	8	66.6
Sanguillen, Manny	-1	41	+2	23	11.1	0.4	29	6	110.5
Scioscia, Mike	+1	32	+4	15	6.0	2.0	4	10	69
Simmons, Ted	+1	32	-2	39	14.1	3.1	36	15	139.2
Sundberg, Jim	+8	2	+6	8	9.6	3.1	15	4	41.7
Tebbetts, Birdie	-5	48	+2	23	6.0	2.5	21	1	101.5
Tenace, Gene	+2	23	+1	29	12.0	3.6	49	22	138.6
Tettleton, Mickey	+2	23	-3	44	9.6	1.4	50	15	143.0
Torre, Joe	+2	23	+2	23	12.9	3.4	39	14	115.3
Triandos, Gus	-2	44	+2	23	15.0	2.9	31	10	125.9
Westrum, Wes	+1	32	+10	4	7.5	1.4	45	8	97.9

Key:

DFA — Fielding Average Differential
RTG — Rating
DCS — Caught-Stealing Differential
PBR — Passed Balls Rating
DWPR — Wild Pitch Differential Rating
DRF — Range Factor Differential
DASSAR — Other Assist Differential Rating

	Final Rating		*Final Rating*
Hartnett, Gabby	1	Rosar, Buddy	16
Campanella, Roy	2	Rodriguez, Ivan	18
Sundberg, Jim	3	Bench, Johnny	19
Carter, Gary	4	O'Dea, Ken	20
Parrish, Lance	5	Freehan, Bill	21
Pena, Tony	6	Battey, Earl	22
Berra, Yogi	7	Cochrane, Mickey	23
Danning, Harry	8	Hoiles, Chris	24
Dickey, Bill	9	Ferrell, Rick	25
Mueller, Ray	10	Lollar, Sherman	26
Crandall, Del	11	Munson, Thurman	27
Ruel, Muddy	12	Lopez, Javy	28
Roseboro, John	13	Westrum, Wes	29
Scioscia, Mike	14	Fisk, Carlton	30
Howard, Elston	15	O'Farrell, Bob	31
Johnson, Charles	16	Tebbetts, Birdie	32

	Final Rating		Final Rating
Sanguillen, Manny	33	Bailey, Ed	42
Posada, Jorge	33 est.	Tenace, Gene	43
Torre, Joe	34	Simmons, Ted	44
Piazza, Mike	35	Lombardi, Ernie	45
Daulton, Darren	36	Kendall, Jason	46
Haller, Tom	37	Tettleton, Mickey	47
Triandos, Gus	38	Porter, Darrell	48
Hargrave, Bubbles	39	Phelps, Babe	49
Cooper, Walker	40	Burgess, Smoky	50
Ferguson, Joe	41		

APPENDIX 5:
FINAL RATINGS AT
2–1 OFFENSE TO DEFENSE

	Offense × 2	Defense × 1	Total Points	Final Rating
Hartnett, Gabby	8	1	9	1
Campanella, Roy	12	2	14	2
Dickey, Bill	10	9	19	3
Berra, Yogi	20	7	27	4
Cochrane, Mickey	6	23	29	5
Piazza, Mike	2	35	37	6
Bench, Johnny	20	19	39	7
Tenace, Gene	4	43	47	8
Torre, Joe	14	34	48	9
Hoiles, Chris	26	24	50	10
Freehan, Bill	32	21	53	11
Posada, Jorge	18	35	53	11 est.
Battey, Earl	34	22	56	12
Carter, Gary	54	4	58	13
Fisk, Carlton	30	30	60	14
Lombardi, Ernie	18	45	63	15
Porter, Darrell	16	48	64	16
Howard, Elston	50	15	65	17
Simmons, Ted	26	44	70	18
Tettleton, Mickey	24	47	71	19
Ferrell, Rick	48	25	73	20
Munson, Thurman	46	27	73	20
Parrish, Lance	68	5	73	20
Ferguson, Joe	36	41	77	23
Hargrave, Bubbles	38	39	77	23
Rodriguez, Ivan	60	18	68	23
Cooper, Walker	42	40	82	26
Scioscia, Mike	70	14	84	27
Kendall, Jason	40	46	86	28

	Offense × 2	Defense × 1	Total Points	Final Rating
Lopez, Javy	58	28	86	28
Roseboro, John	78	13	91	30
Daulton, Darren	56	36	92	31
Lollar, Sherman	66	26	92	31
Phelps, Babe	44	49	93	33
Johnson, Charles	78	16	94	34
Crandall, Del	84	11	95	35
Sundberg, Jim	92	3	95	35
Ruel, Muddy	86	12	98	37
Haller, Tom	62	37	99	38
Burgess, Smoky	52	50	102	39
Bailey, Ed	64	42	106	40
Danning, Harry	98	8	106	40
Mueller, Ray	96	10	106	40
Pena, Tony	100	6	106	40
Tebbetts, Birdie	74	32	106	40
O'Farrell, Bob	76	31	107	45
O'Dea, Ken	90	20	110	46
Triandos, Gus	72	38	110	46
Rosar, Buddy	94	16	110	48
Westrum, Wes	82	29	111	49
Sanguillen, Manny	86	33	119	50

Catchers who were evaluated but didn't make the top 50, and their estimated ratings:

Catcher	Estimated Rating	Catcher	Estimated Rating
Lopez, Al	51	Wilson, Dan	60
Yeager, Steve	52	McCarver, Tim	61
Boone, Bob	53	Wilson, Jimmie	62
Hogan, Shanty	54	Cerone, Rick	63
Edwards, Johnny	55	Hundley, Randy	64
Hegan, Jim	56	Seminick, Andy	65
Davis, Spud	57	Lieberthal, Mike	66
Mancuso, Gus	58	Taubensee, Eddie	67
Santiago, Benito	59		

Appendix 6:
Ratings with Other
Offense to Defense Ratios

	Off-Def @ 1–1	Off-Def @ 2–1	Off-Def @ 4.5–1
Bailey, Ed	47	40	36
Battey, Earl	11	12	15
Bench, Johnny	6	7	8
Berra, Yogi	4	4	6
Burgess, Smoky	49	39	32
Campanella, Roy	2	2	2
Carter, Gary	7	13	20
Cochrane, Mickey	5	5	4
Cooper, Walker	37	26	24
Crandall, Del	23	35	40
Danning, Harry	29	40	49
Daulton, Darren	39	31	31
Dickey, Bill	3	3	3
Ferguson, Joe	34	23	18
Ferrell, Rick	18	20	23
Fisk, Carlton	15	14	14
Freehan, Bill	9	11	13
Haller, Tom	42	38	35
Hargrave, Bubbles	32	23	19
Hartnett, Gabby	1	1	1
Hoiles, Chris	9	10	10
Howard, Elston	13	17	20
Johnson, Charles	25	34	38
Kendall, Jason	41	28	25
Lollar, Sherman	34	31	34
Lombardi, Ernie	24	15	12
Lopez, Javy	29	28	29
Mueller, Ray	32	40	46
Munson, Thurman	21	20	22

	Off-Def @ 1–1	Off-Def @ 2–1	Off-Def @ 4.5–1
O'Dea, Ken	40	46	45
O'Farrell, Bob	43	45	42
Parrish, Lance	11	20	28
Pena, Tony	27	40	50
Phelps, Babe	45	33	26
Piazza, Mike	8	6	5
Porter, Darrell	27	16	11
Rodriguez, Ivan	17	25	27
Rosar, Buddy	36	46	48
Roseboro, John	22	30	37
Ruel, Muddy	25	37	43
Sanguillen, Manny	49	50	47
Scioscia, Mike	18	27	33
Simmons, Ted	29	18	17
Sundberg, Jim	18	35	30
Tebbetts, Birdie	43	40	39
Tenace, Gene	15	8	6
Tettleton, Mickey	34	19	16
Torre, Joe	14	9	9
Triandos, Gus	47	46	40
Westrum, Wes	45	49	44

APPENDIX 7:
THE TOP TEN CATCHERS

Offense	*Defense*	*All-Around*
Mike Piazza	Gabby Hartnett	Gabby Hartnett
Gene Tenace	Roy Campanella	Roy Campanella
Mickey Cochrane	Jim Sundberg	Bill Dickey
Gabby Hartnett	Gary Carter	Yogi Berra
Bill Dickey	Lance Parrish	Mickey Cochrane
Roy Campanella	Tony Pena	Mike Piazza
Joe Torre	Yogi Berra	Johnny Bench
Darrell Porter	Harry Danning	Gene Tenace
Ernie Lombardi	Bill Dickey	Joe Torre
Johnny Bench (tie)	Ray Mueller	Chris Hoiles
Yogi Berra (tie)		

Plus Five More

Mickey Tettleton	Del Crandall	Bill Freehan
Ted Simmons (tie)	Muddy Ruel	Earl Battey
Chris Hoiles (tie)	Johnny Roseboro	Gary Carter
Carlton Fisk	Mike Scioscia	Carlton Fisk
	Elston Howard	Ernie Lombardi

Minimum of 1,000 Games Caught

Offense	*Defense*	*All-Around*
Mike Piazza	Gabby Hartnett	Gabby Hartnett
Mickey Cochrane	Roy Campanella	Roy Campanella
Gabby Hartnett	Jim Sundberg	Bill Dickey
Roy Campanella	Gary Carter	Yogi Berra
Darrell Porter	Lance Parrish	Mickey Cochrane
Ernie Lombardi	Tony Pena	Mike Piazza
Johnny Bench (tie)	Yogi Berra	Johnny Bench
Yogi Berra (tie)	Bill Dickey	Bill Freehan
Ted Simmons	Del Crandall	Earl Battey
Carlton Fisk	Muddy Ruel	Gary Carter

Plus Five More

Bill Freehan	Johnny Roseboro	Carlton Fisk
Earl Battey	Mike Scioscia	Ernie Lombardi
Joe Ferguson	Elston Howard	Darrell Porter
Jason Kendall	Charles Johnson	Elston Howard
Walker Cooper	Ivan Rodriguez	Ted Simmons

BIBLIOGRAPHY

Adelman, Melvin L. *A Sporting Time.* Urbana: University of Illinois Press, 1990.

Allen, Maury. *Baseball's 100.* New York: Galahad Books, 1981.

Bench, Johnny, and William Brashler. *Catch You Later.* New York: Harper & Row, 1979.

Berra, Yogi, with Dave Kaplan. *When You Come to a Fork in the Road, Take It.* New York: Hyperion, 2001.

Bevis, Charles. *Mickey Cochrane.* Jefferson, NC: McFarland, 1998.

Brown, Warren. *The Chicago Cubs.* New York: Putnam's, 1946.

Campanella, Roy. *It's Good to Be Alive.* New York: New American Library, 1959.

Carroll, Bob. "Mitt-igating Circumstances." *Oldtyme Baseball News.* Vol. 7, Issue 3. Petoskey, MI: McKinstry Bros., 1995.

Carter, Craig, ed. *Daguerreotypes,* 8th ed. St. Louis, MO: Sporting News, 1990.

Caruso, Gary. *The Braves Encyclopedia.* Philadelphia: Temple University Press, 1995.

Cochrane, Mickey, and Gabby Hartnett. *How to Catch.* Chicago: International Baseball School, 1941.

Cohen, Eliot, ed. *My Greatest Day in Baseball.* New York: Simon & Schuster, 1991.

Cohen, Richard M., and David S. Neft. *The World Series.* New York: Collier Books, 1986.

Couzens, Gerald Secor. *A Baseball Album.* New York: Lippincott & Crowell, 1980.

Daniel, W. Harrison. *Jimmie Foxx.* Jefferson, NC: McFarland, 1996.

Devine, Christopher. *Thurman Munson.* Jefferson, NC: McFarland, 2001.

Durant, John. *The Story of Baseball.* New York: Hastings House, 1974.

Foster, John B., ed. *How to Catch and How to Run Bases.* New York: American Sports, 1921.

Frommer, Harvey. *Baseball's Greatest Managers.* New York: Franklin Watts, 1985.

Gallagher, Mark, and Walter LeConte. *The Yankees Encyclopedia.* Champaign, IL: Sports Publishing, 2000.

Gold, Eddie, and Art Ahrens. *The Golden Era Cubs.* Chicago: Bonus Books, 1985.

Grayson, Harry. *They Played the Game.* New York, A.S. Barnes, 1945.

Hirshberg, Al. *Baseball's Greatest Catchers.* New York: Putnam's, 1966.

Holway, John. *The Complete Book of Baseball's Negro Leagues.* Fern Park, FL: Hastings House, 2001.

Honig, Donald. *A Donald Honig Reader.* New York: Simon & Schuster, 1988.

Hoppel, Joe, ed. *Baseball's Hall of Fame: Cooperstown, Where Legends Live Forever.* New York: Arlington House, 1988.

Ivor-Campbell, Frederick, Robert L. Tiemann, and Mark Rucker, ed. *Baseball's First Stars.* Cleveland: Society for American Baseball Research, 1996.

Kaplan, Jim. *Lefty Grove, American Original.* Cleveland: Society for American Baseball Research, 2000.

Lane, F.C. *Batting.* Cleveland: Society for American Baseball Research, 2001.

Leonard, Buck, with James A. Riley. *Buck Leonard, the Black Lou Gehrig.* New York: Carroll & Graf, 1995.

Light, Jonathan Fraser. *The Cultural Encyclopedia of Baseball.* Jefferson, NC: McFarland, 1997.

McCarver, Tim, with Ray Robinson. *Oh Baby, I Love It!* New York: Vellard Books, 1987.

McConnell, Bob, and David Vincent, ed. *The Home Run Encyclopedia.* New York: Macmillan, 1996.

McCoy, Alfred, M. "Gabby Hartnett Up." *The Open Road for Boys.* Boston: May 1938.

McCullough, Bob. *My Greatest Day in Baseball.* Dallas: Taylor, 1998.

McNeil, William F. *Baseball's Other All-Stars.* Jefferson, NC: McFarland, 2000.

_____. *The California Winter League.* Jefferson, NC: McFarland, 2002.

_____. *Cool Papas and Double Duties.* Jefferson, NC: McFarland, 2001.

_____. *The Dodgers Encyclopedia.* Champaign, IL: Sports Publishing, 2003.

_____. *The King of Swat.* Jefferson, NC: McFarland, 1997.

Meany, Tom, and others. *The Artful Dodgers.* New York: Grosset & Dunlap, 1954.

Moreland, George L. *Balldom.* St. Louis, MO: Horton, 1989.

Munson, Thurman, with Martin Appel. *Thurman Munson.* New York: Coward, McCann & Geoghegan, 1978.

Nash, Bruce, and Allan Zullo. *Baseball Confidential.* New York: Pocket Books, 1988.

_____. *The Baseball Hall of Shame.* New York: Pocket Books, 1985.

Okrent, Daniel, and Steve Wulf. *Baseball Anecdotes.* New York: Harper & Row, 1989.

Owens, Thomas S. *Great Catchers.* New York: MetroBooks, 1997.

Palmer, Pete, and Gary Gillette, ed. *Baseball Encyclopedia.* New York: Barnes & Noble Books, 2004.

Peary, Danny, ed. *Cult Baseball Players.* New York: Simon & Schuster, 1990.

Pegler, Westbrook. "Cochrane Did Everything but Catch Until the Minors Took Him." *Chicago Daily Tribune,* September 14, 1931.

_____. "Need a Haircut or Apple Pie? Jimmy Foxx Can Fix You Up." *Chicago Daily Tribune,* September 15, 1931.

Powers, Jimmy. *Baseball Personalities.* New York: Rudolph Field, 1949.

Reichler, Joseph L., ed. *Baseball Encyclopedia.* New York: Macmillan, 1979.

Reidenbaugh, Lowell. *Baseball's Hall of Fame, Where the Legends Live Forever.* New York: Arlington House, 1988.

Rickey, Branch, with Robert Riger. *The American Diamond.* New York: Simon and Schuster, 1965.

Ritter, Lawrence S. *The Glory of Their Times.* New York: William Morrow, 1984.

Rovin, Jeff, with Steve Burkow. *Sports Babylon.* New York: Signet, 1993.

Seymour, Harold. *Baseball: The Early Years.* New York: Oxford University Press, 1960.

Shapiro, Milton J. *Heroes Behind the Mask.* New York: Julian Messner, 1968.

Shatzkin, Mike, ed. *The Ballplayers.* New York: William Morrow, 1990.

Singletary, Wes. *Al Lopez.* Jefferson, NC: McFarland, 1999.

Smitley, Al. "Straight from the Horse's Mouth: A Chat with Harry Danning." *Oldtyme Baseball News,* Vol. 7, Issue 4. Petoskey, MI: McKinstry Bros., 1995.

Spalding, Albert G. *Baseball: America's National Game, 1839–1915.* San Francisco: Halo Books, 1991.

Spoerle, Gary. "Buck Ewing: Thinking Man's Player." *Vintage & Classic Baseball Collector,* Issue 4, December 1995. Tacoma, WA: Pretty Panda Publishing, MS #222.

Thomas, G. Scott. *Leveling the Field.* New York: Black Dog & Leventhal, 2002.
Thorn, John, Pete Palmer, Michael Gershman, and David Pietrusza, ed. *Total Baseball,* 5th ed. New York: Penguin, 1997.
Tieman, Robert L., and Mark Rucker, ed. *Nineteenth Century Stars.* Cleveland: Society for American Baseball Research, 1999.
Trimble, Joe. *Yogi Berra.* New York: Grosset & Dunlap, 1956.
Van Hyning, Thomas E. *Puerto Rico's Winter League.* Jefferson, NC: McFarland, 1995.
Van Riper, Guernsey. *Behind the Plate: Three Great Catchers.* Champaign, IL: Garrard, 1973.
Werber, Bill, and Paul C. Rogers III. *Memories of a Ballplayer.* Cleveland: Society for American Baseball Research, 2001
Young, Dick. *Roy Campanella.* New York: Grosset & Dunlap, 1952.
Zanger, Jack. *Great Catchers of the Major Leagues.* New York: Random House, 1970.

INDEX